✧ YO-BDZ-736

The
CONTEXTS
of
LANGUAGE

Fernald Library
Colby-Sawyer College
New London, New Hampshire

Presented by

WALLACE K. EWING

The CONTEXTS of LANGUAGE

ronald wardhaugh
University of Toronto

NEWBURY HOUSE PUBLISHERS, Inc. / ROWLEY / MASSACHUSETTS

FERNALD LIBRARY
COLBY-SAWYER COLLEGE
NEW LONDON, N.H. 03257

Library of Congress Cataloging in Publication Data

Wardhaugh, Ronald.
   The contexts of language.

   Bibliography: p.
   1. Language and languages. 2. Linguistics.
I. Title.
P106.W314   401   75-43973
ISBN 0-88377-051-2
ISBN 0-88377-050-4 pbk.

Cover design by *Lois Jefferson Kordaszewski*

NEWBURY HOUSE PUBLISHERS, Inc.

Language Science
Language Teaching
Language Learning

68 Middle Road, Rowley, Massachusetts 01969

Copyright © 1976 by Newbury House Publishers, Inc. All rights reserved.
No part of this publication may be reproduced without prior written permission
from the Publisher.

Printed in the U.S.A.   First printing: March 1976
                                         5 4 3 2 1

FERNALD LIBRARY
COLBY-SAWYER COLLEGE
NEW LONDON, N.H. 03257

Preface

Very adequate texts exist for teaching introductory courses in language and linguistics. Consequently, this book is not meant to serve as a text which first, or alone, introduces students to language study. Instead, the book is intended to be used in conjunction with an introductory text to provide students with insights into some of the wider applications of their studies and to do so in a unified coherent manner. It addresses itself to many of the questions beginning students ask about language but which introductory texts do not often answer because of their necessary limitations. The book should also prove to be a useful source of information for more advanced students who wish to become familiar with many of the issues that have concerned linguists in recent years.

Each chapter covers a variety of issues related to a central topic. The discussion of those issues is deliberately nontechnical; however, it quite often assumes some familiarity with the kinds of simple technical knowledge which students may readily acquire from introductory texts. Adequate references are provided at the chapter ends and in the bibliography. Students should consult these sources for further information about the topics which particularly interest them.

The central theme of the book is that linguistic issues are related to many other issues in the world. Language study comprises more than the study of technical linguistics. It involves study of the uses of language as well as the forms of language and study of people as constantly changing, psychological, social, interacting beings as well as generators of abstract linguistic forms. Language study as an end in itself is certainly a necessary goal of linguistic endeavor, but not a sufficient goal. Study of the contexts in which language is used and of how those contexts affect and are affected by language must also form part of a fully comprehensive science of language.

November 1975   Ronald Wardhaugh

Contents

The
CONTEXTS
of
LANGUAGE

1

Language and Linguistics

Attitudes and Misconceptions

Although a long tradition of scholarly language study exists, it has had surprisingly little influence on what educated people know about language, even about such a widely spoken language as English. Their knowledge has come from sources largely outside the tradition, from attempts to describe English as though it were Greek or Latin rather than to describe it without such preconceptions. Most educated people still pay a kind of indirect homage to Greek and Latin, though they may not be aware of that fact. For example, if they try to describe how the parts of English sentences fit together, they are likely to use terms much more suitable for Greek and Latin than for English as they assign words to various parts-of-speech classes and label the different types of phrases and clauses. Such parsing never seems to be very satisfactory, For English does not fit the classical mold very well. There is always the ambiguity of a word like *stone* in *a stone wall*—is it an adjective or a noun? It is an adjective if all words which modify nouns are classified as adjectives, but it is a noun if all names of things are classified as nouns. Unfortunately, in this case either principle of classification is possible; consequently, the solution is to say that *stone* is a noun used as an adjective, a solution which is a poor compromise at best.

Moreover, if English does not fit the mold, it must be because it is somehow degenerate compared to Greek and Latin. Languages change, but for the worse we are forced to assume. This concept of degeneracy is often extended to cover all nonclassical languages, particularly their spoken varieties. Even major modern languages like English are regarded as degenerate varieties of classical languages, and people often hold the spoken word in far less esteem than the written word.

Conscious efforts are made to stop or reverse this degenerative process. The result is prescriptivism in matters of language. A grammar becomes a set of caveats, a series of warnings about things not to do and errors to avoid. Authorities are established and appealed to, and occasional attempts are made—some successful, some not—to establish committees and academies to set standards of proper linguistic behavior. France has such an academy; England almost had one. Such attempts result in efforts to control the admission of new words into the language, particularly borrowings (English words into French), to regulate grammatical usages (*ain't*, *like* as a conjunction, and multiple negation), to condemn slang and other such ephemeral expressions (slang like hair- and skirt-length arouses the emotions), to decide on matters of correctness in pronunciation and spelling (the dictionary as bible), and in general to elevate the written varieties of the language at the expense of the spoken varieties. This last point need not surprise us. Most of us are not at all aware of how we learned to speak but are quite aware of the pains we suffered in achieving whatever literacy we possess. What we have won with so much difficulty we must prize and protect.

Educated people often have defensive, self-conscious attitudes toward their language. They know intuitively that systems tend toward chaos if left to go their own way undisturbed, and they regard their language as a system in such danger. Effort is therefore required to stop this natural law of dissolution from taking effect. They fail to realize that countervailing forces are at work, for languages must also be considered within a functional, even evolutionary, framework. Each language has functions to perform; it will continue to perform those functions. so long as they are important to the survival of those who speak the language.

In still other ways we can see how pervasive are misconceptions about language. For many people a language is no more than a conglomerate of words, a kind of huge dictionary. To learn a new language is to learn a new set of words for things and processes, words often pronounced and combined in peculiar ways but words no less. In such circumstances it is not surprising that dictionaries become objects of reverence and that a dictionary which reports on the language in a new but not radically different way—as did *Webster's Third New International Dictionary* in 1961— is greeted with the kind of suspicion and mistrust usually reserved for a new translation of a book of holy writ. Fifteen years later people still continue to discuss the "correctness" of the principles that went into the making of that dictionary.

But words are also acknowledged to be tyrants and communication between people to be difficult. The result is that we are periodically told to straighten out our thinking by taking doses of one variety or another of semantic medicine, for example, to remember that words are potentially tyrants waiting to enslave us. Or we are teased to distinguish between the medium and the message and the message and the massage in McLuhanistic prose which itself requires a considerable teasing out of meaning. Or we are exhorted to forego language entirely in order to substitute touching, feeling, and even primal screaming in an attempt to recover our basic capacities for feeling and expression. Twentieth-century wisemen, gurus, and witch doctors know that words give us problems. The failure to communicate is endemic in society. We know that trying to communicate with someone who speaks another language or who has very different opinions from our own quite often leads to frustration. The noise level of the voices is likely to increase in direct proportion to the level of frustration experienced, but the shouting that results does nothing to overcome the obstacles. Yet, there appears to be no other way of resolving our difficulties than that which language provides, certainly no way with less ambiguity when language is functioning well.

When educated people turn to language experts for help, these experts seem to have little to offer because their interests do not match the needs that are perceived to exist. They expect a grammarian to provide definitive statements on the correct way to say or write something and to give unequivocal answers. They do not expect the grammarian to ask questions and admit uncertainty. They expect a linguist to have a marvelous grasp of numerous languages and display language virtuosity rather than linguistic insight. There is little general realization that language itself can be a fascinating subject of study or even that serious thought can be brought to bear on a wide variety of language-related topics. The popular tradition of language study is not study in any serious sense; rather it is indoctrination into received opinions and myths about language. The result is a kind of folk linguistics. Serious study is possible, but only if questions and concerns of an entirely different kind are made central to such study and if answers are sought through scientific inquiry rather than through reciting seemingly appropriate responses from a kind of language catechism.

The Linguistic Emphasis

One immediate issue confronting anyone who wishes to make a serious study of language is that of deciding what the important questions are and what data exist that bear on the questions. Each discipline is defined by its questions and data. The importance of finding good questions can be shown by listing some that we might be tempted to ask about language. How are the sounds of speech produced and understood? How do words and sentences achieve their meanings? How do the various parts of a language hold together? Is a language built up from sounds, syllables, words, and sentences? What do we mean by *built up, sounds, syllables, words,* and *sentences?* How does language work in communication, for example, between two people in a conversation? How do children acquire language? How does it break down through injury or in old age? How does language change and vary in space and time? Why does it change and vary? What changes and variations are normal? What sets the bounds on normal? Do all languages share certain properties? Do animals also have languages? Could we teach an animal to talk? If not, why not?

Each of the above questions requires a different kind of investigation and data. The questions themselves may not be of equal importance, and there is no shortage of data bearing on parts of all of them. The central issue in linguistic investigation is finding the data relevant to answering a particular question which is of widespread interest, one that furthers our knowledge and understanding of language. By themselves data are valueless in the absence of one or more questions that arise from some kind of researchable hypothesis or theory. The investigator must always have some idea in mind which must be proved or disproved. The idea may emerge from looking at masses of data but it can be proved or disproved only if stated in the form of a hypothesis and then systematically tested against all possible data. As the theory develops and changes so will different questions arise and seem to be answerable and old questions and answers rejected as unscientific or incorrect. The issue of the ultimate origin of language is a good example. In general, it appears to be impossible to say anything useful on the issue, but from time to time faint glimmers of possibility are seen and the issue gets looked at once again.

All linguists are agreed that asking good questions is the cornerstone of any worthwhile linguistic endeavor. They all agree too on the importance of finding just the right data which bear on the questions. The better the data, the greater the certainty there will be about the answers. In this way linguistics has a strong empirical component, that is, it has a great respect for anchoring its conclusions in evidence from the real world. The answers to questions which linguists ask will therefore have a strong empirical basis or be labeled quite clearly as speculative in the absence of such a basis. This requirement follows from a desire to be scientific, that is, to use procedures which other investigators can also use to confirm the same facts independently. If such independent confirmation is not possible, then there has been a failure in the procedures that were used. Speculative solutions, on the other hand, still remain to be confirmed or refuted. If a good chance of doing one or the other exists, they may be considered to be hypotheses waiting to be tested; if there is no chance of doing either, they are quite useless and "unscientific."

Science itself, of course, is not just data collecting. Science is concerned with theory-building, that is, with making general statements about phenomena in the real world. Any findings that linguists wish to present must be accommodated within a theory. In the case of linguistics it is a theory of how language works. Theories also require an explicit statement of both the underlying assumptions and the internal units and operations. Consequently, linguists must constantly ask what the various statements they make about a language really mean, that is, what claims they are making through those statements about the specific language and about languages in general.

A theory is also an abstraction. A good theory about language does not merely offer descriptions of particular linguistic events or individual uses of language but offers an account of language events and uses at some much more general level. To use an analogy, an airline timetable describes more than the route of a particular plane on a particular day; it describes a system of flights. Likewise, a chessboard and the rules of chess are not designed for one particular game but for all games of chess. We must note, however, that a language system is much more difficult to characterize than either an airline timetable or the rules of chess. The system was not designed consciously by one or more people, and the possibilities it allows for seem infinite. Moreover, the linguist must try to reconstruct the whole system from data which are fleeting and partial at best. We need only consider how difficult it would be to reconstruct the timetable for a particular airline from occasional visits to airports and flights around the country or to figure out the rules of chess from a number of photographs of chess games in progress. It is just such a problem that confronts the linguist who tries to construct either a grammar or a theory of language.

Any attempt to discuss language in its various contexts should begin with some discussion of the major assumptions about language which linguists share and the major questions which interest them. It may also be desirable to mention some of the issues about which they disagree. Such disagreements have often been well publicized, particularly those in which linguists such as Noam Chomsky have been involved. However, this publicity conceals the fact that the areas of agreement among linguists are much greater than those of disagreement. It is the shifts in emphasis within linguistics, the sometimes over-eager dissemination of new and still untested ideas, and a decided preference for reporting findings which eclipse previous work rather than confirm it that have captured public attention. What continue to be the shared assumptions and the undisputed findings remain overlooked.

The Systematic Nature of Language

One fundamental agreement among linguists is that every language is systematic, for otherwise speakers could not communicate with each other. Speakers rely on what is consistently structured in language to allow them to say things that will not be misunderstood. Speakers of English rely on the fact that *pin, bin, tin,* and *din* begin with four different sounds and that these sounds occur over and over again to distinguish sets of words, for example, *pan, ban, tan,* and *Dan,* and *pail, bail, tail,* and *dale.* They also rely on words occurring in particular orders to indicate certain meaning relationships systematically: for example, a *houseboat* is not a *boathouse,* and *Jack kissed Mary* is different from *Mary kissed Jack.* Describing how language is systematic is one of the fundamental tasks which linguists face. They agree that every language is made up of two subsystems, a subsystem of sounds and another of meanings. Languages have been described as "double articulated" because they possess these two subsystems which operate concurrently. There are units of different kinds in the subsystems, not just one kind of unit in each, but a hierarchy of units of different kinds. In the subsystem of sounds there are the component parts of sounds, sounds themselves, clusters of sounds, syllables, and tone groups, and in the subsystem of meanings there are component parts of meanings, units of meaning, clusters of meanings, and various phrase and clause groups.

For a long time it appeared the greatest contribution that linguists had made to the study of language was in the new units they used to describe language and in the methods they used to establish the units. Even before the development of modern linguistics students of language had found a need for units with which to describe language and had used such terms as *sound, syllable, word,* and *sentence* in discussing language. However, such terms were never clearly defined for the spoken language, the definitions making appeal to intuitions rather than to specific, verifiable, defining characteristics such as actual articulations, definite grammatical markings, or specific capacities for combining and recombining in various ways. A considerable part of language instruction in schools has been devoted to attempts to develop in children the "correct" intuitions about such matters. It is not surprising that in the heyday of structural linguistics it was just these terms that were most readily abandoned to be replaced by terms like *phoneme* and *morpheme* to describe new language units. At the same time an important methodological distinction was developed in order to distinguish between those things that were *emic* and contrastive in a language and those that were *etic* and variable.

The phoneme is the classical unit of linguistics. *Pin* differs from *bin,* so the sound represented by *p* contrasts with the sound represented by *b.* The contrast is phonemic because it produces a difference in meaning: a pin is not a bin. A phoneme is a recurrent contrastive unit in the subsystem of sounds in a language. The phoneme at the beginning of *pin* also occurs at the end of *cap,* after the *s* in *spin,* and in the middle of *happen.* But it also occurs with slightly different pronunciations in the different environments: for example, it is always aspirated (accompanied by a slight puff of air) in *pin*, usually unaspirated in *cap*, and always unaspirated in *spin* and *happen*. It may also appear to be partially voiced (like a *b*) in *spin*. It is this kind of variation that leads to the distinction for which the terms *emic* and *etic* are used. An emic distinction is one that is structurally important in the language: it is a distinction that results in a different message being sent. *He wants a pin* and *He wants a bin* are different in meaning. On the other hand, an etic variation of a phoneme is the way the distinction is made in a particular context: it is the local variation which occurs and which is quite predictable from the surroundings. Compare the situation of two brothers, John and Fred. They are emically different since they cannot be substituted for each other in every environment and they contrast in certain environments, for example, when they are both present together or when one is doing something the other is incapable of doing. However, John is still John whether he is wearing old jeans on the farm, a surgical gown in the operating theater, or a swimsuit in the pool. Etic differences in appearance are determined by the environment in which John appears.

Linguists have attempted to find units of other kinds than the phoneme using the same principle of contrastive distribution (or distinctiveness) in different parts of the overall language system. The morpheme is the equivalent unit in the subsystem of meanings. *Red* and *good* have different meanings, as have *redder* and *better*. But just as the meaning "red" is found in both *red* and *redder* and the meaning "more" is found in both *redder* and *better*, so the meaning "good" is found in both *good* and *better*, even though considerably disguised in the second word. The three morphemes present in the four words are "red," "good," and "more." Linguists have proposed many such units but none with the same feelings of enthusiasm and certainty that accompanied the initial "discovery" of the phoneme. The search still continues for the set of units which has universal application to all languages. Today, a belief in the usefulness of the principle of contrastive distribution unites linguists rather than any set of beliefs about what phonemes are or are not or what units the overall language system is constructed from. As we shall also see in Chapter Three, there is an accompanying search for the psychological correlates of many of the linguistic units that have been proposed. The hypothesis is that the units have a psychological reality as well as a linguistic one.

Not only are the units of the system important but also how the units combine with each other. The combinations of units that are possible are important because it is such combinations which allow a finite number of units in a language to be combined and recombined in an infinite number of ways. Units such as phonemes and morphemes are used over and over again in different combinations to produce unique utterances. Most sentences are unique, as anyone knows who tries to find the same sentence repeated in a book or any number of books.

Linguistic creativity depends on the availability of systems of combinations as well as systems of units. Therefore, understanding the tactics of languages, that is, the total range of possibilities for combining units of various kinds, is crucially important to achieving a complete understanding of how languages are used to convey meaning. Such understanding is not easy to achieve, but linguists have made considerable progress nevertheless toward that achievement, principally through the advances in theorizing attributed to Noam Chomsky.

English has about forty phonemes—*about* because different decisions as to what does or does not constitute a phonemic contrast produce different inventories. However, the phonemes themselves are combinations of an even smaller number of articulatory events, such as lip closure, use of the nasal passage, placement of the tongue, and so on. The phoneme at the beginning of *pin* is articulated through a combination of lip closure followed by a sharp release and puff of air. There is a concurrent lack of activity in the vocal cords. In addition, there are restrictions on how the phonemes can be combined, restrictions to do with the allowable sequences of vowels and consonants, the structures of syllables, the shapes of possible words, and the patterns of omission and combination of sounds that are required in higher level sequences. *Trem* is a possible English syllable but neither *tmre* nor *trme* is, and *rints* is a possible English plural but *rintz* is not. In the subsystem of meanings, there are equivalent restrictions: *a big car* is possible in English but *car big a* is not.

Linguists recognize that only certain combinations of units are possible; hence they are concerned with the tactics of languages—with phonotactics, the combinations of sounds, and with syntax, the combinations of meanings. They also recognize that the tactical arrangements are not simply linear arrangements. The arrangements exhibit different kinds of depth, and their various parts have definite relationships to other parts. That is, units are often component parts of larger units just as they are themselves often composed of component parts: syntactically *The man left* is composed of two parts, *the man* and *left*, each part of which is also composed of two parts, *the* and *man* and *leave* and "past tense." And, of course, the words themselves are composed of sounds in certain patterns. *The man left*, therefore, is composed of a hierarchy of units and arrangements and has a definite "depth."

The simplest approach to describing the tactics of a language is one that simply lists the various possibilities in sets of different kinds. Such an approach is typical of many of the grammars designed to teach Greek and Latin. These grammars contain exhaustive lists of noun declensions and verb conjugations, words listed according to the typical sets in which they occur, rules and exceptions to rules, and example sentences. The users of the grammars must develop their own intuitions about what goes where in sentences and what is not possible, usually under the guidance of someone who has already developed some such intuitions.

If we were to require that a grammar offer a characterization of the linguistic intuitions of speakers of that language, then such "word and paradigm" grammars would be regarded as linguistically deficient. They would fail to tell us just how native speakers of the language felt their language to work. They would leave learners the task of acquiring the right "feeling" for the language but would fail entirely to offer any characterization of that feeling. They would tell us relatively uninteresting things about the language, while ignoring those which we now regard as much more appropriate to investigation, for example, relationships among sentences, linguistic intuition, and characteristics which all languages have (universals).

Another approach is to classify units by kind and level and then to consider that a language is composed of a hierarchy of units of different kinds at different levels, with each level discrete and each unit inviolate. In such an approach both *man* and *men* would be composed of three phonemes, the middle phoneme being different in the two words. However, *men* is a plural noun whereas *man* is singular. Since *men* is an irregular plural (in comparison to a regular plural like *cats*), the particular way in which it demonstrates its "plurality" creates difficulties in a tactical approach which attempts to keep units and levels inviolate in the hierarchy. In *cats* it is possible to say that the *s* for "plural" is added to *cat* as a suffix. But in *men* the change is from *man*, a change of *a* to *e*. However, that leaves *m-n* in *men* as the phonemic realization of the morpheme "man" (with *e* meaning "plural"). So the morpheme "man" has two variants (or allomorphs), *man* and *m-n*, the first occurring in the singular and the second occurring always (and only) with the "plural" *e*. The phonemic and morphemic levels of statement are kept apart but only in a cumbersome way which at times seems counterintuitive. Irregular plural forms like *men, sheep, houses*, and *wives* and irregular past tense forms like *took, bent*, and *brought* created some serious problems for those linguists of the 1940s and 1950s who tried to adopt this "item and arrangement" approach. They were able to separate various things out from language, but they could not put them back together in ways which seemed to make good sense if they consulted their intuitions. But since the prevailing linguistic climate did not favor consulting intuitions, that difficulty could be avoided.

A third approach, the one which most linguists today have adopted, allows units to change into other units and the various levels of any hierarchy to be mixed through various kinds of processes. *Men* is the plural of *man* through a process of pluralization, the final consonant of *it is* goes through a process of devoicing when elision occurs to *it's*, and the underlying structures of sentences go through various transformational processes on their way to becoming actually pronounced sentences. A "deep" structure such as *SOMEONE past be + en take the book [the book past be red]* underlies the actual sentence *The red book was taken* and becomes that sentence after undergoing various transformational processes which add, delete, or rearrange elements. Linguists today believe that this "item and process" approach to language is necessary if they are to provide economical accounts of observed events, accounts which accord with speakers' intuitions about their language and which also capture certain universal principles.

Any statement about a language, whether about its sounds (a phonological statement) or about its meanings (a grammatical statement), is tantamount to a claim that the language works in a certain way. Linguists realize that phonologies and grammars make such claims. They are, therefore, interested in both the tactical possibilities in each language and the units that take part in the tactics. Linguists are also interested in what determines both units and tactics, that is, in those characteristics which all languages share, either because it is in the nature of every language to have such characteristics, or because it is in the nature of every speaker to be able to use only languages of a certain kind. All linguists assume that any new language investigated will have units of very much the same kind as those that are found in previously investigated languages, and that they will be able to describe the units within systems previously employed for other languages. The assumption is that languages and/or speakers are everywhere much the same. They also assume that nothing new and startling is likely to be found in investigating a previously uninvestigated language. On the whole, new and startling ideas in linguistics have not come from such investigations but have come from asking new questions about language, particularly about the English language, in recent years. To some extent this is a surprising fact, for as recently as a generation ago, a number of people felt that English had been almost completely exploited as a source of linguistic inspiration.

The Abstract Nature of Language

A necessary consequence of any serious concern with units and combinations of units is the recognition that linguists are dealing with abstract systems which underlie the observable phenomena of language rather than with the actual phenomena themselves. There is less interest in actual phenomena than in the systems which underlie the phenomena. However, the actual phenomena cannot be disregarded because linguistics is an empirical science, one with a healthy respect for data. Linguists emphasize their concern for underlying systems in the terms they choose. They use terms like *data, surface* (or *superficial*) *structure*, and *performance* to describe actual observations; on the other hand, they use terms like *facts, deep* (or *underlying*) *structure*, and *competence* to describe underlying systems. Linguists are interested in what Humboldt called *innere Sprachform* and in Saussure's *langue*, the language norms of groups, rather than in his *parole*, the the individual usages and variations. Therefore, they are concerned with the abstract system of language to which all speakers are assumed to have access because they are speakers rather than with particular instances of language, which may be imperfect in any one or more of several ways because of the actual situations in which language is used: in noisy circumstances; while tired; during interruptions; for working out ideas; and so on. However, linguists must construct group norms from observations made on just a few individuals, sometimes even a single individual. The result is a rather interesting paradox in that often the individual is made to represent the whole, but what is actually unique to the individual must remain inaccessible to the linguist in the absence of investigations of numerous individuals, even possibly of all the individuals who collectively are the whole.

In recent years the terms *competence* and *performance* have been used to refer to something like the distinctions between *langue* and *parole*. Competence has taken on the additional meaning of the knowledge of the language system that every speaker is presumed to have, and performance the additional meaning of those things the individual actually does in attempting to make use of that knowledge in communicating. In both sets of distinctions a dichotomy exists between some kind of inner form and outer substance. The inner form is an abstraction—group language norms or knowledge—behind the outer substance of actually observed behavior—the actual usages of individuals on specific occasions. The distinctions are not without their difficulties in interpretation. Does the inability of most people to understand sentences like *The boy the man the gardener met heard saw the car* with its embedding of *The gardener met the man* in *The man heard the boy* and of both in *The boy saw the car* arise from a failure of competence or one of performance? That is, should any grammar of English be written to exclude such a combination of clauses or should the possibility be allowed and the difficulty which arises in understanding the combination be attributed to cognitive rather than linguistic factors? It is not at all clear how such a question can be answered.

Language is abstract in still another sense. A language system is a system for relating meanings and sounds. Meanings, however, are abstractions. They are also complex as philosophers have long known and are unconstrained physically in the ways that sounds are constrained. Sounds must be produced in real time through the physical mechanism of the throat, mouth, and nose. They must also be heard if they are to be understood. Meanings do not have the same limitations. The domain of meaning is the domain of all possible worlds because people can talk about anything, real and imaginary. Meanings are not physical events in the same sense as sounds. Meanings may even be nonlinear, that is, be coinstantaneous in thoughts, but sounds must be linear, produced one after the other as physical events. One possible consequence is that the linguistic structure that expresses meaning may be very abstract and largely nonlinear. It may be very unlike the structure of actually observed sentences. Many linguists believe that extremely abstract units and processes must be postulated to account for the complexities of meaning in language. It is a concern for just such abstractions that predominates in recent linguistics.

However, once abstractions of this kind become readily acceptable because they appear to be necessary, possibilities exist for inventing all kinds of abstractions to explain data. An abstraction is justified only if it offers the most parsimonious account available of the data it is designed to cover. Of two abstractions the one which offers the more parsimonious account is to be preferred. However, in a "soft" area like language and in related soft areas like psychology, sociology, and ethology, parsimony does not always prove to be a completely effective guide since it is not always clear what the relevant data are in each case. A good empirical reason must always exist for creating a new abstraction, but what appears to one investigator to be a sound reason may not appear to be so for another. An overemphasis on abstractions can also easily lead to a kind of scholasticism, just as it readily leads to speculation. Therefore, there is a healthy questioning in contemporary linguistics of the need for any new abstractions which are proposed, together with a continual testing of abstractions with data to ensure the continuance of the empirical tradition in linguistics.

While all linguists agree that language systems are abstract, deciding just how abstract they are remains an issue. No linguist, however, regards language systems as being without depth of some kind. Even linguists who consider that a language is some kind of behavioral system and is learned in ways similar to rats learning the details of mazes, or who propose that every linguistic event has a specific neurological correlate, must have recourse to abstractions: universal principles of learning in the one case and general characteristics of brain function in the other. All good scientific work deals in abstractions, but abstractions which are strongly rooted in empirical observation.

Irregularity and Variability

Linguists have long experienced difficulty in dealing with data that do not quite fit a particular statement they wish to make about a language. Sometimes, of course, the difficulty arises because the particular statement is inaccurate; the recalcitrant data are evidence that a more appropriate statement is required. This difficulty is most apparent when the language under investigation is a little known one. As more and more knowledge is acquired early statements about units and relationships must be revised continually to accord with newly discovered facts. Yet there are still other kinds of data which cannot properly be treated by simply recasting a statement. Such data seem not to require a better, in the sense of a more accurate, statement, but to require a statement of quite a different kind. That is, they force a complete reassessment of the principles which have gone into the writing of the grammar itself.

As we mentioned previously, irregular forms in a language sometimes create problems of description. In English the plurals of *cat, dog,* and *church* are *cats, dogs,* and *churches,* but the plurals of *man, child,* and *datum* are *men, children,* and *data.* Such irregularities are exceptions to a widespread pattern, but they are also invariable in that the plural of *man* is always *men* and never anything else. This kind of consistent irregularity creates problems when rules must be written to describe the distribution of certain data. However, the irregularities can be regarded as the exceptions which "prove" the rule: the rule works for all cases except those specifically mentioned as irregular, and these irregularities are listed exhaustively as exceptions.

As different kinds of rules are written and different levels of abstraction are encompassed or rejected in the writing of the rules, decisions as to what the exceptions are may well change. This kind of irregularity is therefore tied inextricably to the concept of regularity, and as that concept changes so will the irregularities. If the *s* plural type (*cat-cats, dog-dogs, judge-judges*) is regarded as regular in English, then every other plural type (*datum-data, corpus-corpora, mouse-mice*) will be irregular, even though there may be numerous examples of some of the types. However, if some of these other types are regarded as regular in a recasting of the rules of English pluralization, the number of irregularities will be reduced.

Considerable variability as well as irregularity is found in linguistic data. There may be little aspiration at the beginning of *pin,* or the aspiration may be considerable; *stickin'* and *sticking* may alternate as pronunciations of the same word; the vowel in *man* may be considerably nasalized (that is, pronounced through the nose as well as the mouth) or not nasalized at all; and *Did you eat yet?* may be slowly and carefully articulated or sound something like *Jeejet?* It is not easy to devise linguistic systems which can account for variability of this kind and for the variability associated with age, sex, regional, and social class differences in speaking. Partly for this reason some linguists choose to describe only the language of a single speaker—generally referred to as an *idiolect*—through careful elicitation of data in well controlled circumstances, while others describe an idealized linguistic competence rather than the complexities of linguistic performance. In both cases the result is statements about the invariant units and processes which underlie what are readily acknowledged to be the concrete but variable data.

Irregularity and variability have an important consequence for the statements that linguists make about languages. The statements never appear to be complete, for there are nearly always data that cannot quite be made to fit even the most carefully wrought statement: there is a gap somewhere or something left over. The linguist Edward Sapir once declared that all grammars leak. Sapir was actually talking about an intrinsic characteristic of all languages rather than about particular grammars that linguists had constructed for one or more languages. Such leakage seems to be important in explaining not only why linguists suffer some of the frustrations they do over irregularity and variability, but also why it is that any language is like it is at any time and why it changes. A language is not a perfectly wrought system complete unto itself and existing in splendid isolation from everything else. No more than a man is a language an island. Yet linguists often find a certain usefulness in treating languages as though they existed or could exist in splendid isolation from speakers and speaking. They are able thereby to produce descriptions which focus on sets of invariant relationships among fixed and well-defined units. Splendid results have been achieved, and continue to be achieved, in this way, but they cannot possibly exhaust all that can be said about language because the assumption that languages are perfect, independent systems is not really justified.

Variability also creates problems of another kind for linguists. Speakers of a language are aware of variation within the language: their everyday linguistic behavior demonstrates such awareness. They know that people speak differently on different occasions. However, it is an awareness they cannot usually describe consciously. Individuals are well able to make the subtle adjustments in pronunciation, word choice, and grammatical structure that different situations require. They seem to know the correct percentages of occurrence of particular forms and to be able to realize just the right percentages of those forms. They know just how often they must alternate between *in'* and *ing* participle forms, slur words together (*Jeejet?*), omit syllables (*'bout*), and use words like *ain't*. Recently, some linguists have tried to take such variability into account in writing grammatical descriptions, but the resulting statements about the probabilities of occurrence of forms do not fit easily into established ways of writing grammars. These ways require the writing of rules which state that *X* becomes *Y* in certain definite circumstances ("cat" plus "plural" always becomes *cats* and *he* plus *be* becomes *he is* when *be* is stressed). They do not state that *X* becomes *Y* sixty per cent of the time and *Z* forty per cent but that the actual conditions governing the difference are not fully known so that it is not possible to predict that *stickin'* will occur rather than *sticking*.

Statements of probability also create problems of a different order. A grammar of a language is in one sense a claim about the knowledge that speakers of that language have acquired. If some of that knowledge is subtle statistical knowledge about probabilities, how do speakers acquire that knowledge? It is difficult enough to attempt to explain how they acquire abstract linguistic knowledge. How do they also acquire sensitivity to the subtle differences in probability?

What is an organism like that not only acquires abstract categorial knowledge, that is, knowledge that something is or is not in a definite category (something is a *p* not a *b*, is *man* not *men*), but also acquires variable probabilistic knowledge, that is, knowledge that some variant is more appropriate than another (use *stickin'* not *sticking*) depending on certain environmental characteristics which are extremely complex and also highly variable?

In recent years linguists have given more and more attention to issues such as those just mentioned. In Chapter Six we shall examine some of the solutions which they have proposed. For the moment we shall merely note that the concerns for accounting for language variation and for describing how language is actually used in speaking have led to a considerable broadening of the data base of linguistics and several reassessments of the scope of linguistics as a science.

Some Controversies in Linguistics

While linguists share many assumptions and understandings about language and agree about such matters as the importance of system and contrast, they do disagree to a certain extent on a number of issues. These disagreements result from different linguists asking different questions in their work and proposing different answers to some of the same problems. Linguists, like other scientists, sometimes differ about the nature and ends of scientific inquiry. They may even disagree on which concerns are properly linguistic concerns and which are not: Is linguistics concerned with what is in human minds or with what is uttered by human tongues? The generalizability of results, that is, the general import of particular claims, is also a frequent concern. How specific is a particular claim or how general? Does it merely state a local condition in a particular language (English noun plurals are usually formed by adding an *s* ending), or does it make some universal claim (all languages are capable of expressing pluralization in the noun phrases)? Ideas as to what are proper data sources and adequate methods for assembling and evaluating data also vary. Much of the linguistic discussion of the last decade has focused on just such issues as these.

A question fundamental to all scientific inquiry concerns the ends of that inquiry. Are the ends to be construed as truths or hypotheses? Does the scientific quest have for its goal the revelation of the truth of things? Or is making the best hypotheses possible from the data the most any scientist can hope for? In real life, the substantive results of both approaches may be much the same, but their rhetoric is likely to be quite different: in the first case facts are discovered; in the second case hypotheses are postulated.

In linguistics these two approaches have been called the *God's truth* approach and the *hocus-pocus* approach. Some linguists have always adopted one approach or the other, but shifts of allegiance are not unknown. The *God's truth* approach is a very powerful one: it is after all the quest for certainty. On the whole linguists have avoided adopting the God's truth approach. They have recognized how much there is still to learn about language and languages and have resisted the temptation to jump to premature conclusions. So tentative hypothesis formation has predominated rather than assertion that particular discoveries are instances of truth. Of course, such discoveries have been announced from time to time, and it is not unusual for a linguist to announce a program for discovering the truth of things. Those who do have sometimes achieved impressive results, even though all the claims about the importance of those results may not be widely accepted. The hocus-pocus approach has achieved results too: indeed most linguistic work must be regarded as the product of such an approach. The fact that these results are sometimes conveyed in a manner which suggests that one set of conclusions is as good as any other set should not detract from the value of the many insights into language that have been obtained. There is generally a healthy tentativeness and lack of dogmatism which bodes well for the future of linguistics.

The two approaches may not really be so different in respect to the claims that result. Only a small amount of coverage of data may be attempted and no very profound claims made. Data can be inventoried, for example, and nothing claimed beyond the fact, on the one hand, that the resulting inventory is *the* system that speakers know or, on the other hand, that it seems to be the best way of accommodating the observations. For example, a chart showing the phonemic contrasts in English may be said to represent an English speaker's knowledge of the system of English sound contrasts or to be the best hypothesis the linguist can presently make about that system. In both cases a kind of observational adequacy is sought. Only actually observed events are treated, not intuited relationships, if any, among those events, nor underlying causes of the events. However, a further level of adequacy may be attempted, a level of descriptive adequacy which attempts to record observations in a way which agrees with speakers' knowledge and intuitions. Descriptive adequacy is, therefore, an account of linguistic competence. A descriptively adequate statement attempts to show how speakers of a language intuitively relate the bits and pieces of their language: active sentences to passive sentences; questions to answers; embedded clauses to sentences; possible words to actual words; and so on. An explanatorily adequate statement would further claim that the descriptively adequate account takes the form it does because it is in the nature of language that the form must be so. It would provide the reasons for the choice of a particular description over all others in that it would indicate why intuition must take the form it does, for example, because it is in the nature of language that speakers must have the kinds of linguistic intuitions they have and perform the kinds of linguistic operations they do, or it is in the nature of speakers, or both.

In their work linguists always try to achieve observational adequacy, the minimum requirement of any scientific endeavor. Linguistics is an empirical science. Many try also to achieve some degree of descriptive adequacy, and much linguistic discussion focuses on defining descriptive adequacy, that is, on deciding just what kinds of intuitions and relationships must be accounted for. Explanatory adequacy is a much more elusive goal in that it requires a search for universal principles of language and possibly of mind. But it is a goal that is very much the concern of many linguists today. The long commitment to observational adequacy made speculation unpopular for a while in linguistics. The concern for descriptive adequacy which grew out of Chomsky's work freed linguists to investigate new problems and made possible some promising new approaches to explaining why language is the way it is. It also aroused considerable hope that useful linguistic universals, that is, statements applicable to all languages, could be discovered or postulated (depending on one's philosophical viewpoint).

Some of the differences about goals and claims also result from the kinds of methodological differences that abound in linguistics. A preoccupation with methodology has long characterized linguistics and even today forms a frequent subject of scholarly publication. However, no longer are linguists as interested as they once were in writing manuals which, in cookbook fashion, explained how linguistic data should be processed to produce the "correct" solution. For example, manuals on how to use certain procedures to arrive at the phonemic system of a language or at its grammatical system or on how to write grammatical rules are no longer the linguistic "best sellers" they once were. "Discovery procedures" of that kind are quite unfashionable today. They are regarded as making claims which cannot really be substantiated and also as being too restrictive in the issues they address.

Moreover, it is possible to argue that no working linguist ever used them and that they were never more than "pseudo-procedures." The working linguist either did not have the time to use them or could not have used them because they would not work very successfully with real language data in the mechanical way they were supposed to work. They were really too powerful, promising more than they could possibly deliver: the truth about things if only one were to proceed through certain very precise operations in a completely objective manner. Today, linguists are concerned with finding the most useful data sources for their work and with trying to work out how best to exploit those sources. How does one best gain access to linguistic intuition? How can one most accurately assess the extent of variation in a language and describe individual speakers' sensitivities concerning such variation? The methodological issues are still present; the form they take is different.

A continuing topic of discussion is whether linguistic data should be acquired solely through observation or through a combination of observation and introspection. Linguists have long been observers of language events. Recently, many have also examined their own intuitions for further data about those events or have tried to tap the intuitions of native speakers of the language they are investigating. Some have even claimed that linguistic descriptions should be written only by native speakers of the languages in question, since native speakers alone have the intuitions necessary for such a task. Their position is that if linguistics is to achieve descriptive adequacy, then one kind of data that cannot be ignored are the linguistic intuitions of the speakers, the special knowledge they have of relationships in the language and of what can and cannot be said. The further claim is made that such intuitions can be tapped reliably and that conclusions drawn from data acquired from a single speaker may be generalized to a whole population, that is, that the conclusions are valid for the language as a whole. Critics of this position argue that the only reliable and valid data are those that can be acquired through the use of carefully designed procedures which concentrate on language being used for communication. Linguistic data must neither be artificially elicited from one or two individuals nor dredged in some fashion out of the head. They feel that this "secular" origin or linguistic data will bring more valid results than will data which originate in the "closets of the mind."

A second topic of discussion concerns the trust to be placed in either an inductive approach to a problem or in a deductive approach. For a considerable time linguists favored the use of inductive approaches which required extensive data collection prior to the formulation of possible hypotheses. They assumed that given lots of data and certain procedures for handling these data, they would then be able to abstract the system from the data. More recently, a considerable number of linguists have argued for employing a deductive approach to problems, for very early stating alternative hypotheses and then deliberately seeking data to confirm or refute the hypotheses. They believe that scientific inquiry is concerned with hypothesis formation and testing rather than with data collection and systemization. They claim that a belief that data somehow can be collected prior to hypothesis formation is false since some principles of inclusion and exclusion must always operate in the actual selection of the data. Consequently, any procedure used to select data implicitly acknowledges the existence of certain theoretical assumptions. These linguists are oriented toward problems and issues rather than toward classifications and derivative systemizations. Those who disfavor deductive approaches do so on the grounds that sometimes those who adopt such approaches appear to have little respect for real language data. They claim that data are too often selected to fit theories rather than theories built to accommodate data. It is doubtful, however, that a practicing linguist must adopt an either-or approach, that is, be either completely an inductivist or completely a deductivist. The linguist must respect data, must realize that data have no independent existence (except in a rather uninteresting sense), must be prepared to go beyond the data to a level of abstraction which requires theory building, and must constantly test the results of such building. Both inductivism and deductivism find their anchor in empiricism, for their results cannot be at variance with events that are known to exist in the real world.

One possible weakness of either approach is that some of the fundamental experimental concepts found in other sciences are only slowly finding their way into linguistics. Linguists have been much more concerned with "naturalistic" data than with "experimental" data, so they have been slow to adopt some of the concepts from the experimental sciences. They are obviously seriously concerned with the validity of their results, that is, they worry that they are really talking about what they claim to be talking about, which is what the concept of validity is all about. The discussion of different kinds of adequacy shows that validity continues to be a concern of linguists. It may be that overemphasis on the hocus-pocus approach to issues can be interpreted as showing that the concept of validity is not held in high regard in linguistics. However, it is better seen as an expression of tentativeness. On the other hand, the high seriousness of the God's truth approach is a *prima facie* attempt to deal with the issue of validity. Linguists also try to achieve reliability in their results. Reliability means that others should get the same results in similar circumstances. From time to time though, disagreements about the data, inconsistencies in observations (particularly observations of intuitions), and the existence of unexpected irregularities, variants, and counterexamples produce failures in reliability. However, so long as linguistics retains its empirical foundation it will continue to be concerned with improving the reliability of it results.

Linguistic data are often presented in very simple ways, but strong assertions may be made about their import. The graphs, charts, and displays which accompany many discussions tend to present data in simple, fixed categories. Since language makes use of categorial distinctions, that is, items either fit into a category or do not, it should be quite easy to make the necessary decisions and to present data accordingly. That is the assumption behind such presentations. Linguists also tend to say that results are "interesting" rather than that they are "significant," and almost never in the way experimental psychologists do. Statistical tests of significance are almost unknown in linguistics. Instead, readers are invited to inspect the data and agree with the conclusions that are set forth. Many linguists have also adopted extremely powerful devices such as rigid formalisms and rule systems to handle language data. However, there has been a decline in the use of such devices in recent years and a whole array of much weaker devices has been adopted which are more in keeping with the kinds of observations and conclusions that seem feasible given the present state of linguistic knowledge.

The Autonomy of Linguistics

To a considerable extent modern linguistics has developed independently of other disciplines. This autonomous development has occurred partly in reaction to the previous mixture, dating back to the Greeks, of linguistic study with philosophical and literary matters. Linguists have tended to define their area of interest very narrowly, and the development of subspecialties within linguistics has led to even further narrowing. The consequence of such specialization is that often general questions about language with widespread importance are given far less attention than very specific and sometimes quite isolated matters. From time to time attempts are made to relate such matters to things that happen in the mouth, ear, and brain, to psychological and social contexts, to processes of learning, memory, and language acquisition, to other communication systems, and to the issues of change and variation. But these attempts are relatively infrequent. It is much more usual for a linguist to consider a particular set of linguistic data or a particular problem in only the narrowest of linguistic contexts rather than in the broader contexts of language use.

As we have suggested, in part this narrowing was a deliberate reaction to an intellectual climate in which linguistic issues were confused with philosophical and literary issues. The linguist's emphasis on the spoken language and on inductive procedures allowed linguistic concerns to be separated from the concerns of others. Then the apparent uniqueness of language began to stand out: every language appeared to be a self-contained dual system of enormous complexity displaying an arbitrary relationship between its forms and meanings. Saussure in particular regarded language as a well-defined object, something that could be studied for its own sake and as an end itself. Consequently, linguistics emerged as an autonomous discipline, and from time to time workers in other disciplines, for example, anthropology and psychology, looked to linguistics for concepts or for hints on how to proceed. Some anthrophologists found the Whorf hypothesis that language structure influences thought processes, the emic-etic distinction, and systems for analyzing behavior into component parts particularly attractive in their work, just as certain psychologists found the phoneme and transformational processes good topics for their investigations.

While the uniqueness of language is beyond dispute, linguists have found it necessary to temper their strongest claims about such uniqueness. Every claim for uniqueness of any kind, either for language itself or for the methods appropriate to linguistic investigation, must be based on an examination of *all* relevant evidence. Some of that evidence is found to lie outside what have been regarded from time to time to be the proper bounds of language study, particularly when those bounds have been established even more narrowly within a subspeciality within linguistics. The boundaries of language study, therefore of linguistics, have had to be constantly redrawn. Linguists acknowledge that thoroughgoing scientific inquiry rejects special pleading just as much as it rejects ad hoc solutions. "Occam's razor" is as useful in linguistics as it is elsewhere: *Entia non sunt multiplicanda praeter necessitatem* ("Do not multiply entities beyond necessity"). Linguists must demonstrate that what they claim to be unique in language and in their discipline is not just a special plea made from either ignorance or self-imposed blindness. Special pleading, of course, is one of the great dangers of the modern specialization of knowledge: the modern structuring of knowledge with its consequent fragmentation and the modern training of specialists have served to increase isolation, build barriers, and prevent certain kinds of connections to other specializations from being made. The result is a kind of paradox: specialization increases knowledge in one direction only by preventing its increase in others. And attempts to produce interdisciplinary solutions have rarely been successful.

What one proposes to do in linguistics depends on the questions that one considers to be important and on the availability of data that bear on those questions. The scope of linguistics is not obvious in the sense that everyone must agree on what linguistics should be about. No *a priori* grounds exist for making decisions about the domain of linguistic inquiry. In a sense one is neither right nor wrong in specifying a particular domain: such specification is largely a matter of personal preference. The key issue in each case is what the investigator proceeds to do in exploring the specified domain and what insights into language are gained from that exploration. Only if nothing is gained is the search fruitless. Of course, if much is gained the search is extremely worthwhile.

Language is part of total human behavior. Currently, linguistic investigation does not proceed in a vacuum with only language itself the subject of concern. Such a narrow pursuit would have its virtues, but it would also have serious drawbacks, particularly the resulting tendency to consider everything linguistic as unique and qualitatively different from anything else. Exclusiveness and special pleading would be as dangerous in linguistics as they are elsewhere: it would be ad hocness writ large. Language is best considered in relation to a wide variety of human capacities, behaviors, and functions. Principles found valid in the study of those domains can be considered in studies of language phenomena, and vice versa. Parsimony demands no less.

Language is also an instrument of mind. It is a tool like a wheel, hammer, or needle—a tool basic to human survival. In the past, linguists have tended to concentrate on describing the tool both independently of other tools and of the uses it serves. Admittedly, language is a complex tool, largely abstract in its nature, and with a particularly fascinating relationship to its users. It can do no harm to look at the tool, the uses of the tool, and the contexts of its use. As we now know, such an endeavor may even provide some worthwhile rewards.

References

Three "classic" texts on linguistics are those of Bloomfield (1933), Sapir (1921), and Saussure (1959). Two influential texts describing pre-Chomskyan structural linguistics are those of H.A. Gleason (1961) and Hockett (1958). Noam Chomsky's views are set forth in (1957, 1965, 1966, 1972) and summarized by Lyons (1970a). Recent introductions to linguistics include, among others, those of Falk (1973), Fromkin and Rodman (1974), Langacker (1973), Liles (1975), and Wardhaugh (1972). Robins (1968) provides a brief history of linguistics.

Adams (1972), DeVito (1973), Dingwall (1971), Giglioli (1972), Lyons (1970b), Miller (1973a), and Minnis (1971) are useful collections of papers on a variety of linguistic topics. Books by Brown (1958), Burling (1970), DeVito (1970), Farb (1974), and Slobin (1971) also provide broad coverage of issues. The 1973 Summer issue of *Daedalus* entitled "Language as a Human Problem" is a particularly useful collection of papers. It has been reprinted as Haugen and Bloomfield (1974).

For the reception given *Webster's Third* see Sledd and Ebbitt (1962). "Double articulated" is from Martinet (1964). Hockett (1954) discusses "word and paradigm," "item and arrangement," and "item and process" grammars. The *langue-parole* distinction is from Saussure (1959) and the *competence-performance* distinction from N. Chomsky (1965). Hymes (1971) discusses the concepts of competence and performance in linguistic theory. For a discussion of variability see Labov (1972c). The God's truth/hocus-pocus distinction is from Householder (1952). N. Chomsky (1965) discusses problems of adequacy in linguistic statements; Abercrombie (1965) criticizes pseudo-procedures in linguistics; and Labov (1972c) makes the strongest plea for a "secular" linguistics, particularly in his chapter entitled "The Study of Language in Its Social Context."

2

The
Physical
Context

The Primacy of Speech

That language is primarily speech is a basic concept in modern linguistics. In part
the concept results from reaction to a previous overemphasis on philosophical
and literary matters, but mainly it results from the readily observable facts that
while speaking is universal writing is not, that the written forms of languages are
based on their spoken forms not vice versa, and that in the history of both species
and individual the development of speech precedes that of writing. Linguists
consider the primacy of speech to be a well established fact, so the "phonetic
bias" of much linguistic investigation is not at all surprising.

It is of some interest that human communication depends on sounds produced by mouths and perceived by ears rather than on some other sensory system
or systems, particularly the gestural-visual system. Other species communicate
through visual systems (for example, certain species of fishes) or combinations
of visual and call systems (for example, certain species of birds and animals).
Although the human species is predominantly visual, good vision being necessary
to ensure survival in the trees and on the savannas, that part of communication
which depends on gesture—facial expression, posture, movement—is very much
subordinate to and underdeveloped in comparison with that part which shows

no such dependency, language itself. Humans use gestural communication either to supplement speech or sometimes to replace speech; hand waves, blows, kisses, and shrugs may communicate at times even better than words. The universal use of such gestures has led more than one investigator to consider them to be more primitive than speech, even to be the precursors of language.

A communication system which employs gestures and depends on vision has serious limitations. If it engages the hands, they cannot be used for carrying. If there is no light, the gestures cannot be seen. If the potential users are out of view of each other, no communication is possible. Gesture inventories themselves must necessarily be very small because of limitations of production, recognition, and memory. We know, too, how ambiguous gestures can be. On the other hand, the way in which languages use sound allows speakers to send any one of an infinite set of messages and allows listeners to recognize which message has been sent. Information theorists have calculated that the channel which sound provides for human communication is vastly superior to the one which vision would have provided.

The human species, of course, has developed a special means of very efficient communication using vision in its development of writing systems. Such systems are always based on the spoken language in one way or another, and individuals almost always acquire their knowledge of one or more of them after they have acquired the skills of listening and speaking. Certain writing systems—English is sometimes cited as an example—apparently cause some of their learners considerable difficulty; sometimes that difficulty is ascribed to the complexity of the visual and cognitive processes involved in mastering the details and abstractions of the system. On the other hand, children learning to speak their first language usually experience little or no difficulty, even in situations in which severe handicaps exist.

As we shall see in Chapter Eight, the fact that language makes use of sounds in systematic ways differentiates it very clearly from all other kinds of communication systems. Different species can communicate in different ways: visual, tactile, chemical, olfactory, or auditory. The human species alone uses the vocal-auditory channel in a very special way and alone appears to have the capacity for doing so. Humans are also unique in the vast auditory memories they possess. However, the communications systems of certain other species apparently exhibit some of the same general characteristics which provide the foundation for the human system. These characteristics may be present only in greater quantity in language so that the human system is merely quantitatively different from others. On the other hand, the human system may have unique characteristics and be qualitatively different from all others. We shall also return to these questions in Chapter Eight.

Human language makes use of sounds produced through the mouth and nose and perceived by the ears. No more than in dogs and cats do mouths, noses, and ears in humans exist only for making and perceiving sounds. Mouths exist for eating, noses for breathing, and ears for monitoring the environment. Speaking is a secondary "overlaid" function of mouths and noses, and listening to the sounds of speech is a similar overlaid function of ears. Having two ears allows people to locate sound sources and to perceive the environment as a rich auditory texture in the same way that having two eyes allows them depth and richness in vision. Experiments which delay the arrival of sound for a fraction of a second to one ear but not to the other or which increase or decrease the intensity of sound in one ear result in listeners incorrectly locating the source of sound. Creating a slight delay in arrival at the right ear moves a sound source further to the left; however, a slight increase in the intensity of the sound to the right ear will move the sound source back to the right again. Such binaurality, together with the accompanying ability to move the head very slightly in order to compare very slight differences in sound, is not only important to people in locating the sources of sounds but is also important in allowing them to focus on specific sounds and types of sound. Humans can localize a sound source to within about ten degrees in accuracy. They can also pick out one voice from a number of voices or hear two or more sounds together without those sounds necessarily blending to form a single sound. In like circumstances two or more colors always blend to form one.

There appears to be a further interesting consequence of binaurality in humans: the right ear seems to be more responsive to speech sounds than the left, which in turn responds better to musical and environmental sounds. The right ear is also more adept at perceiving consonants than the left ear. If the right ear is given the stimulus word *top* while the left ear is given the stimulus word *pop* under the same conditions, the listener will tend to report hearing the first word rather than the second. However, the words *pop* to one ear and *pip* to the other will produce no trend in responses. There seems to be no ear preference for vowels. These last findings may not be so surprising, because, as we shall see later in this chapter, one important fact about human language is that some of its functions are lateralized in the human brain, that is, located in one side rather than in the other.

The Phonetic Basis of Language

Linguists usually begin any consideration of the use of sound in language with a discussion of the events that occur in the upper respiratory tract during the production of speech. Their previously mentioned phonetic bias causes them to focus very closely on how sounds are articulated rather than on how they are perceived. Such an approach is quite defensible for a number of reasons. Articulations can be observed: it is quite possible to see and feel what happens in many parts of the mouth. On the other hand, ears are quite inaccessible to observation except through the use of sophisticated procedures and devices. Other procedures and devices can also be used to observe what happens in speech, but linguists generally find it quite easy to justify not using sound spectrography, dynamic palatography, electromyography, high speed cinematography, ultrasonic analysis, cineradiography, corrective and experimental surgery, and so on, in order to investigate the physical parameters of speaking and listening. They argue that the really important facts about the sound systems which underlie the observations cannot be established through such use. The devices record only the physical events that are happening: which parts of the articulatory or listening apparatus are moving; what air pressures exist in the various parts of the throat, mouth, and nose; what electrical discharges are occurring as muscles move; and so on. But the really important facts underlie these events: they are abstractions such as phonemes, and no device can actually reveal a phoneme. The observable events are realizations of these abstract facts but cannot be used easily and mechanically to isolate those facts. Hence the failure so far to produce typewriters which automatically type out messages which are spoken to them and other such devices.

The linguistic bias is toward a consideration of how sounds are articulated in a language. The concept of what sounds are is critical. The sounds that interest the linguist are those that can result in a difference in meaning if one is substituted for another, that is, sounds as phonemes rather than sounds as breath groups, accent groups, syllables, or words. Breathing is mentioned only incidentally, with sometimes a reference made to the fact that in speaking the usual rhythms of breathing are quite changed, exhalation dominating inhalation so far as timing is concerned, but without any of the disturbances such as hyperventilation, that are usually associated with changes in breathing patterns. Accent groups, syllables, and words are eliminated as possible units for consideration because they are either too large or units from a different linguistic subsystem, as in the case of words. Units smaller than the traditional phonemes—for example, phonetic features like aspiration, lip closure, or voicing—may be eliminated because they are too small. Phonetics, therefore, concerns itself with the articulation of sounds, and the phonemic principle in one way or another influences the concept of what a sound is. Phonetic notation, the recording in writing of such sounds, has a further bias toward recording sounds and sound types which occur in those languages that were first studied in this way, particularly the major languages of Europe. Even a cursory inspection of the International Phonetic Alphabet (IPA) reveals that bias.

The vocal apparatus itself consists of three basic cavities: the throat, the mouth, and the nose. The lungs are a fourth cavity but are usually ignored in discussions of the sounds of language, even though they do control the airstream. Most speech employs air exiting from the lungs. The air pressure in various parts of the throat and mouth varies considerably during exhalation, and the airstream itself passing between the vocal cords is used to produce any voicing that occurs. However, the precise function of the lungs in speech and their exact relationship to to other parts of the articulatory apparatus are unclear, as is the relationship of breath pulses to units such as syllables and larger intonation groups.

A convenient way to describe sounds is to do so in terms of certain basic parameters that account for the events which occur in the throat, mouth, and nose. One basic parameter is the state of the vocal cords: Are they vibrating so as to set up a condition called voicing (all the sounds in *bathe*), or are they lax and therefore producing voiceless sounds (the first and last sounds in *path*)? A second parameter is the involvement or noninvolvement of the nasal cavity in the production of sounds. If the air exits fully or partially through the nose, then the sounds are nasal or nasalized (the first and last sounds in *Ming*); if no air exits through the nose, then the sounds are oral (all the sounds in *pat*). A third parameter has to do with whether the exiting airstream is noticeably interrupted or whether it is allowed a free passage. Interrupted sounds are called consonants and noninterrupted sounds are called vowels. Some sounds, of course, are marginal, possessing both consonant and vowel characteristics because of the kind of interruption which is involved (the initial sounds of *led* and *red*). Still another parameter is concerned with the types of interruption: a complete stoppage (the consonants in *bat*) or a particular type of frictional interference (the consonants in *this*). The locations of the interruptions and various combinations of type and location are also of interest. With noninterrupted vowel sounds the exact position of the tongue in the mouth, whether it is high (*pin*) or low (*pan*), front (*pan*) or back (*pawn*), and the shaping of the lips are further important parameters.

A large number of sounds can be described by reference to the above parameters. The sound at the beginning of *pin* is a voiceless bilabial stop in contrast to the sounds at the beginnings of *bin*, a voiced bilabial stop, and *thin*, a voiceless interdental fricative. All three words contain a high front unrounded vowel in the middle and end in a voiced alveolar nasal. *Pan*, on the other hand, contains a low front unrounded vowel, and *owe* is merely a mid back rounded vowel. Additional parameters can be employed to make still finer distinctions. For example, the initial sound in *pin* is also aspirated and the vowel of *owe* has a certain gliding quality which can easily be observed if it is compared with the vowel found in the French word, *eau*.

Phoneticians are able to make exceedingly fine distinctions in the uses of various parts of the vocal apparatus in the production of different sounds. The possible combinations and variations are vast. The tongue can be positioned in an enormous variety of ways in the mouth, and each different position results in a different sound not always discriminably different to the ear. As we shall see, listeners can detect fine differences between sounds, especially in controlled laboratory conditions, but most such differences are imperceptible in ordinary speaking and listening, there being too much noise in the environment for exceedingly minute discriminations to be made. However, because each language exploits only certain rather gross phonetic differences through its phonemic system, listeners are not required to make such discriminations.

Sounds may vary in other ways too. They can be spoken more loudly than neighboring sounds: the syllables of *insult* are pronounced with differing intensities in *an ínsult* and *to insúlt*. Different pitch levels may be used too, as in the final syllables of *I asked John* with low falling pitch and *I asked John?* with high rising pitch. There may also be different kinds of transitions between neighboring sounds, as in *a name* and *an aim*, and considerable variation in overriding patterns of pitch, stress and rhythm, the so-called "intonation contours" of a language. Again, minute distinctions can be detected and described, but it is often difficult to decide whether a particular distinction makes a difference so far as communication is concerned, and, if in fact it does, how the whole system of such differences works in the language.

Some Issues

This approach to phonetics owes much of its undoubted success to the linguist having certain ideas about what is likely to be found in a language even before any analysis is begun and also having the skills necessary to carry out the exploratory work. The approach assumes that certain kinds of contrasts exist and are discoverable, that is, it assumes the existence of a phonemic system in every language. It also assumes that certain parameters will be important in that system: for example, there will be a consonant-vowel distinction, almost certainly a voiced-voiceless contrast in the consonants, a set of vowels distinguished from one another through differences in tongue height and frontness-backness, a possible set of nasal vowels contrasting with the set of oral vowels, and so on. The exact contrasts and details for a specific language will have to be worked out rather carefully, but the major characteristics of the system are not likely to be very different from those of previously described systems. The phonemic principle is behind most work in phonetics; it is this principle which leads both to singling out certain events in the stream of sound for attention rather than others and to examining these events to see if they contrast with one another.

But actual speech does not consist of a series of events that can be clearly discriminated from one another in a purely mechanical way. Actual speech requires active interpretation by a listener. Speech is a continuum: the tongue does not move from one fixed position instantaneously, as it were, to another, stop, and then go on to a third, and stop again. Nor does any other speech "organ." The tongue and every other organ is in some kind of motion nearly all the time in speaking, and every study which has examined speaking by the use of mechanical means such as laryngoscopes, spectrographs, and radiography has confirmed this point. The individual sounds about which we so casually speak are as much mental constructs as they are physical events. The phoneme is a mental construct. It is a reference point in a system of abstractions. When we say that the middle sound in *pin* is the phoneme /I/, we are making a claim about how the minds of speakers of English appear to work, not just a claim about some physical characteristics of a particular pronunciation of *pin*.

In recent years some concern has been expressed that the concept of sound which underlies much work in phonetics may not be the most appropriate for describing how systems of sound work. In part, the apparent inadequacy results from some skepticism about the concept of the phoneme—whether there are such things at all, or, if they do exist, how they exist. Some linguists have stated the case for units larger than phonemes to be considered the building blocks of speech and have proposed the syllable as a prime candidate. Others have proceeded in the opposite direction and have searched for the smallest possible component parts of systems of sound. They have tried to analyze the continuum of speech into its smallest component parts, into distinctive features such as voicing, closure types, tongue positions, and so on, and have searched for the smallest set of such features that could be used to describe any language.

They have also searched for principles which would explain how certain sets of such features occur time and time again whereas others do not, occur much less frequently, or seem less stable. The result is the development in linguistics of concerns for *naturalness* and *markedness*. The first term describes sets of features which commonly occur together to establish classes of sounds which tend to undergo the same kinds of processes; the second term describes the difference between the more stable, less complicated sets, the unmarked ones, and the less stable, more complicated sets, the marked ones. The total concern is the development of a new and comprehensive phonetic theory, particularly one which allows for previously disparate facts to be unified, facts from listening as well as speaking, language acquisition as well as adult language use, and language yesteryear as well as language this year.

An adequate phonetic theory must allow something to be said not only about how the system of sounds holds together at any one time but also how it is acquired by the individual and how it changes over the generations. These processes of acquisition and change are gradual as well as systematic, so a phonetic theory which provides a better understanding of the various processes and systems than another theory is to be more highly valued. If a theory which uses distinctive features, "natural" classes of sounds, and "markedness" provides a better understanding than one that uses phonemes, it is to be preferred. However, if the use of distinctive features leads to unwieldy complexity elsewhere in the total account of the language, and "naturalness" and "markedness" turn out to be unmanageable concepts, their use would need to be reconsidered. Already we know that a notational system which employs distinctive features is generally far more unwieldy for some purposes than one which employs IPA symbols, just as Roman numerals are far less satisfactory for arithmetical calculations than Arabic numerals. However, that drawback is not an insurmountable one.

One noticeable gain in recent attempts to work with distinctive features has been the effort made to relate the processes of speaking and listening. Linguists have tended to ignore the ear in favor of the mouth, but those who use distinctive features deliberately seek to show the acoustic correlates of certain kinds of articulations. They relate listening to speaking. It is well known that the ear is important to the voice, not only because people usually talk to others rather than to themselves, but also because they monitor their own speech. Speakers listen to what they are saying: they not only feel the movements of the speech organs, but also are aware of the sounds they are making, even to the extent of being sensitive to the conduction of those sounds through the bones in the head. Such feedback is very important to the production of coherent speech. Anesthesia, deafness, drugs, and deliberate speech delay through experimental procedures can seriously disturb the mouth-ear link. The congenitally deaf do not speak normally because they cannot hear and monitor themselves in addition to not being able to hear others.

On the whole, however, most linguists have ignored the ear. The phonemic principle directed attention to the underlying system of contrasts, to the mouth which produces the contrasts, and to the mind which organizes and uses them. The possibility of easy reference to the vocal apparatus made the difficulty of reference to technical aspects of sound something to be put aside for the attention of communications engineers. There were also enough mysteries contained in the domain already defined for linguistic investigation without seeking to search other domains. But, as we shall see, some of the contents of those other domains is relevant to achieving a full understanding of how systems of sound work and why they possess certain characteristics.

Speech and Sound

One way to study speech is to examine it through techniques used by scientists such as physicists and communications engineers. The vocal apparatus produces sounds in the same way as do trumpets, drums, and collisions between bodies in anything other than a vacuum. We hear the sounds produced if they are within hearing distance and within the range of sounds we can perceive with our ears. Because the sounds of speech differ in their duration, tonal composition and intensity, they can be described with the techniques and apparatus developed by physicists, there being nothing unique to the physics of speech.

The vocal apparatus produces sound much as a trumpet does: an airstream is forced through certain cavities (in the case of speech, the throat, mouth, and sometimes the nose) which act as resonators. In an average adult male the throat and mouth have a length of about seven inches measured from the vocal cords, or glottis, to the lips. A pipe of such length, even a soft, bent pipe, produces a basic set of resonances called a first formant at about 500 cycles per second (cps), or 500 Hertz (Hz), within a total speech energy range of 50 to 10,000 cps (50 Hz to 10 mHz), with the greatest concentration of energy between 100 and 600 cps. Other similar sets of resonances, or formants, characteristically appear at intervals of roughly a thousand cycles per second in pipes of this length. So it is with speech. It is mainly the second and third formants at approximately 1500 cps and 2500 cps in combination with the first formant which give the sounds of speech their recognizable "character."

Modifications within the pipe, in this case modifications in the vocal tract, alter this characteristic relationship of the formants and also shift the first formant. The sounds of speech achieve their individual characters from the specific modifications used in their production. Modifications can also produce "noise" of different kinds, that is, sounds which lack fundamental sets of resonances. Since women and children also usually have shorter vocal tracts than adult males their voices are characterized by formants of higher frequency and greater separation. In addition, women and children tend to have "higher" voices, that is, they speak or sing in a higher register, because their vocal cords are generally shorter and thinner than those of men and vibrate at almost twice the speed, at 200 to 300 cps rather than at 100 to 150 cps.

English vowel sounds are identified by their first three formants. The first two provide most of the information necessary for correct identification; the third eliminates any possible ambiguities that would exist if only the first two were used. A three-dimensional system of this kind is much more efficient than a two-dimensional system, particularly when there is so much individual variation in voices from speaker to speaker. A number of investigations show that the average frequency of each of the three formants for men for certain English vowels is as follows (the averages for women are given in the parentheses): *beet* 270, 2290, 3010 (310, 2790, 3310); *bat* 660, 1720, 2410 (860, 2050, 2850); *boot* 300, 870, 2240 (370, 950, 2670); and *bought* 570, 840, 2410 (590, 920, 2710).

It is of some interest too to note that unround front vowels and round back vowels of similar height have formant structures which are clearly very different and therefore readily distinguishable to the ear. In such unmarked vowels the second formant is particularly responsible for the distinctiveness of the vowels. The marked rounded front vowels and unrounded back vowels of similar height are not so clearly distinguishable from each other, and confusion would probably result, particularly in circumstances which allow for much individual variation, as is the case in everyday speech. It is not surprising that phonological systems are constructed so as to prevent such confusion. Apparently no system uses front round vowels and back unrounded vowels exclusively, that is, only marked vowels, and no system uses front rounded vowels without also having front unrounded vowels or back unrounded vowels without also having back rounded vowels. However, many systems have neither front rounded vowels nor back unrounded vowels, for example, English. French is an example of a language with the expected front unrounded vowels and back rounded vowels, together with an additional set of front rounded vowels. Vowel systems therefore owe some of their characteristics to what ears can hear and clearly distinguish.

Hearing and Sound

Speech is not only produced; it must also be heard. In some ways it seems surprising that speech is heard because it has so little intrinsic power and is so evanescent. It has been said that fifteen million people each speaking in a large auditorium without the assistance of amplification would together generate only a single horsepower of acoustic energy. Likewise, a hundred men hammering on steel plates would produce only enough acoustic energy to light a single one hundred watt bulb if that energy were convertible to electric power. However, the human ear is a very sensitive instrument, well able to respond to sounds of different intensity and frequency. In fact, it is so sensitive that in ideal conditions the ear can detect differences not much greater than the random movements of individual molecules of air. The weakness and evanescence of speech actually have advantages for communication. Sounds can coexist without losing their individual identities and they also disappear quickly. The result is that more than one person can talk at a time, voices can be heard against other noises, and the channel of communication does not become cluttered up with old information. Instead, the channel constantly maintains its availability to all who wish to use it and allows considerable freedom in that use.

The intensity of sound is commonly measured in decibels (db). A whisper source at four to five feet is about 20 db, night noises in a city about 40 db, quiet speech about 45 db, conversation on the telephone or at a distance of three feet between 60 and 70 db, loud shouting about 85 db, and a pneumatic drill at a distance of ten feet about 90 db. People experience hearing discomfort beginning at about 110 db and actual pain at about 140 db.

A subtle relationship exists in hearing between the frequency of a sound and its intensity. A sound at a particular frequency must have a certain intensity before it can be heard: there is a hearing threshold. Whereas 90 per cent of a normal population can hear a pure tone of 1000 cps at 30 db in ideal conditions, none can hear a pure tone of 100 cps at 30 db. Less than 50 per cent can hear a pure tone of 10,000 cps at 30 db. However, if the intensity of a pure tone of 100 cps is increased to 55 db and one of 10,000 cps is increased to 65 db, then over 90 per cent can hear the tones at these new levels of intensity. People also vary in their hearing thresholds, revealing different ability to detect low intensity sounds: whereas 90 per cent can hear a pure tone of 1000 cps at 30 db, only 25 per cent can detect a similar tone at 10 db. However, people are fairly consistent in reacting to sounds of high intensity: any sound within the normal frequency range of human speech that achieves an intensity of about 140 db causes them pain. While the hearing threshold varies considerably, the pain threshold is much more uniform. Frequency and intensity are related in still another way. A pure tone of 100 cps at 50 db will be judged to be as loud as a pure tone of 1000 cps at 20 db and one of 10,000 cps at 30 db. However, at 90 db the first two tones will be judged to be still equally loud but the third not so loud. At 60 db the tone at 1000 cps will be judged a little louder than the tone at 10,000 cps, and the tone at 100 cps will be judged considerably less loud than either.

It has been estimated that the human ear can detect variations in pure tones as small as two or three cycles per second in tones below 1000 cps. Altogether as many as one thousand differences are distinguishable in ideal experimental conditions using pure tones. Together with nearly three hundred perceptually different intensity levels in the same conditions, this number of differences would allow for the existence of as many as one third of a million potentially distinguishable pure tones.

Speaking and listening occur in less than ideal conditions: all kinds of noises exist in the environment; the tones of speech are not pure tones; and individuals differ from each other in their realizations of different contrasts. So a particular sound system exploits only a few of the many possibilities and exploits these without a great deal of finesse. The possibilities actually exploited are derived from only part of the total acoustic space that is available. The human ear is most sensitive to differences of sound when the tones are 50 db above the hearing threshold and have a frequency range of from 500 to 4000 cps. At the upper end, sounds in excess of 20,000 cps fall outside any useful range for speech. The sound systems of languages make maximal use of exactly that part of the total acoustical space which human ears prefer to use.

Although speech has a general low intensity, the individual sounds of speech vary considerably in their intensities. In English the vowels are "stronger," or louder, than the consonants, with the low back vowel in a word like *talk* the strongest vowel of all. High vowels, front or back, as in *beet* and *boot*, are weaker than low vowels, possessing no more than a third of their intensity. This difference in vowels is attributable to the intensity of the first formant which is stronger in low vowels than in high, the mouth being more open in their production. The strongest consonant is the initial consonant of a word like *red*, but

FERNALD LIBRARY
COLBY-SAWYER COLLEGE
NEW LONDON, N.H. 03257

S2104

it is no stronger than the weakest vowel. However, it is more than twice as strong as the initial consonant of *ship*, six times as strong as the initial consonant of *no*, and over two hundred times as strong as the weakest consonant of all, the initial consonant of *thin*. It should not be surprising therefore, that words containing this last sound cause certain children difficulty in both listening and speaking.

The human ear is undoubtedly an amazing instrument. It can detect subtle differences in frequency and intensity, distinguish between periodic (resonated) and nonperiodic sounds and between tones and noise, and catch exquisite differences in timing, as, for example, the different onsets of voicing at the beginnings of *tan* and *dan*. The brain obviously plays an important part in any such activity, but what the ear itself does must not be underestimated. It could handle a communication channel of enormous complexity. That it is not required to do so is an interesting fact. The constraints on the language systems people use are not imposed solely by the peripheral "organs," the mouth and ear. The constraints are also central, arising from characteristics of the brain, the nervous system, and the mind, whatever the latter is.

The brain must somehow guide the mouth and ear in selecting what they are to do. Certain properties and relations must be present if a particular message is to be produced or detected. To take one obvious example: a child, a woman, and a man will all pronounce a word differently, yet they are all perceived to have said the same word. Just about every one of its parts may be shown to be physically different in each case, but the overall relationship of the parts demonstrates a pattern which is recognizably the same at some level or levels of abstraction. The linguist is interested in this abstraction because that is where the structure of languages is presumed to be located.

That many apparent inconsistencies do exist in the acoustic information the ear and brain must process is well confirmed. We know that people are more hesitant in identifying vowel sounds than consonant sounds. The latter are usually perceived as being either clearly one sound or another, but the former must be assessed in relation to each other for purposes of identification. We may be quite sure that we hear *pat* not *cat*, but we may not be so sure that we hear *pat* rather than *pot*. The same sound, that is "same" so far as its acoustic properties are concerned, may even be identified differently in different environments. Even consonant sounds can be so affected. For example, the same noise burst produced by a speech synthesizer before *eep*, *oop*, and *op* may be identified as a *p*-like sound in the first two cases (*peep* and *poop*) and a *k*-like sound in the last (*cop*). While the ear is extremely sensitive to the various frequencies, intensities, and relative durations it hears in speech, how the brain interprets that information is another matter.

Overcoming Noise

Numerous experiments have also shown that speech is remarkably resilient. These experiments have employed either a treated sample of natural speech or speech which has been synthesized artificially. If certain intensities usually present in a message are omitted, the message can still be understood. It seems to make little difference to the intelligibility of speech that the sounds of very high and low intensity are not transmitted: the message remains intelligible in the absence of the two peaks because the majority of its "information" is contained between the peaks. A small amount of such peak-clipping can even make a message more intelligible: the consonants become more discriminably different as the intensity of the vowels is reduced. On the other hand, center-clipping, that is, cutting out sounds of middle intensity, leads to unintelligibility and distortion.

Other kinds of filtering and masking sometimes have little effect too: eliminating certain frequencies; interrupting by regularly excising minute parts of a message along the time axis; varying the intensity levels in different parts of the sound spectrum; changing the fundamental frequency of the voice; slowing down or speeding up the message with or without accompanying changes in frequency; and even systematically delaying one part of the signal. Experiments show that speech is relatively impervious to many such experimental changes. So far as the need to hear one's own voice is concerned, however, experiments with delayed auditory feedback show that a delay of as little as one-fifth of a second in hearing one's own voice can disconcert a speaker, putting speech production out of phase and inducing hesitations, repetitions, stammering, and sometimes even shouting.

Normal speech is massively redundant and contains much more information than listeners really need in order to decide what is being said. Consequently, speech can be used in situations which contain many different kinds of potential hindrances to communication. But listeners do not simply perceive the sounds of language without any involvement of the mental processes; they must interpret what they hear. This interpretation occurs centrally in the brain not peripherally in the ears, for it is the brain which guides and for the most part controls what it is the ears hear.

The Brain and Aphasia

While the brain is obviously important in the production and reception of language, much remains to be discovered about its internal structure and functions. We well know that the importance of the human brain does not derive entirely from its absolute size: an elephant has a larger brain, and a dwarf's brain may be no bigger than that of a chimpanzee. Its importance derives from its complexity: the massive number of connections, the alternative pathways, the redundancies, and even the overall asymmetry. It has been said that human brains are qualitatively different rather than quantitatively different from the brains of other species. However, only a very small part of the human brain is involved with language activity.

A brain is a difficult object to study in a living person. It is impossible to probe into and experiment on a living brain for linguistic purposes alone. Any understanding of the relationship between language and the brain must be gained in indirect ways, principally from the incidental and accidental effects of research and experimentation primarily conducted for medical reasons. Or it must be gained through trying to relate particular kinds of linguistic evidence to evidence provided by autopsies, as in the case of aphasia, that is, language loss brought about by brain damage through accidents, tumors, or strokes. Millions of people suffer varying degrees of such damage, which is often accompanied by other physical and intellectual deficits.

The linguistic characteristics of aphasia can vary considerably. They can range from total loss of language ability to just a slight impairment in one or more of the abilities to name objects, to recall vocabulary, to repeat items, to use normal sounds and syntax, to comprehend spoken or written language, to speak, to read, and so on. Aphasia may result in what sounds like a "foreign" accent or some kind of "word salad" being produced instead of coherent speech. It also produces effects which appear to be less like problems of retrieval, that is, inability to get something out of the head, than like problems of programming in the gaps, confusions, and production difficulties that are exhibited. The aphasic condition itself may be temporary or permanent.

The various symptoms of aphasia have proved to be very difficult to classify. Broad classifications such as receptive aphasias and expressive aphasias have sometimes been used. So also have classifications employing a linguistic basis. However, no classification is entirely satisfactory because of the wide range of symptoms that exist, their interrelationships, their range of severity, and their relationships to deficits of other kinds, for example, to the previously mentioned physical, particularly motor, and intellectual deficits.

Since aphasia results from brain damage, it should be possible to relate specific linguistic deficiencies to particular kinds of damage as these are revealed through autopsy. The findings should lead to a gradual increase in understanding of how the brain functions with regard to language. The evidence from aphasia should provide a growing body of information about such matters as the storage of linguistic information, the localization of linguistic function, the interrelationships of the various functions, and possibly even the reality of the language systems that linguists postulate. A century of work has produced a considerable amount of evidence on each of these topics, but much more remains to be discovered before truly definitive statements can be made. Many people believe that brain research is still in its infancy and that most of the discoveries are still waiting to be made.

One of the most important discoveries in the history of research in aphasia was made by the French physician, Paul Broca, in the early 1860s. Broca discovered that a particular kind of speech loss was associated with damage to a particular area in the brain. This area, part of the left frontal lobe (located a short distance above and in front of the left ear), has become known as Broca's area. It is associated with certain kinds of expressive and motor difficulties which affect the ability to speak. There is a loss of articulation and grammatical skills but not of vocabulary and comprehension skills. A person may understand what is said but may not be able to reply except with disconnected words. In the 1870s Carl Wernicke identified another area, known as Wernicke's area, which is associated with a different kind of aphasia. Damage to Wernicke's area, the posterior part of the left temporal lobe (behind and above the left ear), results in sensory aphasia. In this kind of aphasia, control of articulation and grammar is retained but control of vocabulary is lost. The result is loss of the ability to comprehend both the spoken and the written language. The ability to monitor one's own utterances for their sense is also impaired.

Lateralization

It was soon apparent that damage to the left side of the brain more often resulted in aphasia than damage to the right side. It is now generally accepted that the two halves of the brain function quite differently in human beings and that for most people language is located in some way in the left side (or hemisphere) of the brain. It is not distributed equally in both hemispheres. Moreover, within the left himisphere it is located toward the front rather than toward the back. Language is, therefore, lateralized in the brain with the left hemisphere the dominant hemisphere. This kind of lateralization of function is almost unknown outside of the human species. While it is common for the right sides of bodies to be controlled by the left sides of brains and left by right, it is rare for one side of the brain to control a total function of the whole system, in this case language. It has been shown that the singing ability of chaffinches is also lateralized in the left side of the chaffinch brain, but any similarities between human beings and chaffinches are almost certainly quite accidental.

The human brain is not symmetrical. The left hemisphere is usually larger than the right, and this difference is noticeable at birth. Evidently the left hemisphere takes the lead in language acquisition and most people have left dominance so far as language is concerned. The left hemisphere may also be the side that controls many learned movements, for example, movements used in working with tools. Humans are the world's best tool users as well as the world's only language users. A young child who experiences damage to the left side of the brain may lose all ability to use language for a while but can relearn what was lost by using the right side of the brain. However, the right hemisphere remains available in this way for no more than about the first ten years or so of life. Early brain damage followed by such a switchover also usually produces no discernible negative results so far as the acquisition of language is concerned. The right side of the brain can do anything the left can do but usually is not required to and cannot, after the first years of life. Unfortunately, very little is known about why this ability to switch over is lost when it is.

The left hemisphere also controls the right side of the body. If language is localized in the left hemisphere in the vast majority of cases, then the possibility exists of close relationships between handedness preferences and language. Human beings are predominantly right-handed with about 93 per cent having such a preference. They are also predominantly right-footed and right-eyed, though to a lesser extent. It is well known that aphasia is often accompanied by physical disturbances such as paralysis in the right side of the body, and it is also the case that deliberate interference with handedness preferences can disturb language development. An interesting question concerns people who are naturally left-handed: Do they exhibit left dominance or right dominance so far as language is concerned?

While the evidence from aphasics gives consistent support for the connection between right handedness and left dominance for language, it shows that left handedness is associated only to a limited extent with right dominance. Damage to the right side of the brain rarely produces aphasia in right-handed people but does so significantly more frequently in left-handed people. However, damage to the left side of the brain produces aphasia with just about the same incidence in both right-handed and left-handed people. Only about one third of naturally left-handed people appear to be right dominant so far as speech is concerned or to give evidence that both hemispheres are involved in their use of language. Even if we add to these those who have substituted use of the right hemisphere for the left because of injury or disease experienced in early life, it is likely that no more than one adult in twenty-five is right dominant so far as language is concerned. Human beings are, therefore, overwhelmingly left dominant.

Language in the Brain

Even though for most people language is localized in the left hemisphere of the brain there is considerable difficulty in further localizing specific linguistic functions. As we have observed, Broca's area is associated with certain motor and expressive difficulties and Wernicke's area with certain receptive and sensory difficulties in reading, writing, and self-monitoring. However, injuries in other areas of the left hemisphere can produce similar consequences, and, conversely, injuries that might have been expected to produce a particular kind of aphasia sometimes do not.

Maps of the brain which try to associate particular areas with specific language functions have limited usefulness. They are based on experimental procedures which tend to produce very general, and often ambiguous, results, for example, procedures that use electrical stimulation. The brain is exceedingly complex, much more complex than any existing maps indicate. Brain systems appear to be highly redundant, and there is a considerable plasticity which allows functions to be taken over when parts die or cease to be serviceable. Brain cells are not replaced like skin cells: they die, and already existing cells must be pressed into service if the brain's capability is to be maintained. This plasticity makes attempts at localization of specifics extremely difficult. Human brains are obviously alike in many respects, but it is an interesting problem at what point they differ in their internal structures. Certainly the evidence from aphasia suggests wide individual variation.

In recent years brain researchers have turned to different kinds of hypotheses to account for how language is stored and functions in the brain. One proposal is that linguistic information is not stored as a series of wholes, that is, in the form of discrete units, but is stored holographically. This suggestion obviates any need to be concerned with extreme localization, but it must be recognized for what it is, little more than an analogy. As such, the suggestion does not easily generate hypotheses which are subject to experimental validation and may, therefore, have little practical value. Other proposals have tried to relate memory of linguistic information to such things as RNA molecules, proteins, and amino acids in the brain, but the various searches for engrams, that is, for the physical correlates, or neural memory traces, of bits of linguistic information have been unsuccessful. There must be some ultimate units and language structures in the brain, but these may well be characterized by a massive redundancy which allows language itself to function as various parts die. The human brain can afford such redundancy. The whole system does not break down usually until extreme old age and sometimes not even then, and when it does, it often breaks down in a fashion that seems to testify to this very redundancy. It is bits and pieces which disappear randomly, not whole systems.

Recently, particularly as the result of work by the psychobiologist, Roger Sperry, some attention has been given to the nondominant hemisphere of the brain. The two hemispheres are connected by the corpus callosum, which is sometimes severed as a surgical procedure in treating epilepsy. The result is a split brain, that is, a brain whose two parts function independently. Studies of split-brain patients indicate that the nondominant hemisphere controls certain visual and spatial capabilities, is the locus of certain musical and artistic abilities, and plays an important part in emotional behavior. Apparently too the dominant hemisphere controls the nondominant hemisphere in a variety of ways through the corpus callosum. Split-brain patients lack such control; they cannot integrate certain kinds of visual and linguistic information, nor can they control emotional and affective behavior through language.

If the nondominant hemisphere is surgically removed, the result is likely to be a loss of emotional response and some of the patient's musical and artistic ability, but little or no language impairment. Surgical removal of the dominant hemisphere, however, drastically affects language capability. A few commonplace expressions sometimes remain, particularly the emotional swear words, and there is likely to be evidence of comprehension of a considerable amount of speech and knowledge of how the world works, for example, knowledge of its social conventions. But full, expressive speech is lost. The nondominant hemisphere obviously knows certain kinds of things that it cannot communicate through language: artists of all kinds have frequently spoken of knowledge that is too deep for words. Split-brain research confirms the fact that while different ways of knowing do exist, language provides the principal way of expressing such knowledge.

Neural Transmission

Whatever it is that happens during the production and reception of speech, it results in signals being sent through the central nervous system. These signals originate in the brain in the case of speech and eventually cause various muscles of the jaw, larynx, tongue, lips, and so on to move. In the case of listening, most of the activity proceeds in the opposite direction from the periphery to the center. However, in both speaking and listening, it is the brain which exercises control of the various activities of the nervous system. The brain is particularly well adapted to controlling the muscles used in speech. It has been demonstrated that the motor activities of the lips and tongue are regulated by areas of the brain much greater in size than those which regulate the motor activities of many other parts of the body. Likewise, the areas of the brain which regulate the motor activities of the hands and fingers are also large in contrast to those which regulate the feet and toes.

Speaking is particularly sophisticated in the very fine signalling that is involved in speech production and in the programming of those signals. Minute differences must be produced in extremely precise sequences. Listening requires equally fine detection capabilities. We know that one essential way in which *den* and *ten* are articulated differently is that in *ten* there is a delay of as little as four hundredths of a second in voicing the vowel, that is, in setting the vocal cords in motion after the tongue is removed from behind the top teeth, but there is no corresponding delay after the removal of the tongue in *den*. These movements are controlled through the nervous system, and normal articulated speech requires a large number of such movements each second. Therefore, the nervous system is actively involved in the production of speech under the control of a very sophisticated central source, the brain.

As more becomes known about the neural transmission of language signals, the more we are likely to find out about how the structure of the nervous system imposes limitations on both the production and reception of speech. The system has characteristics which limit its capability; it can do only so much, and it must do what it does in certain ways. For example, electrochemical neural impulses take longer to travel over long nerve fibers to the effector cells than they take to travel over short nerve fibers, everything else being equal. Impulses that must travel over thin nerve fibers also travel more slowly than those that must travel over thick nerve fibers. Facts like these are inescapable and must be recognized in any serious consideration of how the brain is involved in the production of language. The brain's instructions to the various speech organs have to be programmed in a way that allows for the desired sequences to be realized. Yet, the various signals do not always travel at the same speed because their neural pathways differ. Therefore, the brain must have the ability to regulate the instructions it gives so as to take such differences into account.

The brain still remains much of a mystery; many of its properties and processes are obscure. If the live brain resists investigation and tells us little directly, the dead brain tells us even less, particularly about linguistic functioning. Language certainly begins and ends in the brain, but, as for many beginnings and endings, we can make little more than educated guesses about the facts. We do know that language is extraordinarily complex. The brain is much more complex. We understand certain gross characteristics of the brain. However, any connections we proceed to make between what we know about language and those characteristics must be regarded as conjectural. They depend on taking many things on trust, not the least of which are beliefs about what language is and how useful one or another analogy is so far as the functioning of the brain is concerned. Some linguists believe that knowledge of language will offer insights into the structure and functioning of the brain. Such may be the case. But we must also remember that brain research too can provide linguists with insights into language structure and functioning which they may find extremely useful in understanding how language works.

References

Four general books of interest are those by Denes and Pinson (1963) on speech, Lindsay and Norman (1972) on information processing, Miller (1951) on communication, and Rose (1973) on the brain.

For ear preferences for sounds see Kimura (1967), Shankweiler (1971), and Studdert-Kennedy and Shankweiler (1970). Fry (1970), Kim (1971), and Laver (1970) provide good reviews of recent work in speech production and reception, discussing the various units and processes that have been proposed and experiments that have been conducted. The data on average frequencies of formants are from Denes and Pinson (1963), p. 118. The observation concerning formant structures and roundness is from Wang (1971). Miller (1951) and Denes and Pinson (1963) are the sources for most of the data on the power of speech, the hearing of pure tones, and the relative strengths of sounds. The categorial perception of consonants is discussed by Liberman (1957), Liberman, Cooper, Harris, MacNeilage, and Studdert-Kennedy (1967), and Stevens and Halle (1967). Identification of the same sound as being different according to environment is described by Liberman, Delattre, and Cooper (1952). Miller (1951) describes numerous experiments which demonstrate the resilience of speech.

Geschwind (1973), Rose (1973), Whitaker (1971), and Zangwill (1971) describe various aspects of aphasia. For a discussion of possible lateralization of bird song in chaffinches see Nottebohm (1970). The data on handedness are from Zangwill (1971). Pribram (1969) discusses the possibilities of holography, and Sperry (1964) and Sperry and Gazzaniga (1967) work in split-brain research.

3

The Psychological Context

Investigating the Mind

As we indicated in the previous chapter, language is controlled by the brain just as are the mouth and ears. The mouth, ears, and nervous system also constrain certain language possibilities, but we must not underestimate the importance of the central control which the brain exercises. Constraints exist at the center too, constraints of attending, perceiving, remembering, planning, and processing, and these central constraints are even more difficult to investigate than the peripheral ones. They are much less amenable to probes, rays, and other forms of physical manipulation and experimentation. Instead, the central constraints must be studied inferentially with all the attendant consequences of such study, particularly that of possibly drawing the wrong conclusions from time to time.

In general, the "higher" the mental, or psychological, process we wish to investigate the more difficult that process is to study, the greater the ingenuity that is required, and the less confidence we can place in our results. Remembering, or memory, is much more difficult to investigate than attending, or attention. These higher processes are sometimes called processes of the mind rather than of the brain. Minds and their characteristics are much more difficult to study than brains and their characteristics. Psychology itself has often been defined as the science which investigates behavior, particularly the prediction and control of behavior, rather than the science which investigates mind. Some psychologists have gone so far as to deny the usefulness of mind as a concept in psychology, but such denials are less frequent now than they once were.

It is not surprising, therefore, that the issue of how language relates to mind is one of the most interesting and exciting issues in modern linguistics. Language is possibly the highest "process," or set of processes, of all. It is unique too in the sense that only humans possess language. But that very uniqueness itself creates a difficulty: If language is uniquely human, how far can one generalize findings about behavior from animals to humans and then proceed to apply these findings to language? Since this question recurs constantly, some immediate discussion of the issues it raises is necessary.

Behaviorism and Mentalism

In recent years there has been a continuing debate among students of language between those who are behaviorists in psychological matters and those who reject behaviorism in favor of mentalism. A generation or so ago there was hardly any such debate. At that time most linguists were able to subscribe concurrently to beliefs in the uniqueness of language and in the relevance of behavioristic psychology to studies of language learning and language use. They regarded language as a sophisticated stimulus-response system learned much like any other habit system through the building up of associations and through the success of schedules of reinforcement. Except for its complexity, language behavior was not really different from the kinds of behaviors that rats and pigeons exhibited in laboratory conditions. The psychologist B. F. Skinner even went so far as to write a book entitled *Verbal Behavior* which claimed that principles derived from laboratory work on small animals were also quite adequate to account for human language behavior. What the psychologists described as verbal behavior also appeared to be synonymous with all that others described as thought, speech, and language.

Many people found such a view of language attractive. It encouraged both linguists and psychologists to treat language just like any other kind of behavior. The same principles were applied and special pleading was completely avoided. Investigators of language behavior did not begin their work by assuming that such behavior was different in kind from all other types of behavior. They assumed the opposite: that language behavior was no different.

While not everyone agreed with such an approach to language and language behavior, its first major linguistic critic was Noam Chomsky, who published a widely read, quite devastating review of Skinner's book. Chomsky denied the validity of Skinner's claims, asserting instead that language is a uniquely human possession and that behaviorist principles cannot explain even the simplest facts about human language behavior. Language is unique in that the human species is specially, that is, uniquely, equipped to use language: the human mind is structured in a special way as a result of evolutionary development. This structure accounts not only for the resemblances that all languages have but also for the processes through which all languages are learned. The human mind is, as it were, programmed to learn and use languages of a certain kind—in fact, just the kind that human beings actually do use.

Chomsky's mentalist views on these matters have won over many linguists, perhaps even a majority. The result has been something of a revolution in linguistic thinking and investigation. Many influential psychologists have also adopted some or all of Chomsky's ideas. Numerous investigators now believe that close examination of the structure of language may reveal interesting facts about the structure of the human mind. Finding out how languages work may be equivalent to finding out what human minds are like, language serving as a window into the mind. Chomsky is by no means alone in his belief that in a number of respects linguistics has become a branch of cognitive psychology.

Linguists and psychologists who investigate language behavior while subscribing to this mentalistic view deny that concepts such as reinforcement contingencies and stimulus generalization adequately explain anything of interest about language behavior. They argue that such concepts are extremely vague at best and tend to beg the very questions they claim to answer. Why should reinforcement work with language, and what is a language generalization? They themselves do not propose different answers to the questions; rather they propose different questions, asking how all languages and minds are the same rather than if all things are learned in the same way. In turn, they must pay a price for treating language behavior as a unique kind of behavior. That price is a certain decrease in parsimony. Their premise is that particular language behaviors exist because they are "innate" in human beings, but the end result is something less than a parsimonious, totally integrated view of all kinds of behavior, human and animal, language and nonlanguage. Particular claims have also proved to be very difficult to test. Mentalism requires as much "faith" as behaviorism; however, they differ considerably in their articles.

The debate between the behaviorists and the mentalists continues to occupy attention. As we have said, perhaps a majority of linguists consider the mentalists to have been victorious, but many behaviorists feel that their views have been misunderstood rather than superseded. As in many debates, perhaps the issues were incorrectly formulated and the opponents have argued about different things. There may well be merit on both sides. Language certainly has some unique properties, and linguistic behavior is so extraordinarily complex that simple laws of behavior derived from laboratory study of lower animals do not seem to be anywhere near adequate in explaining that complexity. On the other hand, languages must be learned, language behavior does not occur in a vacuum, and that behavior does share many characteristics with other kinds of behavior. While adopting an either-or position, that is, taking one side or the other, is the strongest position one can take over this issue—and there is considerable merit in taking the strongest possible position—pursuing a middle course which seeks the best from both views may ultimately bring more productive results.

Attention and Perception

Speech must be attended to and perceived if there is to be any possibility of communication. In the previous chapter we noted how it can be attended to and perceived under very adverse conditions; we can understand distorted and mutilated speech. Language stimuli are also fairly readily distinguishable from nonlanguage stimuli. Experiments show that in very adverse conditions people can tell whether a human voice was present or not, whether it was a man's voice or a woman's voice, and when a pure tone was substituted. But they cannot recognize the language, a change in the language, the message, or distinguish sense from nonsense. There is also the well-known "cocktail party effect": we can follow one voice among many, and our attention may also be caught by something relevant to us in another conversation to which no attention was being paid. Like a voice-actuated recording device which works only when speech begins, the human mind is capable of attending to and perceiving information only when it is somehow relevant. It can ignore what is not relevant.

Attention and perception refer to the immediate processing of the sensory experiences of organisms: experiences of sight, sound, smell, taste, and touch. Cognition refers to the less immediate central involvement of the organism at some later stage in the processing. It is, of course, impossible to say precisely when one kind of processing ends and the other begins. Speech also has its own peculiar perceptual puzzles. The sounds of speech are not clearly discriminable from each other and vary considerably from utterance to utterance and person to person.

How do we learn to attend to and perceive speech? A simple answer is that we do so on the basis of experience alone. The British associationist psychologists, for example, Hartley, Mill, and Berkeley, believed that people learn to associate elementary sensations because such sensations tend to co-occur. People build up hierarchies of experiences that enable them to make more and more complex perceptions. The Canadian psychologist Donald Hebb went even further, claiming, for example, that when people notice the lines and corners of objects, sets of brain cells are activated. These sets of brain cells eventually form cell assemblies which are brought into play in visual perception. The availability of such cell assemblies increases according to their frequency of usage. This is a template view of perception, one that maintains the importance of matching something in the world with some kind of stored inner representation of that thing. We do know that people and animals deprived of the opportunity to perceive certain kinds of things, for example, humans born with cataracts and animals raised in the dark, experience difficulties in seeing for a while after all sources of visual deprivation have been removed. Some learning or experience is a necessary part of perception. However, template-matching is generally acknowledged not to be a feasible hypothesis for perception.

Something more than learning and experience is required. There is a strong likelihood that organisms possess perceptual mechanisms of different kinds which predispose them to perceive various things. Studies of animals such as frogs, cats, and rabbits show that their visual systems are organized in ways that help them to perceive certain very specialized characteristics of the environment. They seem to have feature detectors built right into their perceptual systems. Frogs have detectors which enable them to perceive the edges between light and dark regions, the movement of such edges, and changes in illumination. They also have a fourth kind of detector, one which allows them to perceive movements of small dark objects in their field of vision, a "bug detector." They depend on this last detector for survival, for a frog will starve to death in the presence of freshly killed but motionless flies. Cats and rabbits have detectors which allow them to respond to angles and motion in the environment. Evidence exists, therefore, that the innate structures of organisms may predispose them to perceive certain kinds of things. Human beings may have very specialized systems of speech detectors. But even stronger claims than the existence of detector systems have been made. Gestalt psychologists, for example, claim that minds are innately disposed to search out patterns and to organize stimuli in the environment into patterns. Special perceptual mechanisms or detector systems could be regarded as providing no more than the means by which such an end is accomplished.

This claim is similar to the one many linguists make today. They acknowledge that people may indeed employ a variety of perceptual and processing strategies determined by the nature of the human organism, but they insist that the perception of language requires them also to have both an innate knowledge of the general form of all languages and the acquired knowledge of the special rules of the particular language that is being attended to. Such knowledge "guides" them not only in their production but also in their perception of speech. Speech perception is under the control of this central language ability which all humans possess.

That view is very different from the associationist view, for there is a great distance between a belief in some abstract and innate predisposition or knowledge which guides perception and a belief that the same perceptions are built up entirely from the growth of associations among stimuli. However, the evidence available to us seems to support neither position to the complete exclusion of the other. An experiential basis must exist to the perception of language; certainly it must exist to the perception of a specific language. The existence of certain kinds of receptor cells and perceptual processes is also of importance and may well have a considerable effect on what is perceived. What we know, no matter how we define knowledge, must also predispose us to perceive certain things, as a wealth of studies which have explored ambiguous stimuli have shown: we often see what we expect to see and hear what we expect to hear. In such circumstances a theory of perception which encompasses all the facts is obviously more desirable than one which attempts to force recalcitrant data into the theory or which asserts that certain things must exist because the theory requires that they exist.

In one specific area of language perception there are some particularly interesting problems. Do people perceive speech so well because they actually speak themselves? Is speaking somehow basic to listening? Do people understand what they hear by using a process which requires some kind of access to the systems involved in speech production?

The available evidence does not support in any very solid way the claim that a speech base exists to language perception. The strong claim that speech is perceived through reference to articulation, that is, that listeners subvocalize what they hear when they listen, cannot be supported. Likewise without support is the weak claim that individual sounds in utterances are recognized through some kind of association to the neural surrogates of articulation rather than directly from their acoustic properties, that is, that sounds are associated directly to some representation of these sounds in the brain. There are cases of people who cannot speak because they lack the necessary muscular control to do so; however, they are able to understand what they hear quite well. As we saw too in the preceding chapter, there is considerable disagreement concerning the fundamental units and processes out of which speech is constructed. Consequently, we cannot be sure exactly what aspects of sound are relevant to perception. And, of course, this claim requires another cumbersome kind of matching model. There is considerable evidence, therefore, against some kind of motor theory of speech perception. However, evidence from the perception of foreign languages and from the ability to hold unclear utterances in temporary storage so as to resolve the unclarity also shows that certain parts of the speech production system do have a role to play in speech perception. They cannot be dismissed entirely. Perception of any kind is an active process: it demands considerable central involvement of the organism in the various perceptual systems that operate.

Memory

Memory must play an important role in language use. However, memory itself is not a unitary concept, for it involves a number of different characteristics and processes. We must also exclude from consideration any characteristics which we believe are entirely genetic in origin. It seems inappropriate to describe as memory any program an organism must obey because it is an organism of a particular kind. As we have indicated, many linguists and psychologists consider that human beings are programmed genetically to learn languages of only a certain kind. If we believe that certain linguistic characteristics are innate to human beings, for example, that they can learn only certain kinds of grammatical entities and perform only certain kinds of grammatical operations, then it makes little or no sense to say that such characteristics either are learned or must be remembered. In exactly the same way a person does not have to remember to have blond hair and freckles or to grow up to be six feet tall. Memory refers to active learning and remembering. Innate knowledge neither has to be learned nor remembered in this sense; in fact, it may be regarded as providing a guide to the organism in its learning and remembering.

No one working on problems of language learning and language behavior can fail to attribute innate knowledge or ability of some kind to the learner or user. A researcher may not wish to attribute innate linguistic knowledge to people but must still attribute to them an innate ability to learn in certain ways, with language learning one consequence of such ability. The particular learning theory would have to allow for the learning of language as well as the learning of other kinds of things. The ability to learn in certain ways would be innate. Likewise, with language behavior: it would be regarded as being under the control of certain universal laws of behavior that people are predisposed to follow.

There appear to be three different kinds of memory of interest to us: a sensory-information store; a short-term memory; and a long-term memory. The sensory-information store allows information gathered by the senses to be retained very briefly, only for a fraction of a second so far as vision is concerned. However, we can remember sounds a little longer than we can remember sights. This ability is very useful, for it allows us to hold sounds briefly in that store, which is probably of fairly high capacity, until we are in a position to deal with them or decide not to deal with them. It is in this sense that hearing may be regarded as a necessary prerequisite to understanding.

Short-term memory is a store of limited capacity in which information is retained during the processing of messages. This information comes from the sensory-information store, but the items may vary considerably in size. Very little information can be held in short-term memory: its capacity is limited to about seven unrelated items, or "chunks." When about seven chunks of unrelated information are in short-term memory and more chunks need to be added, either the chunks already present must be reorganized by grouping two or more together into a still bigger chunk, or something must be squeezed out to allow the new information to enter. Space may be provided by shifting material into long-term memory or just discarding it. Short-term memory achieves its turnover in these ways. Of course, items can stay there for a considerable time but must be rehearsed to do so. Unrehearsed items are dropped rather quickly. The whole process of entry to and exit from short-term memory is one of "easy in" and "easy out" to ensure rapid turnover.

Long-term memory seems to offer fairly permanent and seemingly unlimited storage capacity for everything that was held long enough in short-term memory to be processed, understood, and deemed worth remembering. However, precisely how information is stored in long-term memory is still much of a mystery. As we noted in the last chapter, the search for the engram, the neural memory trace of a linguistic datum, has been fairly unsuccessful, and even less ambitious attempts at localization of systems have been inconclusive. Information is most certainly stored, and it appears to be stored in different schemata or hierarchies in the brain. The key issue so far as memory is concerned is one of retrieval from storage. All kinds of approaches have been used, including the use of drugs and hypnosis, to study the access system or systems that humans employ. Entry to a specific bit of information can be achieved both directly and indirectly. In everyday language use we do pull all kinds of information out of long-term memory without the slightest difficulty or hesitation. But occasionally we cannot find exactly what we want: our search procedure seems to get us close to where we want to be in our search, but that search is not always ultimately successful. Somehow access was gained to the right schema or hierarchy, but the particular piece of information sought still escaped discovery. We recognize our failure as partial not total.

The "tip of the tongue" phenomenon is an instance of this last kind of failure to bring an item immediately and completely out of long-term memory. Sometimes we cannot recall a name, word, or phrase but know that it is on the tip of the tongue. We may even be able to give a paraphrase or synonym or say of a forgotten word that it has such and such a number of syllables or some other peculiarity or feature. In other words, we know certain properties of whatever it is we are searching for, but we cannot immediately recall the total set of properties, that is, the item itself. Eventually the item may come: *Hartmann* may come after *Hauptman, Heinemann,* and *Rinehart* are each rejected in turn, and the desired *Sanderson* may supersede *Ferguson* and *Richardson.*

This phenomenon argues for items, particularly words, being stored in longterm memory in different places with different properties "filed" in each entry. No particular entry would necessarily contain every bit of information in such a highly redundant system. Different search procedures would then give access to different sets of properties: associative, syntactic, semantic, phonological, and so on. Successful resolution of a tip of the tongue experience requires a search for alternative procedures to the one or ones initially creating the experience. For example, information about how many syllables a word has, or what some of its sounds are, or what one of its syllables is may have to be supplemented by a review of associations of meaning if the word is to be retrieved in its entirety.

We should note that this phenomenon applies only to a limited range of linguistic information, mainly retrieving the right word or the right pronunciation. For a speaker of English that a particular sound is or is not English makes demands of quite a different kind. These demands are demands on intuition. Intuition and memory are not the same. But memory does seem to influence intuition; otherwise everyone's intuitions about things would be very much the same as everyone else's, particularly intuitions about language. As we shall see later in this chapter, speakers do not necessarily share the same intuitions about language, and the fact that they do not creates problems for any theory of language which relies heavily on the use of intuition as a heuristic, that is, as a device which is used in making decisions about what is or is not part of the grammar.

Planning Speech

Language itself may be studied intensively for its usefulness in providing some kind of window into the mind. We can look closely at linguistic evidence and then theorize about the kind of mind that would be necessary to produce such evidence. What does the linguistic evidence we have suggest to us about the organizational units of language in the mind? Does the mind organize language into phonemes, or into syllables, or into some still larger unit or units? Speech must be planned; it does not just happen.

In the preceding chapter we indicated that certain instructions to the speech organs must be extremely precise in their detail and timing, for example, the instructions to produce the initial sounds of *den* and *ten* so that no confusion results. Likewise, the timing at the ends of *ax* and *ask* or *apt* and *act* must be extremely delicate. Timing differences of as little as one fiftieth of a second are critically important in ensuring that the right phonemes occur in the right sequences. Such evidence might seem to favor a hypothesis that speech is planned and organized phoneme by phoneme and that words themselves are stored as sequences of phonemes. But still other evidence refutes that hypothesis. While there is evidence that the phoneme may be an important unit in planning and producing speech, other evidence indicates that it is not the only unit, nor even possibly the most important unit. Units both smaller and larger than phonemes also appear to be involved.

Phonetic features smaller than phonemes are important. Their importance may be seen from the way in which particular segments tend to assimilate (that is, become more like) to neighboring segments or, much less frequently, dissimilate (that is, become less like). The speech organs are constantly moving in the direction of following sounds: lip rounding and frontness-backness of vowels, voicing, nasal quality, and so on are all anticipated. The *k* at the beginning of *Kansas* is produced in a different position (more forward) from the *k* at the beginning of *Kootenay*, and the vowel of *pin* is much more likely to be nasalized than the vowel of *pit*. Such assimilations are a basic linguistic fact. At some stage in the production of speech, therefore, subphonemic features become important: they influence each other.

Evidence from pauses, hesitations, false starts, and slips of the tongue shows that phonemes and units other than phonemes are involved in speech production. Slips like *Merle* for *Pearl, rip lounding* for *lip rounding, trite rack* for *right track, florn cakes* for *corn flakes, shoe snows* for *snow shoes,* and Dr. Spooner's famous *queer old dean* for *dear old queen* illustrate that entities such as features, phonemes, permissible phonemic clusters, grammatical endings, and even units of meaning play a part in speech production. Such slips usually do not violate the sound system of the language: they do not result in the production of "foreign" sounds or nonpermissible sequences of sounds such as English words beginning with *ng* or *lk*. Quite often too there is a semantic similarity between the slip and what was intended: *proception* may result from trying to convey the idea of both *production* and *perception* at a time when less than full attention is being given to the precise words being chosen. Slips of the tongue have also always been regarded as an important source of data in Freudian psychology.

Syllable units appear to be very important in planning speech. We do not usually stop in the middle of a syllable, and even babbling and stuttering show a characteristic syllable structure. Studies have also shown that syllable structure appears to control how certain phonemes are prolonged in relation to each other: a consonant which follows an intrinsically long vowel is given a briefer pronunciation than one which follows an intrinsically short vowel in an otherwise identical syllable. The final consonant of *mace* is therefore shorter in duration than the final consonant of *mess* because the vowel in *mace* is longer in duration than the vowel in *mess*. This temporal compensation suggests that whole syllables act as the organizational units of speech production rather than individual phonemes: it is the only way to explain the phenomenon. However, there is no truly conclusive evidence about the size of the organizational unit used in planning speech. Possibly more than one such unit exists between the central thought and its final realization in sounds. The use of language seems to require an initial ideation stage, that is, a state at which a person decides to say something. At this stage the speaker must have access to certain permanent stores of linguistic information in long-term memory. Planning processes allow language units of different kinds to be assembled so that ideas can be communicated. As we shall see, the units that participate in these processes and the processes themselves are of considerable interest to both linguists and psychologists. The planning results in orders being issued to the nervous system to do certain things which produce actual speech. Finally, during the actual production of that speech a considerable amount of self-monitoring occurs.

This self-monitoring, which generally goes on below the level of consciousness, also throws light on certain obscure processes. Speakers do detect errors made in the execution of a plan to speak: they sometimes know that the plan is apparently not working out, and they attempt to salvage it in the course of its execution. Self-monitoring does not go on co-instantaneously with planning so that speakers stop before they make errors. It works concurrently, but with a momentary delay. This delay allows some of the planning to be observed indirectly through the mistakes in execution which occur and the attempts made to rectify those mistakes. This notion of "mistake" is not without its difficulties in that it suggests that mistakes are planning failures. It would therefore tend to make mistakes as much competence errors as performance errors. Elimination of the competence-performance distinction or some redrawing of that distinction would, of course, remove that apparent difficulty. Brains do not appear to be maximally efficient systems as efficiency is usually defined; they seem to be unnecessarily redundant, even underused. But that redundance and reserve of resources is also the source of their resilience and adaptability, hence their peculiar efficiency. The match between what actually goes on in human brains and the linguist's idealized linguistic competence is still far from a perfect one. But it is one which may be expected to improve as both brain research and linguistic research make new discoveries.

Processing Speech

Just as the planning involved in saying something is complicated, so is the processing of what is said. Sound waves come to the ears, and the listener must distinguish speech sounds from other sounds and assume that what is being said makes sense. We rarely question this last assumption and often take a great deal of convincing that what we are listening to is either gibberish or nonsense of some kind. Listening and understanding require people to have at their disposal various kinds of information about the world, the language being used, and the probability that certain kinds of things will be said and others not said. Listening and understanding do not simply require some kind of passive perception and recognition of sounds and words as a preliminary to active interpretation. Such a two-stage model is quite inappropriate. Listening and understanding, that is, the processing of language, require the active involvement of the listener at *all* stages of contact with what is being said. The signals that reach the ears contain such a variety of information and noise that only a receiver actively committed to getting sense out of the signals, and with some kind of foreknowledge of what the message is likely to be, could succeed.

Experiments show that people cannot identify individual words or even very short sequences of words when these are presented out of context even in optimal conditions. To achieve 90 per cent intelligibility, they must hear sequences of seven to eight words produced in no less than about two seconds. If listeners recognized words from their component sounds, they should have recognized even single words in such circumstances. Context is very important, even to the extent of affecting how particular combinations of stresses are heard. *Lighthouse keeper* in *The life of a lighthouse keeper was formerly very lonely* and *light housekeepr* in *Our maid weighed 180 pounds, but the Joneses had a light housekeeper* have stress and timing patterns which are noticeably different if they are analyzed using a sound spectrograph which shows all the component frequencies and intensities of sounds. However, if the pairs of words in the sentences are switched electronically, listeners do not detect the switch or any change at all in the sentences. If people are presented with normal grammatical sentences, anomalous sentences, and random strings of words all of equal length in varying conditions of noise, they will not be able to repeat the random strings of words in conditions in which they can repeat the normal sentences quite accurately. They will have an intermediate degree of success with the anomalous sentences. Therefore, both syntactic and semantic clues are used in the processing. Again, this evidence suggests that processing is as much an inside-out process as an outside-in one, that is, that speech signals are interpreted and evaluated as part of the process of perception, not perceived and then interpreted and evaluated.

This inside-out characteristic of speech perception and understanding accounts for how deviant utterances tend to be interpreted as though they were not deviant: the listener projects his own regularity on them. Slips, hesitations, false starts will tend to be overlooked, gaps will be filled in, and even a certain amount of semantic and syntactic confusion will be tolerated if the overall gist is acceptable. Some of the best cases to illustrate this phenomenon are sentences spoken to us by people who do not know our language at all well, but who must say something in it. Such sentences often make a lot of sense, because we make them make sense. Unfortunately, sometimes the sense we make of them is not the intended sense.

The assumption that what they are listening to makes sense leads listeners to occasional misinterpretation of what was said. For example, listeners frequently do not attend to many of the details of what is said to them since they are aware that speech is highly redundant. They also pick and choose what they want to hear according to strategies which have proved to be useful, but which are by no means infallible. If they hear words *man, drove,* and *car,* they may well assume that what was said was something like *A man drove a car.* Likewise, the words *man, struck,* and *car* may be heard as something like *A man struck a car* rather than *A man was struck by a car,* which may have been what was said. People know that men drive but cars do not. With the verb *struck,* on the other hand, they are also likely to take the grammatical subject of the sentence *man* (the noun that appears before the verb) as the conceptual subject or agent (the person or thing that causes the event), even though the actual utterance employed a passive construction. Both men and cars can strike all kinds of things. Just as in speaking people tend to make a verb agree with the nearest preceding noun, so in listening they tend to interpret grammatical subjects as conceptual subjects if it makes sense to do so. On the whole this is a useful strategy. It does not always work, but when it does not, the level of redundancy in what is being said ensures that little misunderstanding generally results. Additional comments cause the listener to make any necessary corrections. The listener corrects the original interpretation.

As we shall see, experimental work has demonstrated the existence of certain phenomena that occur during the processing of sentences. These phenomena are few, but they do allow us to describe some of the processes and strategies that must be operating in the production and reception of speech. However, we are still far from being able to build a theoretical model of human speech processing, and even further from constructing the hardware of an automatic speech decoder. There was a time in the not too distant past when such decoders, mechanical translation devices, and voice-actuated typewriters seemed to be just on the verge of becoming realities. Now, they are remote possibilities at the best. Human beings far exceed any mechanical devices we have for doing all such tasks. At present only human brains can carry out the "computing" that is required to recognize and understand even the very simplest of sentences that are used in everyday speech.

Most attempts to construct models of the process of recognition and understanding have used an analysis-by-synthesis approach. That is, they have been based on the assumption that understanding an utterance results from the listener constructing an internal representation to match what is heard. The attempts have led to models which contain complete grammars of the language, the assumption being that understanding could not be achieved without such a store of grammatical knowledge. A competence model is held to be an essential component of a performance model. However, as we have seen, the assumption that a two-stage process exists (recognition followed by understanding) is not borne out by the evidence. In addition, it makes little sense, even for a large computer, to adopt a process which requires matching something which is recognized to something which is generated randomly. That process of generation would be impossibly cumbersome, even if every sentence were twenty words or less in length. It would take far too many years to carry out the simplest matching tasks. But brains work in split seconds! A knowledge of the language heard is essential to understanding what is being said, but the process of understanding also requires access to strategies which will achieve results quickly and almost always correctly rather than access to sets of rules which will achieve completely correct results but take forever doing so. People behave in the first way not the second.

We must work within an infinite set of possibilities both in planning and saying what we want to say and in processing what is said to us. Most sentences have such little probability of occurrence that any model which uses probability estimates as one of its components, for example, an information theory model, cannot hope to account for the language processes that go on. However, even if particular messages are quite unpredictable, some of the units and processes that go into their composition are not. In every human language only certain sounds are used over and over again, only certain kinds of structures and semantic arrangements occur, and throughout every message there exists a pervasive redundancy. Messages usually occur in situations which tend to reinforce whatever sense they have. They are also spoken and listened to by people who, though they act much more slowly than computers, act much more intelligently. Obviously, much remains to be learned about how people use their language abilities to get through even a simple telephone call or to read a page in a book. As we shall see in a later chapter, linguists have begun to turn their attention to such matters.

Psychological Investigation

Given the basic seriousness of explaining what kind of thing a human mind is that can learn to use language, psychologists would seem to have almost endless opportunities for discovering interesting facts. However, some of the limitations of psychological interests and methods tended to curtail discoveries for a long time. The most important was the refusal to investigate the black box of the mind because of a preference for overt, easily manipulatable behaviors. In addition, many of the issues appeared to be obscure, and the results of those investigations that were conducted tended to be quite ambiguous.

Psychologists have often avoided examining complex behavior. Psychologists try to isolate discrete variables and work with these in the hope of achieving objectivity. Rigid procedures are used in highly controlled laboratory conditions, but there is serious doubt that many of the results can be applied to language as it is learned and used outside the laboratory. For example, there is a long history of verbal-learning studies, and an extensive literature exists on different kinds of learning and forgetting, on interference, and on patterns of word association. But almost none of this work has anything to tell us about how language is learned or used in everyday life. Vast gaps exist between the findings of laboratory investigations and the everyday use of language, between highly controlled learning situations and natural learning, and between the word lists that are employed and the words and combinations of words that people actually use. Yet psychologists have sometimes not been afraid to extrapolate from their results. In the soft sciences *any* extrapolation of findings from the laboratory into real life must be done with extreme caution. The likelihood of error is considerable.

A corollary to this last observation is that the results of many investigations are either inconclusive or contradictory. Since the gaps between different findings and between projections of the results of these findings to natural language are so wide, it is difficult to bridge them. An illustration may be useful. It is possible to time how long it takes a person to produce a particular response to a given stimulus, for example, to produce a negative sentence corresponding in some way to a particular affirmative sentence. It might be argued that the greater the length of time taken to produce a particular response the less available, or more difficult, was that response. If the various stimuli can be controlled in such a way that every conceivable variable is accounted for, then the different response times should indicate very directly the effects of the variables (such as sentence length or the number of transformations required) as these are manipulated one by one in an experimental procedure. Just such a strategy was used for a while to find out what happened when people were required to manipulate various combinations of affirmative, negative, active, and passive statements and questions. However, the results were not at all clear. It proved impossible to account for all the variables present in the stimuli or to be sure what the various response times indicated, because they did not depend only on linguistic stimuli but also on the particular kind of judgment required by the task: sameness or difference; truth or falsity; and so on. Since the results of the experiments were not clear, it was therefore impossible to be very certain about what bearing they had either on the processes used to produce sentences or on the "correctness" of the grammar which generated the sentences.

The problem of how the results are to be interpreted is important. In their experiments linguists and psychologists have not always been crystal clear as to what it is they are actually testing: how language is produced; or how items are learned; or how sentences are remembered, comprehended, or judged; or how "real" a particular grammar is. In recent experiments there has been widespread agreement that it is linguistic competence that is being investigated rather than linguistic performance. But numerous performance variables exist in every experiment. Consequently, it is not surprising that conflicting results continue to be reported and that a consensus has been slow to develop regarding what is important and what is not, and what is really known and what is mere conjecture.

Before 1957 psychologists had shown little real interest in the kind of language behavior that interests linguists. Their principal interest in language lay in the area of word associations explored through verbal-learning tasks of various kinds. Language was regarded as some kind of complex set of word associations built up through reinforcement, the view expressed in B. F. Skinner's *Verbal Behavior*. A few psychologists were excited by certain linguistic "discoveries," particularly that of the phoneme. For a while it even seemed that these new concepts from linguistics, together with concepts from information theory, would revolutionize psychological investigations of language. Then, in 1957, the publication of Noam Chomsky's *Syntactic Structures* changed the direction of linguistic work drastically: new issues came to the fore, and old issues and findings were discarded as "uninteresting." One of the first psychologists to see the relevance of the new linguistics for the psychology of language was George Miller, and it was he who promoted the initial psychological investigations of Chomsky's ideas.

Investigating the Reality of Grammars

The earliest investigations were based on the view of language described in Chomsky's *Syntactic Structures*, a view modified considerably in his later publications. The 1957 version of generative-transformational theory focused on syntax rather than on sound and meaning. The immediate result was a shift away from investigations of phonemic structure, word associations, and information content. However, only certain kinds of sentences were discussed in *Syntactic Structures*, mainly simple one-verb sentences comprising statements and questions, affirmatives and negatives, and actives and passives. Transformations were of two kinds: obligatory, to manipulate elements in sentences; and optional, to change a sentence of one type into a sentence of another type, for example, an active into a passive or a statement into a question. Two-verb sentences were built up from combinations of one-verb sentences through generalized transformations, so that *He has a red book* would originate from two separate sentences: *He has a book* and *The book is red*.

In 1965 Chomsky changed the theory considerably with the publication of *Aspects of the Theory of Syntax*. The new version specified a deep structure–surface structure distinction in language, required transformations which did not (later modified to only rarely) change meaning, and established procedures for dealing more clearly with the actual meanings of words and sentences. Later still, some of Chomsky's critics demonstrated to their satisfaction that issues of meaning were more important and more central to understanding how sentences work than issues of syntax. They questioned the deep-surface distinction which had been proposed and substituted a generative semantics for Chomsky's generative syntax. Most recent psychological investigations have been based on one or another of these last two approaches to language and have attempted to find out how real their "fictions" are, that is, to investigate the reality of the units and processes that are postulated.

Many of the investigations have tried to assess the reality of transformational processes. The assumption is that sentences employing few transformations in their generation should take less time to recognize, judge, or manipulate in some other way than sentences requiring more transformations. Even the effects of the use of a single transformation should be measurable, for example, the difference between an active and a passive sentence, or between an affirmative and a negative. One immediate difficulty is with the term *generate*. Speakers produce sentences and grammars generate them, but whether production and generation are the same or in what ways they are the same are much debated issues. Any measure of complexity is also fraught with difficulties. Is complexity to be measured by numbers of transformations, types of transformations, kinds of conjoining and embedding, or what?

One investigation which measured reaction times in a sentence-matching task found that it took subjects longer to match active sentences to corresponding passive sentences (for example, *Jane liked the woman* to *The woman was liked by Jane*) than it did to match affirmative sentences to corresponding negative sentences (*Jane didn't like the woman*). The time required to match active-affirmative sentences to their corresponding passive-negative sentences (*The woman wasn't liked by Jane*) was also roughly equal to the sum of the times required to match active sentences to passives and affirmative sentences to negatives. However, another investigation which measured motor responses using a tachistoscope rather than reaction times on a pencil-and-paper test found active and passive sentences more closely connected than affirmative and negative sentences. A similar additive effect was found for combinations of passives and negatives.

Several other investigations required subjects to determine the truth values of different active-affirmative, passive, negative, and passive-negative sentences in relation to a variety of pictures and imaginary situations. They measured response times. All found that passive sentences required more time to evaluate than active sentences, negative sentences more time than either active or passive sentences, and passive-negative sentences most time of all. The evidence also appeared to support an additive effect. Again, too, actives and passives were found to be more closely connected than affirmatives and negatives, although the passive transformation has usually been regarded as linguistically more complex than the negative transformation in that it requires subjects and objects to be switched and the introduction of *be*, the past participle, and *by*: *John will do it* becomes *It will be done by John.*

However, sentences containing negatives do not always produce such results. Negation produces consequences not only for the syntax of sentences but also for their meanings. Two investigations of negation showed that negative sentences are generally more difficult to understand than affirmative sentences which convey approximately the same information, possibly because people must recast them as affirmatives to verify their content, as we see if we compare *Nine is not an even number* and *Eight is not an even number* with *Nine is an odd number* and *Eight is an odd number.* Still another study suggested that the actual plausibility of the negation creates part of the difficulty. Sentences such as *A pig isn't an insect, A spider isn't an insect,* and *An ant isn't an insect* cause people to react differently. The first sentence is not very likely: such a denial would seem to be rarely called for. In contrast the second sentence is very plausible: spiders are classed with insects quite frequently. The third sentence is untrue in contrast to the first two. Consequently, real-life usefulness and truth value may well be confounding variables in any task that investigates negation.

Further investigations which employed sentences containing words such as *some* and *all* in contexts like *All philosophers have read some books* and *Some books have been read by all philosophers* and required their meanings to be explained found that the form of the sentence tended to control the explanation which was given to it. Even though each of these two sentences is ambiguous in exactly the same ways as the other, the first is generally understood as "some books or other" and the second as "some books in particular." It is no longer surprising that problems of interpretation were found with the results of experiments on negation and on quantifiers such as *some, all, none,* and *any.* Just as sentences containing negatives and quantifiers were producing unexpected results in psycholinguistic investigations, linguists were discovering independently through their own attempts to explain grammatical relationships among sentences that negatives and quantifiers required a major recasting of the grammars they were attempting to write. They found that they had to take underlying meaning relationships into account in their rule writing and that many of their assumptions about the form and power of those rules required modification.

Investigating Psychological Processes

Today we see investigators adopting a much weaker approach to the problem of trying to relate grammatical descriptions to mental operations. No longer do they try to find close correspondences between the derivational history of a sentence, as that history is described in a grammar, and mental operations, as these may be revealed through some kind of response-oriented task. They rarely attempt to equate linguistic complexity directly to possible mental operations. There is general recognition of the unlikelihood of such a simple equation. A sentence like *He put his hat on* is linguistically more complex than *He put on his hat* since it requires an extra transformation to move the *on* to the end of the sentence; however, neither sentence seems more "difficult" than the other. Likewise, the sentences *The book was taken* and *The old man died* are more complex linguistically than *The book was taken by someone* and *The man who was old died* because both require deletion transformations removing *by someone* and *who was* respectively. But the first two seem to be even easier to understand than the last two. Faced with such problems, investigators today have largely abandoned the former search for direct correlates and are attempting instead to discover some of the ways in which sentences are processed. They also tend to approach the task piecemeal rather than wholesale as they attempt to locate specific strategies and processes rather than some all-encompassing principle which might explain everything in a very simple way.

Short-term memory processes are among those which have been investigated, particularly the processes which are involved in moving information into and out of short-term memory. For a while, as we might have expected, the concern was with remembering and forgetting sentences of various degrees of grammatical complexity: actives, passives, negatives, and so on. The general conclusion of such investigations is not surprising: less complex sentences are easier to remember than more complex sentences, but no fine gradation employing a complexity measure works consistently. Sentence length is important, and semantic factors and real-life conditions are again subtly involved. Actual quantity, meaning, and context, therefore, play important parts in remembering and forgetting.

A short-term memory experiment with a more restricted goal has led to conflicting results. The assumption behind the experiment is that sentences take up space in that memory, simpler sentences less space, and more complex sentences more space. The subjects in the experiment were given a sentence followed by a string of eight unrelated words and asked to recall the sentence and the words immediately following the last of the eight words. Then they were asked to repeat the task with another sentence of different grammatical complexity and another set of eight unrelated words, and so on for eleven different sentence types. The initial results indicated that when sentences were recalled before words, the number of words recalled from each set of eight indicated very accurately the grammatical complexity of the accompanying sentence. The more complex the sentence the fewer the words that were recalled: active-affirmative statements like *The boy has hit the ball* produced an average of 5.27 words; negative questions like *Has the boy not hit the ball?* 4.39 words; and passive-negative questions like *Has the ball not been hit by the boy?* 3.85 words. These results were interpreted to mean that transformations took up storage space in memory, questions taking up more such space than longer active sentences, for example. However, in conditions which required the words to be recalled before the sentences no such effects were observed. So the issue seems to be one of the relative ease of retrieval from memory rather than one of storage; one kind of retrieval task must interfere with the other. While it may be easy to get things both into and out of short-term memory, the two processes are apparently not mirror images of each other.

There is some evidence to suggest that semantic and syntactic information are not treated alike in short-term memory. The meanings of sentences are easier to recall than their exact grammatical shapes. If subjects are told that after listening to a short story, they will be asked to judge whether a particular sentence they will hear is identical to one they will hear in the story or, if changed, whether it is changed in "meaning" or "form," they produce an interesting pattern of replies. Given a sentence in the story like *He sent a letter about it to Galileo, the great Italian scientist,* they will generally fail to detect changes in form like *He sent Galileo, the great Italian scientist, a letter about it* or even *A letter about it was sent to Galileo, the great Italian scientist* as little as seven to eight seconds, or forty syllables, afterwards when those extra syllables have continued the narrative. But a meaning change to *Galileo, the great Italian scientist, sent him a letter about it* is readily detectable as long as three quarters of a minute after the original sentence. These findings suggest that the exact grammatical form of the original sentence is rapidly forgotten but that the information it contains is not: people remember the substance of what was said much better than they remember exactly how it was said.

The grammatical structure of a sentence must still play an important part in how it is perceived and remembered, even though many of the details of the structure are not retained. A series of experiments has used a task which requires subjects to locate where a click occurs during a spoken sentence in order to discover how people perceive units of grammar and meanings. The subjects are asked to listen to tape recordings in a dichotic listening test. In one ear they hear sentences; in the other ear they hear a click at some point during each sentence; they must report the point in each sentence at which the click occurred immediately after they hear the sentence. In one experiment sequences of words such as *George drove furiously to the station* and *hope of marrying Anna was surely impractical* were spliced to form pairs of sentences such as *In order to catch his train, George drove furiously to the station, The reporters assigned to George drove furiously to the station* and *In her hope of marrying, Anna was surely impractical, Your hope of marrying Anna was surely impractical.* In these pairs the syntactic break is before *George* and *Anna* in the first sentence of each pair and after *George* and *Anna* in the second sentence. The subjects heard a click timed to occur with the vowel in *George* and the first vowel in *Anna*. Most of them reported that the clicks occurred at the syntactic breaks; the remainder between some other pairs of words; and none actually during a word.

Working in this way, investigators can be sure that it is not the acoustic stimuli which produce the differences in response. Any differences which are observed must result from the perceptual strategies that the subjects are using. The real controversy appears to be over whether such strategies require listeners to recognize characteristic types of superficial structure, for example, phrasal modifiers or nominalizations, or certain sequences of words in the surface structure which correspond to underlying sentence types. Since many of the relevant characteristics of superficial "surface" structure reflect underlying "deep" sentences, no easy resolution of the controversy may be possible. In both interpretations, however, the grammatical structure of the incoming sentence plays an important role in allowing listeners to make decisions about the actual physical events that occurred. Grammatical structure is projected as well as recognized, and listeners use specific strategies in making their projections. Since language stimuli fade so rapidly, people must have processing strategies which work quickly and fairly reliably if communication is to be effective.

A few specific strategies have been suggested. Events spoken of will be assumed to have occurred in the sequence mentioned; the sequence of clauses will tend to mirror the sequence of events. Consequently, a sentence like *He left after I spoke* will create difficulties in comprehension that a sentence like *After I spoke he left* will not create. Passive sentences like *The woman was wounded by the man* which allow subjects and objects to be switched readily and still make sense (*The man was wounded by the woman*) are harder to verify through reference to the actual events described than sentences like *The ticket was bought by the man* which do not allow such switching. (*The man was bought by the ticket* is not possible.) Noun-verb-noun sequences are usually interpreted as actor-action-object sequences. Therefore, a sentence like *The pitcher tossed the ball tossed it* will almost certainly seem to be ungrammatical on first hearing. It is a good sentence if *tossed the ball* is interpreted as a participial phrase, but the most productive strategy, that is, the strategy which usually produces the correct result most quickly, requires *pitcher* to be the subject of *tossed* and *ball* to be its object.

Successive nouns or noun phrases at the beginning of a sentence will be interpreted as coordinate in structure. Embedded clauses will therefore be troublesome on that account. *The girl the rat bit screamed* is less easy to grasp than *The girl that the rat bit screamed*, the relative pronoun *that* effectively interposing between the two noun phrases. *The pen the author the editor liked used was new* is almost totally incomprehensible; however, inclusion of the two relative pronouns *which* and *whom* radically improves comprehension: *The pen which the author whom the editor liked used was new.* We should note that English requires use of the relative pronoun in just those cases where noun and verb phrases fall together to produce possible confusion. Consequently, *who* or *that* is mandatory in *The player who scored the touchdown was injured* to prevent *player* being interpreted as the subject of *scored* and leaving *was injured* with no subject. But in *The book I want is missing* a *which* or *that* between *book* and *I* is optional. It does sometimes help, particularly in long or complicated sentences. Today, investigations are more likely to be concerned with the strategies and heuristics which listeners appear to use in processing sentences than with the reality of grammatical processes. They are also likely to be concerned with the way in which sentences themselves are structured so as to give listeners the best chance of arriving at correct interpretations.

Over the years attention has been given from time to time to such concepts as "grammatical" and "acceptable," to how ambiguous sentences are interpreted, and to the ability to paraphrase. Studies of grammaticality and acceptability have been rather inconclusive because no clear distinction can be made between what is grammatical and/or acceptable and what is not for just those sentences that are worth investigating. Is Chomsky's famous sentence *Colorless green ideas sleep furiously* grammatical or not? Acceptable or not? It is not at all clear how one can decide such questions. So far as ambiguous sentences are concerned, people assign only one meaning to a particular sequence of words at any one time, just as they assign only one interpretation to an ambiguous figure or picture at any one time. Consequently, when a sequence of words takes an unexpected turn, the listener must reprocess both meaning and structure from a suitable back-up point, an experience all of us have had. Sentences in isolation are highly ambiguous. They have many potentially different meanings. Context decreases the ambiguity considerably but generally does not eliminate it completely.

Tests of paraphrase ability can produce results which bring into question the whole concept of linguistic competence. Twenty-five subjects were given 144 three-term compounds and asked either to paraphrase the compounds or to choose one of several alternative paraphrases. It is generally agreed that such compounds have a syntactic base and result from transformational processes, for example, *a birdhouse* from *a house for birds* and *a bath house* from *a house which has a bath.* The compounds used were made up from the words *bird* and *house* and one of twelve words such as *bath, black, boot, eat, foot,* and *glass.* The result was compounds such as *bird-house bath, bird housebath, bird bathhouse, housebath bird,* and so on. Many such compounds were obviously bizarre in meaning. The seven advanced graduate students and holders of the doctoral degree (no linguists) in the group did significantly better than both the seven undergraduate students and the eleven people without a college education. The undergraduate students performed only a little better than these eleven. Everyone was able to do the paraphrase task to some extent, and no one questioned its validity. It seems safe to conclude that some kind of linguistic knowledge or ability was being tapped. However, the differences among the groups and some of the differences in specific responses raise important questions concerning the nature of that knowledge or ability. It is not clear whether the differences demonstrated a different linguistic competence or a different linguistic performance within the groups, or whether the findings suggest that the competence-performance distinction may not be particularly useful in describing what is going on.

Some Limitations

Even a brief, nonexhaustive review of part of the work in experimental psycholinguistics bearing on certain aspects of language production and processing provides evidence that while much has been discovered, considerably more remains unknown. The experimental methods used require the manipulation of discrete variables, but the problems under investigation are so complex that such manipulation tends to produce ambiguous results. There must still be many variables not yet accounted for. Results are not only ambiguous on occasion; many times they are completely contradictory to other results. So progress tends to come by fits and starts and there is much backtracking. The mind still remains the blackest of all black boxes. Its inner workings are not directly accessible, and all the knowledge we have of those workings comes through inference. Making inferences about deep mental processes from any kind of memorization and reaction-time tasks is a hazardous business: the chances of being wrong are usually much greater than those of being right. Hence the caution with which most results are announced.

An alternative approach would downplay the role of experimentation, except to confirm claims, in favor of building hypotheses about the innate structure of the black box. In such an approach the investigator says that language is like this or like that and that the human mind must be like this or like that in order to use language. If language is a rule-governed system, then the mind must work like a machine in handling the rules; and if language is a complex network of relationships, then the mind must be built to accommodate such a network. The fundamental assumption behind this approach is that it takes a theory of language to be a theory of mind, claiming as it does that any grammar that is postulated must be both linguistically *and* psychologically real. While there is some evidence to support such a claim, we do not yet have available a theory of language that allows us to make very strong claims with any degree of confidence. Existing theories and all the derivatives of such theories—the units, rules, processes, and so on—are sufficiently tenuous that the search for the psychological correlates of any parts or processes must be regarded as still in the planning stage rather than in a stage of productive achievement.

A necessary part of any search is an investigation of the limiting psychological constraints that *any* theory of language use must observe. Such constraints would also apply to the theory of language structure which would form part of a theory of language use. Consequently, investigations of memory limitations, perceptual strategies, redundancy utilization, and the relationships between syntactic, semantic, and real-life situations are mandatory. If every conceivable experiment shows that certain kinds of psychological constraints must operate, for example, that human beings can deal with only a certain number of possible surface structures in a language or only certain kinds and depths of syntactic embedding, then any grammar written for the language must heed those constraints. In recent years linguists have somewhat modified their earlier position that such constraints are performance constraints of little interest. They now acknowledge that if no one apparently has the competence to ignore the constraints, the original competence-performance distinction requires reexamination.

It has sometimes been argued that language itself can be used as a window into the mind. It can even be argued that the kinds of containments which can be explained within language in linguistic terms (no matter how awkwardly) reveal properties of mind. Such arguments have a certain attractiveness in that they leave the linguist largely free to ignore psychological matters. However, they can lead to linguistic investigation proceeding in a vacuum of its own making. Language is certainly self-contained in one sense. As we noted in Chapter One, that it is so is a fundamental assumption of linguistics. But the reasons for the self-containment may not all arise from within language. That is a highly unlikely proposition. Linguistics may be a branch of cognitive psychology, but it is certainly not the main stem. If it offers a window into the mind, it is a window into only part of that mind and still a rather unclear one.

References

Rose (1973) contains much valuable material on a number of topics discussed in this chapter. Skinner's (1957) book on verbal behavior is reviewed by Chomsky (1959). MacCorquodale (1969, 1970) reviews both Skinner's and Chomsky's views.

See Hebb (1949) for his views on perception, Cherry (1953) for "shadowing," and Hubel (1963), Hubel and Wiesel (1962), and Lettvin, Maturana, McCulloch, and Pitts (1959, 1961) for feature-detector systems. Lane (1965) and Studdert-Kennedy, Liberman, Harris, and Cooper (1970) present opposing views on the motor theory of speech perception. Lenneberg (1962) describes the presence of language ability in the absence of speaking ability. Miller (1956) discusses the capacity of short-term memory, Brown and McNeill (1966) the "tip of the tongue" phenomenon, and Boomer and Laver (1968) and Fromkin (1973) slips of the tongue.

Ladefoged (1967) and Taylor (1966) report on babbling and stuttering respectively, and Fromkin (1968) on syllables as basic units. The pronunciation of consonants after vowels of various length is in Lehiste (1970). For speech perception in general see Wanner (1973). The experiment on the intelligibility of short sequences of words is described by Pollack and Pickett (1964), that on *light, house,* and *keeper* by Lieberman (1967), and that on grammatical and anomalous sentences and random strings of words presented against noise by Miller and Isard (1963). For the impracticality of analysis-by-synthesis see Thorne (1966), and for a discussion of general issues in performance see that paper and the papers by Wales and Marshall (1966) and Fodor and Garrett (1966) in the same volume, Lyons and Wales (1966).

Greéne (1972) provides an overview of psychological work based on generative-transformational theory. Miller (1962) discusses the very early work and Johnson-Laird (1970) focuses on more recent work. The use of reaction times in sentence matching is described in Miller and McKean (1964) and of motor responses in Clifton, Kurcz, and Jenkins (1965). Gough (1965), McMahon (1963), and Slobin (1966) report on the effects of truth values on responses. The first two investigations of negatives that are cited are Eifermann (1961) and Wason (1961); the third is Wason (1965).

Two articles by Johnson-Laird (1969a, 1969b) discuss ambiguity in the presence of quantifiers. Savin and Perchonock (1965) and Epstein (1969) report on the use of sentences plus unrelated words to test memory space for transformations. The "Galileo" sentences come from Sachs (1967) and the "George" and "Anna" sentences from Garrett, Bever, and Fodor (1966). Bever (1970) discusses possible strategies that are involved in language processing. The paraphrase investigation is the subject of Gleitman and Gleitman (1970).

4

The
Personal
Context

Individual Variation

One possible way of studying language would be to try to say everything we can about the language of a specific individual in an attempt to exhaust a single source of data. Admirable though such an approach may appear to be, it does have an obvious weakness: many of the conclusions will not generalize to the population at large. Certain variations and characteristics will be quite idiosyncratic when considered in relation to the distribution of those variations and characteristics in the total population. What interests linguists are those characteristics which everyone shares with everyone else and which together function as a total language system: certain phonemic contrasts; particular patterns of word order; regular meaning relationships; and so on.

Such individual characteristics as how loudly or how softly someone generally speaks, the pitch range of a particular voice, a person's verbosity or lack of it, a listener's habits of interruption, or a speaker's patterns of hesitation and change of direction generally hold little interest. They seem to be distributed normally over the total set of language users. One person may speak extra loudly and another extra softly, but most speakers fall somewhere in between near the middle of a range of loudness-softness. Each individual's language derives some

of its uniqueness from the particular combination it exhibits of characteristics which appear to be normally distributed.

Even though a wide range of personal variation exists, it is still quite
possible to be aware of departures from individual norms. These departures
can also be used for special kinds of communication. For example, a person
may speak overloud or oversoft or may drawl out words or clip them. Such
behavior is likely to be interpreted as indicating something about the speaker's attitude either to the listener or to the topic or about the speaker's general state of mind or physical condition. A beginning has been made in attempts
to characterize this kind of behavior in which the voice is used alongside the
spoken words to convey messages by paralinguistic means. People moan and
groan out words, they yell and whisper, laugh and cry, and their voices whine,
break, and vary in pitch, intensity, and duration of the various sounds. What
they do in these ways reinforces or subverts their words, and listeners know
that. So a system of some kind seems to be operating. Likewise, people are
sensitive to the postures of others, to the kinds of eye contact that are maintained during conversations, to touching of varying kinds, to distances between
the participants when any words are exchanged, and even to the physical
warmth and smell of others.

A beginning has been made in investigations of such systematic uses of
the voice, space, gesture, and a number of interesting discoveries have been
made. Different parameters can be isolated and manipulated experimentally
so as to produce consistent results. Overall, though, progress has been slow
mainly because many of the characteristics being investigated seem to demonstrate a normal curve distribution (that is, they are quantitatively distributed with a peak around a norm) rather than a categorial distribution
(that is, they are qualitatively distributed, either present or not). Linguistic
methodology is much more comfortable with distributions of the second
kind. However, softness-loudness for voices and near-far for distances may
be two continua rather than two binary choices. Since linguists have only
very recently made any serious attempts to deal with noncategorial distributions, it is likely that new investigations will produce still further findings
of interest.

Whatever the results of such investigations, language remains a personal
thing in many respects. Each individual uses it to mediate the world in
some way. Each person thinks more or less successfully. Each person expresses through language a capacity for dealing with the world intelligently
and logically or fails to do so either because that capacity is limited or the
ability to display it is limited. Language is the primary tool for mediation,
thought, and expression. It would be useful, therefore, to consider what we
know about these important uses of language.

Language and Thought

The relationship between language and thought has been a persistent theme in philosophy, psychology, and, to a much lesser extent, linguistics for many years. The problems are legion ranging from how specific individuals use language to solve different kinds of problems to how the structure of a language might possibly determine how speakers of that language think and behave. The issues are many, and, as we shall see, some of them are still hotly debated.

A necessary preliminary observation is that certain kinds of thinking appear to go on without language, for example, those kinds of artistic thought which find expression through movement, music, painting, sculpture, and so on. Certainly no animal has such expressive abilities: they are unique to human kind. As we saw in the second chapter, such abilities seem to be associated with the nonlanguage hemisphere of a brain which is partially lateralized for function. Since the products of artistic expression show form and symmetry and "say something," they can hardly be regarded as "thoughtless." But they are probably "language-less," certainly in any sense that the term *language* has for linguists. What grammars they have are their own grammars, an entirely different species from the one which interests linguists. The term *grammar* in *grammar of music* or *grammar of dance* bears only a superficial resemblance to the term *grammar* in *grammar of English*.

Writers on thinking and the processes by which thought becomes speech have sometimes expressed the view that thought is really some kind of speech itself: thought is language. Certain behaviorist psychologists, for example, have considered language to be speech and have concentrated their research on the physical manifestations of language rather than on any abstract characteristics language might have. Thinking itself has been regarded as a kind of subvocal speech, a position stated in different ways by John B. Watson, who considered thinking to be largely subvocal talking, a set of motor habits in the larynx, and by B. F. Skinner, who asserted that man thinking is simply man behaving. In this view, language behavior is just like any other kind of behavior and subject to the same laws, the language-thought dichotomy is a false one, and there is possibly even little need for a linguistics with its own unique set of beliefs and assumptions.

The counterevidence to such a view is considerable. Paralyzing the muscles of speech should result in a total loss of the ability to think, but an experiment which induced total paralysis in subjects through an injection of a form of curare brought about no such loss. Likewise, a child suffering from a complete neurological inability to talk was observed to be able to comprehend spoken English quite well. Neither result should have been possible according to the extreme behaviorist view stated above. Linguistically, of course, as Chomsky and others have demonstrated, such a view is not tenable. Language is not just speech:

it is also some kind of abstract system that speakers share. Thinking makes use of the abstract system in ways we have only begun to explore, as we saw in the last chapter. Speaking itself it just one part of total language ability, and not necessarily the most critical part.

The Whorf Hypothesis

A very different point of view and one which has attracted considerable attention among linguists, psychologists, and anthropologists is associated with the linguist Edward Sapir and his student Benjamin Lee Whorf. This view is that thought processes are more or less determined by linguistic structure. It is not easy to be quite sure where Sapir stood on this issue. He said both that human beings are very much at the mercy of a particular language, their language habits predisposing them to make certain choices of interpretation, and also that it was difficult to see what causal relationships could be expected to subsist between particular experiences and the manner in which a society expresses its experiences. Like his eighteenth- and nineteenth-century predecessors, Herder and Humboldt, Sapir was obviously intrigued with the connection between language structure and thought processes, but he was somewhat equivocal in describing the connection.

Whorf had no such hesitancy. A professional engineer and insurance adjuster, Whorf lacked Sapir's considerable caution in linguistic matters. As a result of comparing what he called Standard Average European (languages like English, French, and German) with American Indian languages, particularly Hopi, Whorf proposed that the structure of language determines thought and that speakers of different languages experience the world differently. This proposal has become known as the Whorf hypothesis. For some of his examples of how language influences thought Whorf drew on his own experience in looking for the causes of fires. "Empty" gasoline drums were often treated quite haphazardly whereas "full" ones were not; the fact that they were often full of fumes, and, therefore, dangerous fire hazards was completely ignored. The word *empty* was the culprit; according to Whorf, it gave people entirely the wrong idea about the situation.

The strongest statement of the Whorf hypothesis is that language structure determines thought completely and controls the way a speaker views the world; consequently, different languages produce different "world views" in their speakers. A much weaker position is that the structure of a language makes certain kinds of perceptions easy and others difficult but does not make anything impossible. Each language acts as a kind of filter for reality. It makes certain kinds of things more likely to be commented on than others, but it does not necessarily leave the latter unnoticed. Language structure predisposes rather than determines certain kinds of thought and behavior.

In attempting to confirm or refute any version of the hypothesis, a linguist can use a variety of evidence. However, that evidence cannot consist merely of casual observations about how strange an exotic language sounds or how peculiar are its words and grammatical structures. Greater objectivity than that is required. The words and grammatical structures are the important evidence, but the key issues have to do with the interpretation of the evidence. What conclusions can one draw from the fact that in one language a certain distinction, for example, a singular-plural distinction, *must* be made in all "naming" words (nouns) but in another language it *may* be made? Or from the fact that adjectives must precede nouns in one language rather than follow them in another? Or from the fact that one language has a word for a particular concept but another must use a phrase if it uses anything at all? The interpretation is all.

German has words like *Gemütlichkeit, Weltanschauung,* and *Weihnachsbaum;* English has no exact equivalent of any one of them, *Christmas tree* being fairly close in the last case but still lacking the "magical" German connotations. Both people and bulls have legs in English, but Spanish requires people to have *piernas* and bulls to have *patas.* Arabic has many words for types of camels; English does not. Speakers of English have many words for different kinds of automobiles, just as Eskimos have many words for different kinds of snow and the Trobriand Islanders of the South Seas many words for different kinds of yams. The Navaho of the Southwest United States, the Shona of Rhodesia, and the Hanunoo of the Philippines divide the color spectrum differently from each other in the distinctions they make, and English speakers divide it differently again. English has a general cover term *animal* for various kinds of creatures, but it lacks a term to cover both *fruit* and *nuts;* however, Chinese languages have such a cover term. French *conscience* is both English *conscience* and *consciousness.* Both German and French have two pronouns corresponding to *you,* a singular and a plural. Japanese, on the other hand, has an extensive system of honorifics. The equivalent of English *stone* has a gender in French and German, and the various words must always be either singular or plural in French, German, and English. In Chinese, however, number is expressed only if it is somehow relevant. Kwakiutl speakers in British Columbia must also indicate whether the stone is visible or not to the speaker at the time of speaking, as well as its position relative to one or another of the speaker, the listener, or possible third party. Some Japanese sentences are almost completely the reverse of corresponding English sentences in their word order.

Given such a range of evidence, the linguist is faced with the task of assimilating it and drawing defensible conclusions from both it and any experiments that seem to bear on the issues. The conclusions are generally different from those that Whorf drew. For example, the words *fist, wave, spark,* and *flame* are nouns in English, so we tend to see the events or actions they name as having some kind of objective existence. But we also know that this existence is of a different kind from that of houses, rocks, cats, and trees. We can, therefore, understand that words for the same events or actions can appear as verbs in Hopi: we know that houses and rocks comprise a different order of "things" from fists and waves. One language refers to certain characteristics of the real world in terms of one possible subset of characteristics; another favors a different subset. However, speakers of both languages may still be aware of all the characteristics. They are not required to refer to all of them.

Syntactic evidence can also mislead investigators. Much of the evidence is provided by literal translation, as though *breakfast* were understood as a "break in a fast," or *cats* as "cat" plus "plural," as though in a group of cats one cat were noticed independently of, and before, the presence of the other cats. Over-literal translation is very dangerous, particularly of metaphoric language. English, for example, is full of metaphors: *I see what you mean, He grasped the idea, You're behind the times*, and so on. At best, the syntactic evidence suggests that languages allow their speakers to make certain observations more easily in some cases than others. An obligatory grammatical category, for example, tense-marking in English verbs, will lead to certain things being said in English that need not be said, for example, in Chinese; an available vocabulary item, for example, various words for snow in Eskimo, will have the same result.

It may be the case that recognition, recall, problem solving, and concept formation are influenced by the particular language that is used. One experiment showed that different names given to twelve briefly presented figures resulted in these figures begin reproduced differently on a later occasion. A line drawing that was somewhere between a bottle and a stirrup would very likely be reproduced to resemble a bottle when a person heard it referred to as a *bottle*. However, another person would reproduce it to resemble a stirrup when the word *stirrup* was used. The word labels guided the participants in remembering the original drawings but not in remembering them absolutely correctly. Just what effect the labels had on the actual perception of the drawings is much less clear.

Experiments with the perception of the color spectrum show that speakers of various languages do favor referring to certain parts of the spectrum, but that they can also make distinctions they do not usually make if they are required to do so. Different languages have also been examined for the basic color terms they use in dividing the color spectrum. A basic color term must be a single word (not *light blue*), not a subdivision of another term (like *crimson*), not highly restricted in use (like *blond*), and not highly specialized (like *puce*). Although different languages contain different numbers of basic color terms a natural hierarchy appears to exist for referring to the parts of the spectrum. An analysis of the basic color terms of nearly a hundred languages revealed that if a language has two color terms, these are for *black* (or *dark*) and *white* (or *light*); if it has three, these are for *black, white,* and *red*; if it has four, the additional term is for either *green* or *yellow*; if it has five, the additional term is the remaining one of *green* or *yellow*. Then the terms for *blue, brown, purple, pink, orange,* and *grey* are added, although not necessarily in that order. There is apparently a connection between the first few terms and the colors in nature that are most noticeable: black, white, red, green, yellow, and blue. Languages differ in where they place in such a hierarchy with the languages of more technologically oriented and complex societies having more terms. The different placements therefore account for the different color naming practices of speakers.

The most valid conclusion to all such studies is that it appears possible to talk about anything in any language provided the speaker is willing to use some degree of circumlocution. Some concepts are more "codable," that is, easier to express, in some languages than in others. The speaker, of course, will not be aware of the circumlocution in the absence of familiarity with another language that uses a more succinct means of expression. Every natural language provides both a language for talking about every other language, that is, a metalanguage, and an entirely adequate apparatus for making any kinds of observations that need to be made about the world. If such is the case, every natural language must be an extremely rich system which readily allows its speakers to overcome any predispositions that exist.

Language and Culture

So far we have considered the issue of linguistic determinism and relativity only from the perspective of the individual: how far a particular language constrains a speaker of that language to a certain view of the world. The Whorf hypothesis, however, was extended to cover whole cultures. For example, one writer argued that what he identified as some of the worst traits of the German character could be blamed on what Mark Twain called the "awful German language" because of the extensive use of nominalizations and the capitalization of nouns. More recently, others have argued that the postpositioning of French adjectives, as in *les plumes rouges*, reflects deductive habits of thought, whereas the prepositioning of English adjectives, as in *the red pens*, reflects inductive habits, and that Navaho grammatical structure, which does not clearly separate actors, actions, and objects in the way that English does, reflects the underlying passivity and fatefulness of the Navaho. In each case a close relationship is postulated between certain cultural characteristics and certain linguistic forms or structures.

If language does not control thought but merely inhibits thought processes, it should not control any aspect of culture either. The evidence we have tends to show that there is no such control. There is no evidence that language type correlates with culture. Speakers of different agglutinative languages, that is, languages like Turkish and many American Indian languages which build up very complex words rather than complex sentences to express ideas, can be associated with very different cultures. So can inflecting languages, those with a balance of morphology and syntax, and isolating languages, those with complex syntax but relatively little morphology. Speakers of very different languages can also share much the same culture, and a single language—English is a good example—can be spoken by members of very different cultures. While it is a truism that each language is different from every other just as is each culture, singling out a few isolated forms or structures where this difference is most obvious —as in the examples in the previous paragraph or in attempts to show how different Japanese is from English by exploiting the system of honorifics—results in highlighting the peculiar at the expense of illuminating the usual. The result is a collection of language curiosities rather than a set of linguistic insights.

Two important experiments have cast serious doubts on the proposition that the language people speak binds them to a particular world view. In one, speakers of English and Hopi were presented with twelve sets of three pictures of actions or events. From each set they were asked to select the two pictures that went best together. For example, one set consisted of a picture of peaches being poured from a box, another of coins being spilled from a pocket, and the third of water being spilled from a pitcher. English uses the words *spill* and *pour*, the first for an accidental action and the second for a deliberate one. Hopi uses the words *wehekna* and *wa:hokna*, the first for an action involving liquids and the second for an action involving solids. The twelve sets dealt with situations which could be described differently in Hopi and in English. Fourteen Hopi-speaking adults, many of whom also spoke English quite well, twelve rural New England adults of an educational level comparable to the speakers of Hopi, and fifteen graduate students sorted the sets of pictures. The results showed only a rather small nonsignificant difference in the expected direction between the speakers of Hopi and the speakers of English. The Hopi actually favored the unexpected English groupings more often than they did the expected Hopi groupings by a ratio of not quite three to two. In contrast, the ratio for speakers of English was three to one. The fact that most of the Hopi were also speakers of English might have accounted for the lack of a significant difference. Of course, it did not account for the fact that approximately twenty per cent of the responses by the speakers of English supported Hopi categorizations of the pictured actions or events.

The other experiment investigated grammatical categories that must be expressed in Navaho. Navaho verbs of handling require an obligatory grammatical marker which indicates certain characteristics of the shape of the object handled: a request to be handed a long and flexible object such as a piece of string requires the verb to have one marker, *sanleh*; a long and rigid object such as a pencil another, *santiih;* and a flat and flexible object such as a piece of paper a third, *sanilcoos*. Would Navaho children therefore tend to classify objects on the basis of their shape rather than on some other basis, for example, on the basis of their size or color?

Navaho children aged between three and ten were used. Since the children were bilingual, they were tested for language dominance and grouped as either Navaho-dominant or English-dominant. White middle-class children from Boston, who spoke only English, were also given the same task. They served as a control group. The task itself was quite simple. Each child was shown pairs of objects differing in both color and shape, for example, a blue stick and a yellow rope. Then the child was shown a third object, either a blue rope or a yellow stick, and asked to match it with one of the previously shown objects. The Navaho-dominant and English-dominant children performed significantly differently in the predicted direction; however, the control group from Boston out-Navahoed the Navaho-dominant group. When a further group of black children from Harlem was tested, these children resembled the English-dominant Navaho children in their performance. All the children who participated, regardless of language and ethnic backgroud, relied more and more on the shape of the objects rather than on their color as they became older. If a reliance on shape rather than on color is interpreted to be a sign of cognitive development, then such development seems aided both by having a necessary grammatical category in the language which requires reference to shape and by factors in a middle-class environment. It appears to be hindered when both are absent. The overriding conclusion is that the grammatical structure of a language is but one of the variables which influence cognitive development. Culture itself and the experiences provided by the culture are at least as potent factors in the development of cognition and thought.

There is still a further corollary of the hypothesis that culture and language are intimately related, with cultural patterns to some extent determined by language structure. It is that individuals are constrained in their cultural behavior and opportunities by the language of their subculture. Very young children are obviously constrained by the language they speak, but these constraints seem to be of a differen kind; developmental rather than behavioral. The constraints at issue are those that are said to arise from the sexual, social, and racial biases which have been built into languages. The claim is that a language can be "sexist," "classist," or "racist" *within* itself, predisposing its speakers to have certain attitudes to others within society. We will have more to say on this subject in Chapter Six. For now, suffice it to say that just as the main thesis has never been proved, neither has this corollary. Both thesis and corollary have been asserted to be true; both are provocative; both seem to offer explanations for phenomena in the outside world; but conclusive data to support either do not exist.

Finally, there is no justification for the existence of beliefs in either primitive languages or primitive patterns of thought. The former do not exist in the sense in which *primitive* is always intended, that is, in the sense of "inferior," and the evidence cited for the latter generally ignores the complexity of the linguistic issues and short-changes the culture which is being considered. When the linguistic evidence has been assessed, it has generally been within a superficial Whorfian perspective: since there are few or no grammatical markings for tense, time must be unimportant to the speakers; since there are no obvious words for logical operations, reasoning and problem solving must be minimal and complex scientific thought an impossibility. Such conclusions are quite invalid, betraying as they do preconceptions about how time relationships must be expressed or what forms argumentation must take. They also fail to take into account the complexity that any language must have if it is to function as a cohesive bond in a group that lasts for any length of time in even the starkest living conditions. We know today how difficult it is to provide anything like an adequate account of the language *and* culture of any group no matter how small. Explaining the relationship that is presumed to exist between language and culture is a task of still another magnitude of difficulty.

It is not unreasonable to say that an individual's language acts as a guide in thinking about the world in certain ways and in thinking about it in much the same way as others who speak the same language. But the language does not determine either thought or behavior. New ways of thinking and behaving remain possible. The history of Western science is a particularly good example of individuals and groups developing new patterns of thought. Western science is also exportable, though not without some inconvenience at times, to "non-Western" languages and cultures. Admittedly, language is intimately related to thought and culture in subtle and pervasive ways. But at the same time every language has resources which allow its speakers to talk about language, thought, and culture. It is this capacity, above all, that must make any belief in linguistic determinism highly suspect.

Words and Concepts

It is sometimes argued that a capacity for thought and language most clearly differentiates humans from other species. Thought and language allow people to act or not to act, to analyze the consequences of their own and others' actions, to consider past and future as well as present, to take into account the real and the imaginary, and to think about their own thinking and talk about their own talking. Thought and language allow humans to create and manipulate symbols of all kinds. Whether the need to symbolize is a human being's most basic need beyond those which must be satisfied to ensure survival is a philosophical matter. But beyond dispute is the fact that language is the symbol-using system *par excellence*. Certain capacities for symbolization, thought, and language must be innate in the human species. How unique the species may be in possessing these capacities we will examine in Chapter Eight. For the moment we will consider only how words, thoughts, and language appear to function in the regulation and development of certain aspects of human behavior.

Although any view of a language which regards it as a set of words each of which stands for a concept is oversimplified linguistically, nevertheless studies based on such views have furnished a number of useful insights into specific aspects of concept formation. Studies of the development of simple concepts in children have shown that children generally must refine the initial concepts they arrive at. For example, a concept such as "dog" must be progressively narrowed so as to exclude a whole range of inappropriate instances. Neither cats nor ponies are dogs. Eventually the concept "insect" must also exclude that of "spider." Children find abstract concepts such as "brother" and "mother" very difficult to learn because they must be mediated through other concepts and depend on sets of relationships. A child may understand that John is his brother but not that he is also John's brother. He may extend the concept of "mother" to include that of "wife." Young children have difficulty with tasks requiring the sorting of objects such as spoons, knives, hammers, matches, pipes, apples, cigars, and balls into various groups by material, use, color, and so on. They cannot manipulate the necessary abstract concepts easily. Asked in what way are an orange and a grapefruit alike, young children are more likely to respond that they are alike in that they are round (a concrete characteristic) rather than that they are fruit (an abstract characteristic). That they are fruit is typically the reply of older children and adults.

Words and phrases do not always stand for simple concepts, either concrete or abstract. Many stand for derived concepts, that is, concepts formed out of combinations of existing concepts. Three basic kinds of derived concept have been proposed. A conjunctive concept shows the joint presence of several attributes, as in *foreign diplomat, service station operator,* and so on. A disjunctive concept shows a lack of commonality in its members except in the named characteristic, as in *children* (boys and girls), *round* (oranges and balls), and *red* (traffic signals and tomatoes). A relational concept shows a relationship between attributes, as in *right side, taller,* and *underneath.* Experiments with invented concepts show that adults find relational concepts harder to learn than conjunctive concepts and disjunctive concepts hardest of all. It is not surprising therefore that children often misuse words like *brother* and *mother* as they learn to use the language.

Piaget and Egocentric Speech

The Swiss psychologist Jean Piaget has long been interested in how concepts develop in children and how children acquire their knowledge of the world. Piaget has tried to show how various aspects of human behavior develop in sequences of stages. According to Piaget, what children do at a particular age and what they say and think is limited by their innate capacity for doing, saying, and thinking at that age. This capacity both limits and prescribes their ability to deal with the world. It is the biological nature of the human organism which determines how that capacity changes and develops over time.

Piaget observed two kinds of speech in kindergarten children: egocentric speech and socialized speech. He defined egocentric speech as speech lacking in communicative intent. It can occur in solitude or in the presence of others, but in the latter case shows no regard for possible listeners. It is speech bound up with the activity of the moment. Children also assume that any listeners are also bound up in that activity and see it in exactly the same way they do. Egocentric speech is therefore a kind of thinking out loud, and listeners are considered to be parties to the thoughts. Children cannot step outside of themselves in order to adopt another's perspective. They are at the centers of their own universes, and no one, particularly the children themselves, can do anything about it. According to Piaget, there are also three kinds of egocentric speech: repetition or echolalia in which children merely repeat themselves or others; monologue in which they talk to themselves in a kind of thinking out loud; and collective monologue in which individuals within groups talk aloud in turn but do so without any real communicative intent. On the other hand, socialized speech does try to take the listener into account; it also leads to criticizing, commanding, stating, and questioning, and brings about a real exchange of information.

As a result of his various investigations Piaget claims that nearly half of kindergarten speech is egocentric. In one study involving kindergarten children, one child was given information to relate to a second child. The study showed that young children do not communicate material very clearly because they fail to consider the needs of the listener. However, they believe that they have been understood. They do not even understand very well what they are told, even though once again they almost always believe that they have understood. Children are quite unaware that their gestures, their pronouns without clear referents, and their abbreviated utterances are failing to communicate. They do not realize that the intended communication is not the one that is actually received. Piaget's investigations convinced him that egocentric behavior is a pervasive characteristic of cognition in very young children. According to Piaget, egocentric speech is gradually replaced by socialized speech as children grow older and develop both cognitively and socially. Egocentric speech gradually atrophies from growing disuse and eventually disappears.

In this view much of the language development of children therefore depends on their cognitive development. Children's intellects develop as part of a natural process in which interaction with the environment plays an important part. Language is used in part of that interaction, but it is not the development of language ability itself which leads to increased ability to interact and think. Rather it is the natural growth in the ability to think, that is, cognitive development, which leads in the development of language and of the skills necessary for successful social behavior.

Vygotsky and Socialized Speech

The Russian psychologist Vygotsky disagreed considerably with Piaget's views of the relationship between language and thought and of the functions of language in childhood. Vygotsky's major concern was with the development and function of what he called *inner speech*. By inner speech he did not mean verbal memory, that is, the storage of words and concepts, or subvocal speech, that is, covert laryngeal motor habits, or the interior aspects of speech activity, that is, the mental processes involved in ideation. Nor is inner speech just talking to oneself. Vygotsky defined inner speech as speech for oneself as opposed to external speech, which is speech for others. Inner speech, being for oneself, turns inward to thought; external speech, being for others, turns thought into words. External speech is therefore social speech. Because of its function, inner speech is highly abbreviated and dominated by predicates (often unmodified verbs and objects) when it employs language at all. Topics are already known and need not be stated because people know what they are thinking about. In social speech, topics must be stated and comments made about the topics; predicates alone are not enough.

Vygotsky differed with Piaget on the nature of egocentric speech. He regarded egocentric speech as a phenomenon of the transition from the social, collective activity of children to more individualized activity. According to Vygotsky, individual speech has its origin in collective speech. Egocentric speech, like inner speech, does not merely accompany activity; it helps to produce conscious understanding and is closely connected with the development of thought. Egocentric speech develops and becomes inner speech; it does not atrophy. All speech is therefore social in origin; part of it becomes inner speech.

Vygotsky argued that at the age of three there is no difference between egocentric and social speech; however, at the age of seven the two are quite different. It is the differentiation which accounts for the lack of vocalization and the structural peculiarities of egocentric speech and gives it the appearance of dying out. But, according to Vygotsky, saying that it has died out is like saying that children stop counting when they cease to count on their fingers and use their heads instead. What has happened is that egocentric speech has developed into inner speech. External social speech continues as before in order to support communication. Vygotsky, therefore, conceived of all speech as social in origin but subject to a bifurcation, moving in one direction toward inner speech and thought and continuing in the other direction to serve the needs of social communication.

Vygotsky attempted to demonstrate the essential social basis of speech, particularly of egocentric speech, in several series of experiments. In one series he tried to destroy any illusion children might have of being understood. The amount of egocentric speech children used was measured in a situation similar to that used in Piaget's experiments. Then the children were placed in new situations, either with deaf-mute children or with children speaking a foreign language. In the majority of cases the amount of egocentric speech that the children used in the new situations declined to zero. Vygotsky concluded that children need to feel that they are being understood when they speak.

The second series of experiments examined collective monologues and egocentric speech. Children's use of egocentric speech was measured in a situation that permitted collective monologues. They were then placed one by one in a group of strange children, or each was required to sit or work completely alone. Once more the amount of egocentric speech declined in the new situations to about one sixth of the original amount. This decline was not as large as that revealed in the first series, but it was still a very considerable decline. If Piaget's theory were correct, argued Vygotsky, the new situations should have led to an increase in egocentric speech rather than to such a large decrease.

The third series of experiments examined the vocal nature of egocentric speech. Either an orchestra played extremely loudly outside the laboratory where the children were gathered or they were allowed to speak only in whispers. Once again the amount of egocentric speech declined to about twenty per cent of the original amount. The various experiments eliminated one or more of the characteristics of egocentric speech which make it like social speech, particularly the characteristic that somebody apparently understands what is being said. In every case the amount of egocentric speech declined. Vygotsky concluded that egocentric speech must be a form of speech which develops out of social speech. His experiments indicated that it was not yet separated from social speech in its manifestation, even though it was already distinct in function and structure. It had not yet gone "underground."

Vygotsky's conclusions may well be questioned since none of the experimental conditions was particularly conducive to any kind of speech activity, nor have the actual experiments been replicable since the details necessary for replication were not provided. It would also be particularly difficult to test many of Vygotsky's other assertions, provocative though some of them are: for example, that inner speech is to a large extent thinking in pure meanings; that the processes of thought and speech are not identical; that thought, unlike speech, does not consist of separate units, individual thoughts being wholes which must be developed successively in speech; that thought must pass first through meanings and then through words; and that some thoughts may be completely inexpressible. The inexpressibility of certain thoughts and the ways in which certain thoughts have originated have interested philosophers and artists from time immemorial, but little systematic evidence exists. It is not possible to proceed very far in accounting for how thought originates in the mind, even from reports by such reputable, yet different, persons as the poet Coleridge in his well-known account of the genesis of "Kubla Khan" under the influence of a drug and Albert Einstein in his discussion of scientific creativity. Vygotsky's views must be placed in the same category.

Luria and Regulatory Speech

Vygotsky's pupil Luria was interested in the problem of how language might or might not regulate or be related to motor behavior. We know that very young children talk to themselves, saying *walk* as they walk, *away* as they push objects away, *blow* as they try to blow their noses, and so on. What exactly is the relationship between the two kinds of behavior? Luria distinguished nonverbal behavior from verbal behavior, declaring that the first preceded the second in the development of the child. Eventually the second comes to regulate and inhibit the first as speech takes on a directive function which is gradually internalized.

In early childhood only the speech of others, particularly adults, can direct the behavior of children. Later, children's own overt speech becomes directive, and, still later, their inner speech. Initially, speech, like any other physical stimulus affecting behavior, acts through its physical properties alone; only later do its symbolic characteristics come to dominate when development of the speech system makes possible verbal control of motor behavior. Since the speech system matures more rapidly than the motor system, Luria maintained that it was also easier for children eventually to speak on command than to act on command.

Luria tried to show the validity of his claims in a series of experiments which employed commands given to young children. He found that children in the middle of their second year who were asked to give the experimenter one of a number of objects lying on a table in response to a command like *cat* or *fish* reached out their hands to the object but would often be distracted by a nearer or brighter object and pick it up instead. The physical setting was a much more powerful influence on behavior than the verbal instruction. Likewise, asked to retrieve a cat three or four times in a row, the children would retrieve it once more even if that time the command were *fish*. Once very young children begin to repeat the same action, a verbal command alone generally cannot stop it: verbal behavior has little or no inhibitory effect on motor behavior. At three, though, children can exercise positive control over their motor behavior by means of their own verbal cues. They can be taught on seeing a light flash to say *squeeze* and then press a bulb. The self-given command *squeeze* controls motor response. Three-year-olds seated before two lights, one red and the other green, and told to say *squeeze* and squeeze a hand-held bulb only when the red light flashes can do this task quite successfully. But if they are told to say *squeeze* and squeeze when the red light flashes and to say *don't squeeze* and not squeeze when the green light flashes, they squeeze when either light flashes. The word *squeeze* in both commands controls the behavior. If someone else gives the commands *squeeze* and *don't squeeze*, there is no such difficulty. By four this difficulty in following commands is overcome and children can use their own speech to regulate or inhibit their behavior. Luria also notes that older children and even adults give themselves overt verbal commands in difficult situations, not only to help work things out but also to help them control their behavior.

As with Vygotsky's and Piaget's work, Luria's experimental findings have sometimes proved to be difficult to replicate. That such difficulties arise is not surprising. Each theorist is working on problems which are immensely complicated. Each begins with a different set of assumptions and proceeds to build a theory. Each finds evidence to support his theory. But the components of each theory are so general and unspecified that it is quite difficult to define what a really critical test would be like. How would an investigator test to be really sure that cognitive development takes place in orderly stages and that each stage sets the limits on possible behaviors at that stage? Or that every child is a social being from birth? Or that speech behavior develops faster than motor behavior and eventually gains control of that behavior? However, the underlying issues are worth considering: the connection between language and cognition; the relationship of language function to language expression; and the connection between language behavior and other kinds of behavior. Any serious and comprehensive study of language must confront such issues.

Language and Intelligence

Just as language, thought, and cognition are related in some sense, so are language and intelligence. But again the relationship is not entirely clear. Just as there have been many attempts to define language and to write grammars of specific languages, so there have been many attempts to define intelligence and to describe instances of intelligent behavior. The result in both cases has been considerable controversy, particularly within the last few years.

In one sense it does not require intelligence to speak. In the absence of some congenital deficiency or injury, everyone speaks. Languages are so complex that no comprehensive account of the structure of even a single language exists anywhere. Yet people speak and are understood; they listen and they understand. Naturally, there are better speakers and there are worse speakers; and there are situations in which an individual speaks well and other situations in which the same individual speaks badly. It is quite possible to consider variations of these kinds as being distributed over a set of normal curves, each curve representing a particular group of speakers or a particular set of circumstances.

In a like sense it does not require intelligence to live. Anyone who has lived any length of time has demonstrated the intelligence required to adapt to the environment. Different circumstances require different kinds of adaptation, and some individuals are more successful at making required adaptations than others. Again, the various abilities required to adapt may be assumed to be distributed over a set of normal curves. It is somewhat unfortunate that many psychologists who have investigated intelligence have taken a much narrower view of it than the ability to adapt to a wide variety of circumstances. They have regarded intelligence as the ability to solve problems of a certain kind, and they have developed measures of intelligence which assume a normal curve distribution of ability to solve a rigidly prescribed set of problems. That the problems chosen tend to reflect the various kinds of *status quo* in society is largely ignored as are the consequences to many of such a choice. Objectivity, particularly in the sense of the reliability and consistency of results, has been the concern rather than validity. We must not forget that intelligence is not something like height or weight: a statement that someone has an "I.Q." of 115 must be regarded very differently from a statement that that person is six feet tall and weighs two hundred pounds.

It would be quite possible to consider that language ability and intelligence, whatever each is, are quite independent so that in a sufficiently large population all possible combinations of high and low language ability and high and low intelligence would occur. But such appears not to be the case. Certain kinds of language ability become indicators of the kinds of behavior that societies reinforce. Certain kinds of behavior are regarded as "intelligent." Those who exhibit such kinds of behavior tend to be successful; those who do not tend to fail. The particular kinds of language ability can vary from time to time and place to place: retelling legends, conjuring up spells, persuading crowds, solving crossword puzzles, writing books, diagnosing mental ills, and so on. As societies become more complex, they also become more language conscious, and the ability to manipulate language becomes highly valued. Complex societies depend heavily on the ability of people to manipulate symbols, and language provides just the kinds of symbols and the infinite means for manipulation that are needed. Highly complex societies cannot exist without highly complex languages, that is, languages whose inner resources are continually being exploited to meet new demands.

Earlier the existence of primitive languages was denied. A statement that highly complex languages exist does not resurrect primitive languages in a different guise. Languages are only as developed as they need to be. Likewise, intelligence is only as developed as it needs to be, taking the form that best ensures the survival of the group. Languages must develop differently to meet different cultural needs and so must intelligence. Different languages, therefore, will develop inner resources differently: a language such as English has many more developed linguistic resources than a language such as Cree. Different cultures likewise develop different types of intelligence: survival on Wall Street or in political office requires a different set of behaviors from survival in a rain forest, and almost certainly a set which is far more complex and dependent on the ability to manipulate symbols of various kinds, including language symbols.

What emerges is a possible classification of societies by degrees of complexity. All cultures value language, but some cultures depend on it in sophisticated ways. All cultures maintain themselves through the intelligent behavior of their participants. But some cultures impose greater demands for language sophistication than do others. North American society is extremely complex. One of its characteristics, therefore, is to favor those kinds of language behavior which seem conducive to the survival of the society and to label them as "intelligent." Unfortunately, we cannot be sure that those behaviors which actually lead to survival are the ones that psychometricians measure on intelligence tests. However, whatever it is that they measure it is only a part—possibly even a very small part—of the total array of abilities by which a society continues itself.

There are some interesting consequences for different groups in society. As a result of different cultural conditions one group may not have developed certain kinds of language abilities valued by the dominant group or groups and tested on standardized tests. The members may even disfavor such behavior setting higher value on certain other kinds of behavior. Consequently, at any one time a group in society may on some measure such as a traditional standardized intelligence test, *as a group*, perform differently from the dominant group toward whom the test is biased. The difference will show the group to be "disadvantaged" with respect to whatever was measured. However, within the group the total range of abilities will so overlap the total range of abilities in the dominant group that predictions about individuals will be next to impossible.

Recent, sometimes quite bitter, discussions of the relationships, if any, between language and intelligence have not clearly separated out those things that can properly be said and those that cannot. Intelligence has been narrowly defined. Individual and group differences have been confused. Race has been made an issue. Implications of all kinds have been asserted but not proved. The place of scientific investigation itself in society has also been made an issue as attempts to investigate possible connections between race and intelligence have been opposed on the grounds that such attempts are inherently racist.

Individuals vary widely in their ability to use language. Linguists have generally considered such variability to be performance-based rather than to be an indicator that linguistic competence varies from person to person. They tend to assume that linguistic competence is very much the same everywhere in all people. What interests them is what everyone shares, linguistic competence, not what everyone does, linguistic performance. On the other hand, psychologists have concentrated on what it is that separates person from person, variable human intelligence, rather than on what it is that everyone shares with everyone else. It should come as no surprise then that the relationship between what we currently know about language and what we currently know about intelligence is tenuous at best. Investigations of language and intelligence find their origin in radically different assumptions about what is to be explained. It may be wise, therefore, to treat with caution any statements which casually relate the two or any schemes which propose to investigate or develop one through the medium of the other. Such schemes are likely to be based on assumptions about language which linguists cannot share and often feel they must oppose. Linguists do not believe that certain children are "nonverbal" and "lack" language or that children can be "taught" language in the usual sense of the word *taught*.

Language and Logic

Likewise to be treated with caution are attempts to make any language more logical. As we know, it is decidedly difficult to make speakers behave logically, that is, to use coherent argumentation. Languages have their own structures. The more linguists find out about these structures, the more coherent and "logical" they become. In this sense there is already a logical basis for the structure of English noun phrases, relative clauses, and nominalizations: the various parts fit together into a coherent whole. Attempts to remove double negatives, or to regulate uses of *will* and *shall* for futurity and volition, or to insist on subjunctive verb forms in certain types of conditional statements are no more than tinkerings with inconsequential trivia. Each language has its own structure which its speakers "know," which allows them to say what they wish, and which is its own logic.

It is possible though that language structure has a logical basis in another sense of the term *logic*, the more technical sense familiar to philosophers. In fact, in recent years several attempts have been made to devise logical bases for linguistic structure and to show that deep structures can be expressed in logical form. However, three caveats are in order. The first is that systems of logic were developed because of the inadequacies of language for certain purposes; consequently, it is not easy to conceive how a "perfect" logical base would relate to an "imperfect" language. Why it should be expected to is a related issue. The second is that a variety of logics exist, but there are no adequate criteria for choosing among them so far as their use with natural language is concerned. The third is that no one has yet succeeded in relating even one system of logic to natural language in a fully explicit way. Even courses in logic devote much of their time to developing in students the "correct" intuitions about logical form. That such intuitions can be developed consistently argues that the task of explicating the relationship is not in principle an impossible one. It is just extremely complex.

Linguists make their major contribution to understanding the logical basis of linguistic structure through describing the formal structure of language, that is, the grammatical relationships that exist. They acknowledge that they are on much less secure ground when they attempt to relate that structure to problems of meaning or to construct abstract systems to deal with meaning. Nevertheless, linguists have discovered quite independently of logicians that it is words like *some, none, all, any, every, only, because, and,* and so on—that is, quantifying words, relational words, and negatives—which produce interesting grammatical effects. However, it is the concepts associated with such words which interest logicians rather than the grammatical consequences of particular choices.

As for making people more logical, or judging how logical they are through their use of language, psychologists have long been aware that a mixture of factual conditions and emotions controls responses. A person may readily agree that the syllogisms *All men are mortal; John is a man; John is mortal* and *Heroin is a drug; Drugs are bad for you; Heroin is bad for you* are logical, but reject *All men are immortal; I am a man; I am immortal* and the substitution of *marijuana* for *heroin* in the second syllogism on the grounds that the last two syllogisms are illogical. It has been pointed out too that almost nothing about a person's logical abilities can be discovered by making inferences from poorly elicited verbal data, particularly data which adult investigators elicit from children who suspect their motives. Data which are carefully elicited, on the other hand, generally reveal surprisingly good logical ability. Language training exercises having as their purpose the development of logical thought must obviously be suspect linguistically, logically, psychologically, and pedagogically. An individual's language has a system of its own, the system shared with all other speakers of that language. That it also has an abstract logical basis is still an untested claim. That speakers sometimes behave illogically with language is an undisputed fact. That attempts have been made to devise logical notations that are free of some of the properties of natural languages is still another well attested fact. Various mathematical notations, varieties of symbolic logic, and computer languages are good examples of attempts to achieve precision and explicitness. But each depends on natural language in ways that natural language does not reciprocate. Each was brought into existence through natural language, the midwife to them all. The resulting systems may, of course, be used as bases for investigations of natural language, just as they are used for investigations of nonlanguage data.

A beginning has been made with such investigations, but much more work remains to be done before any kinds of conclusions can be drawn concerning their ultimate productivity.

Language and the Individual

There is undoubtedly an intimate relationship between language and thought. However, no one can be sure of the precise form which the relationship takes. Language enables the individual to share in the experiences of a culture and also to step beyond its immediate demands. It also enables experiences to be shared and, in doing so, provides people with the opportunity to live vicariously through participating symbolically in the experiences of others. And all the possible worlds of the imagination lie open too. Language and thought allow for the present moment and its experiences to be transcended.

The human species has made much of the tool that language provides. Humans have used it to create complex societies which depend on language and thought. The human world is a world of verbal constructs as well as of physical constructions. What success the individual enjoys in that world depends to a considerable extent on mastery of those verbal constructs. The various educational processes, both formal and informal, that a person is subject to are largely indoctrinations into sets of such constructs. For many, the manipulation of words becomes more important than the manipulation of objects. Objects are manipulated through words—through commands, laws, contracts, rituals, instructions, pleas, and so on.

Individuals vary in their ability to deal with such constructs; hence the ranges of individual differences that interest many psychologists. But no one is without the fundamental capacity that language itself provides for survival, except the congenitally or pathologically afflicted. There do, however, appear to be different capacities for original thinking, different strategies for attaining concepts, different skills in reasoning, and different types of cognitive styles in resolving indeterminacies. As a result, individuals vary widely in how they react to their environments and use the language competence they have.

It would be unwise to underestimate the place of language in such reactions. A cultural system which places a high value on language for what it can do and which has developed systems for looking at language draws the individual's attention to language. For example, the development of new words encourages the development of new concepts. The constant use of language to probe and question leads to probing and questioning. Instruction in the methods and vocabulary of different kinds of inquiry, both scientific and speculative, and attempts at resolving conflicting interpretations likewise lead to further use of language for similar purposes. It therefore comes as no surprise that complex cultures place the emphasis they do on language skills in their various systems of acculturation.

Whatever its basis in the individual—genetic, social, or behavioral—language comes to transcend that origin as the demands made on thinking increase, change, and develop. It may well be, as more than one writer has observed, that thought may be too deep for words. But the major avenue we must follow in investigations of thinking is that provided by the language used in thinking. No other avenue is likely to be so rewarding. However, since the relationship between language and thought is symbiotic, each depending on the other in many ways, certain cautions must be observed in investigations of the one conducted independently of the other. As we shall see in the following chapter, when people use language in communication, they do not express all their thoughts. They assume that others share some of those thoughts and state only what they assume is not shared. A meeting of minds is achieved through a shared language system *and* through thoughts which are also assumed to be shared. Thinking is not just an individual matter; each of us assumes that others think much the same way as we do. Much of our use of language can be explained only on the basis that this assumption is valid.

References

Most of the papers in Adams (1972) and much of Brown (1958) and Slobin (1971b) are relevant to issues discussed in this chapter. Knapp (1972), Harrison (1974), and Miller (1973b) provide overviews of nonverbal communication and Birdwhistell (1970) and Hall (1959, 1966) more specialized treatments of gesture, space, and so on.

Jenkins (1969) provides an overview of the issues on the relationship of language and thought. For Watson's views on thinking see his (1913, 1924) and for Skinner's his (1957). The experiment with curare is described in Smith, Brown, Toman, and Goodman (1947), and Lenneberg (1962) reports on the case of the child who was unable to talk. Whorf's views are expressed in Carroll (1956). The experiment with ambigious stimulus figures is described by Carmichael, Hogan, and Walter (1932). Berlin and Kay (1969) provide the analysis of the data on basic color terms. The two experiments using English and Hopi and English and Navaho are reported in Carroll and Casagrande (1958). Bruner, Goodnow, and Austin (1956) provide a view of concept formation.

Piaget's works are numerous and now readily available: Evans (1973), Flavell (1963), and Gardner (1973) provide useful overviews. See also Piaget (1972). The experiment in which children related information to other children is recounted in Piaget (1950). Vygotsky (1962) is an account of his ideas; part of the account is reproduced in his (1972). For Einstein's and others' views on the origin of thought see Ghiselin (1955). Luria's views are most accessible in his (1971).

The writings on language and intelligence, particularly the possible connection of both to racial differences, are numerous: representative are Deutsh, Katz, and Jensen (1969), Eysenck (1971), Herrnstein (1973), Jensen (1972, 1973), Richardson and Spears (1972), and Scarr-Salapatek (1971). Fodor (1970) discusses language and logic and Labov (1970, 1972a) the logic of different kinds of English and the danger of drawing false conclusions.

5

The Functional Context

System and Communication

Language is both an individual and a group possession. As we have observed, linguists have been much more interested in the language systems to which members of a group have access than in the idiosyncrasies of the speech of individuals. The general rather than the particular has claimed their attention. The result has been called a paradox: linguists usually attempt to describe the system *all* speakers of a language presumably share by using data gathered from very few individuals—sometimes only a single individual—and do not attempt to describe individual variations unless they have access to data from many individuals. Since these last kinds of data are extremely difficult to acquire, few such attempts have been made.

The interest in system has been pursued within the kinds of limitations discussed in the first chapter. The major emphasis has been on explicating the formal characteristics of the system, the internal units and processes, rather than its various functions. Attempts to deal with the communicative uses of language, that is, how any group makes language work for it, have seemed far less important than attempts to make more exhaustive statements about phonemes, morphemes, rules, transformations, and so on. While linguists have readily acknowledged that language is speech, they have tended to ignore the actual act of speaking.

We will leave the question of variation to the following chapter; the issue of immediate concern is communication through the various acts of speaking. A number of questions come immediately to mind. What function does language have in the total system of human communication? What relationships, if any, are there between the linguistic forms of a language and the functions which the language must perform? How do particular bits of communication work, for example, how does a particular conversation succeed or fail? Answers to such questions can be sought only in a linguistics that is concerned with form *and* function, with speech *and* speaking, with language *and* language use. Contemporary linguistics is developing just such concerns.

A well-justified initial assumption is that every language is a system which allows its speakers to interact with each other. The system provides speakers not only with a code within which to conceptualize events both in the outside world and in individual "minds" but also with a means for conferring about the resulting concepts with those who also have access to the system. The system can be understood in its entirety only if this transactional aspect of language is considered, that is, only if a study of functional uses complements the study of formal properties.

A second assumption is that linguistic function is no less systematic than linguistic form. Just as individual speech is not haphazard, neither is collective speech. Monologues, dialogues, conversations, narratives, and language used for thinking, imagining, speculating, ordering, questioning, and answering will reveal certain systematic features. A simple illustration of the validity of this assumption is that people quite consistently recognize failures to use language properly: words that are inappropriate; stories that are incoherently confused; jokes that fall flat; and many other kinds of aberrant language use.

Linguistic Communion

One of the simplest yet most essential functions of language is that of social maintenance; language helps to define a particular community. Two people who share the same language are able to communicate with each other. Without a common language they experience a host of difficulties in conveying any but the simplest messages, and even these are likely to be highly ambiguous. Gestures, as we have noted, have a high cultural "load"; consequently, various kinds of pointing, nodding, and gesturing with the hands can easily be misunderstood. A shared language provides a channel for communication which is far less ambiguous. And within certain social bounds anything can be said.

The availability of a shared language does not necessarily mean that only new and original things are said, that is, that only genuine information is transmitted from one to another. Language also serves people for the purposes of "phatic communion." It allows them to know that they are in touch with others and that a channel of communication is open if it should really be needed. Exchanges of *How do you do*'s and *Hi*'s function in this way, as do many comments about health, feelings, weather, relatives, and even events such as ball games. Requests for matches, the time, and simple information also fall into this category. Idle gossip is another manifestation: the "small talk" of an office, assembly line, or party, which although often "job talk" is not usually serious job talk. No real information is exchanged, and shared knowledge and understandings are rehearsed while essential contacts are maintained. There is a kind of continual checking to see that the channel remains open, and the same rituals occur time after time.

Phatic communion has an additional function: it establishes the worth of the participants by acknowledging that they *could* talk to each other about important things if that were necessary. They are not strangers to each other. They have not been excluded from sharing. They do not threaten each other with their silences or by their failure to indulge in "meaningless" exchanges and small talk. They participate in a communion of words and achieve a form of group solidarity through that communion. In some ways, therefore, language functions for humans as grooming behavior functions for animals. Grooming behavior brings animals together and helps them to maintain social relationships. An ungroomed animal is a rejected animal, one that for some reason is not able to participate in general group activities. Who can talk to whom and how easy or not it is to talk are important in human society in much the same way: a word of approval or a snub can have a powerful effect on a person's self-esteem.

Much of this kind of communication is not directly related to linguistic events at all. Voice quality, posture, distance, and other kinds of behavior are also important. Eye contact is a particularly good example. Glancing, looking, staring, glaring, and complete eye avoidance all produce different effects. Both looking at someone and returning a look are social acts, often regulated in extremely complex ways. English has numerous expressions indicating the importance of eye contact, among them *to stand eyeball to eyeball, to recognize a speaker, to catch someone's eye,* and *to be downcast.* Speakers also relate to each other in very subtle ways. In conversation they vary their rates of speech, their loudness, their rhythms, their habits of pausing and interrupting, their amounts of talking, and even their accents in relation to other participants. In these ways they demonstrate that there is more to speaking than just words, and more to a record of conversation than a transcript of the words that were spoken.

Watching two people talk to each other is like watching a dance. In how they perform the dance the participants show whether they are in harmony or in con-

flict with each other, and they may also show who is leading and who is following. The amount of eye contact, the quality of the voices, the gestures, the movements, and the conversational rhythms will all reflect the participants' feelings
about what is happening during their conversation. A conversation felt to be ·
"good" or "useful" by both participants will be accompanied by a different kind
of dance from one that both feel to be "bad" or "destructive." There will be a
harmony of words and gestures among the participants. An effective communi-
cator is one who is capable of getting others to dance with him rather than
against him. And not to get anyone to dance at all indicates complete failure.

This function of language, then, is a socially supportive one. The claim is very
different from the Whorfian claim that language forms determine certain kinds
of intellectual and social behavior. That claim arose from a superficial examination of linguistic forms and from generally unwarranted philosophical extrapola-
tions from literal translations of those forms. The claim made here is that many
linguistic forms used in everyday speech must be largely ignored as forms because they are fixed, ritualistic, and so conventional as to be meaningless so far
as their substance is concerned. It is the ritual uses of these forms, their functions, the dance of speaking itself, and the place of that dance in society which
must be understood.

Language also allows for communion of still another kind. It allows for
memory, particularly the collective memory called history, in contrast to instinct, or genetic memory. Language allows people to build communities not
bounded by either the past or the immediate circumstances but on the basis of
abstractions and speculations about the past, present, and future, and of ideas
and ideals shared by a community. Linguistic communion forms the cornerstone of all "higher" behavior and of whatever freedom humans enjoy from
genetic constraints. Language has given mankind new powers of adaptation to
the environment. Through the communion that language affords, cultural evolution is possible in addition to genetic evolution. As we shall indicate in Chapter
Eight, a number of ethologists have argued that this consequence is fraught with
danger to the species, in that language has allowed humans to develop complex
systems which they are genetically ill equipped to control.

Speech Acts

Any attempt to discuss how language functions in communication requires that
a clear distinction be made between linguistic form and linguistic function. Linguistic form refers to the phonological, semantic, and syntactic properties of
language; linguistic function, in the sense used here, refers to the uses speakers
make of linguistic form in communication. Certain forms are often clearly related to certain functions. Forms like *Let's go* and *Please sit down* generally func-

tion as requests; forms like *What would you like?* and *Are you ready?* generally function as questions; and forms like *He scored a touchdown* and *He didn't come* generally function as statements. The important word here is *generally*. In actual language use, linguistic forms do not correlate exactly with linguistic functions on every occasion.

A sign saying *Dangerous Dog* is a warning, not just some kind of statement. *I like that one* may be a request for someone to buy the object that occasioned the remark. *I would like that dress* said to a sales clerk is a request to buy the dress. Said to a companion during window shopping it may be no more than a fanciful comment. *You've changed!* said about someone changing clothes may be a request for a reason for an unexpected action. *Your room's a mess!* said by a mother to a child is usually taken not as a simple statement about the room's condition but as a command to tidy up the room. *I can't find my glasses* may well be an indirect request for assistance, just as a teacher's comment that *It's warm in here!* may lead to a student opening a window. *Will you send me your trial offer?* in a letter to a mail-order house is a request, though the form is that of a question. *Can you do it for me?* may get one of two answers: *Yes,* or the doing of the action previously indicated. *Don't tell me he's done it!* will usually lead to an act of telling that he has indeed done it, in spite of the form of the command, an apparent prohibition of any such telling. The question *Are we going to let them do that to us?* cannot appropriately be answered *Yes,* so it is a rhetorical question rather than a genuine question requiring either *Yes* or *No* for an answer. A child who asks another *Why is a Volkswagen like an elephant?* expects not an answer to his question, but a reply such as *I don't know. Tell me.* Moreover, the second child asked knows that this answer is expected and is in fact the "best" answer possible.

Any attempt to classify linguistic forms which disregards the linguistic functions of those forms must miss a good deal that can and should be said about language. It must certainly miss the fact that listeners know that they treat particular forms used in certain contexts in different ways from the same forms used in other contexts. Data such as those just cited are not therefore in dispute. They must be accommodated in a comprehensive statement about English. The key issue is one of deciding on some principled basis which linguistic functions are important within communication, that is, which are significant and contrastive, and then to relate, so far as it is possible, linguistic forms to those functions. As we shall see, some interesting work has been done on this problem, initially by philosophers but more recently by linguists too as emphasis on linguistic form alone proved to be unsatisfactory in dealing with certain kinds of language data.

A basic assumption behind any attempt to understand linguistic functioning is that most utterances have a purpose, that is, that they are spoken with an intent to communicate something. We must ask what a speaker intended by an utterance before we can fully understand what the utterance itself meant. Intention therefore is part of meaning and use. It is necessary to make hypotheses about what is going on inside the black boxes that are people's minds. In contrast, we do not usually inquire about the intentions of the sun, rainbows, rivers, and trees. For that reason, speaking may be regarded as a series of acts of a particular kind rather than as a series of events, the difference between an act and an event being that an act has an element of purposefulness or intent to it, whereas an event is just something that happens. If speaking did not consist of acts but of events then it would be empty, for communication would cease. Speech would be a set of artifacts rather than a set of utterances. An undeciphered writing system offers just such a set of artifacts in the absence of any knowledge of the meaning and intent of the writing. Speech must also use acts systematically; otherwise communication would break down through sheer unpredictability.

According to the philosopher of speech acts, John Austin, there are three different kinds of speech acts: locutionary acts, illocutionary acts, and perlocutionary acts. A locutionary act is an utterance with a certain sense and reference, that is, the utterance is meaningful. All meaningful utterances are locutionary acts. But a speech act may also be an illocutionary act in that it may do one of a number of different things: announce, state, assert, describe, admit, warn, command, congratulate, comment, request, reprove, apologize, criticize, approve, welcome, thank, promise, regret, and so on. Or it may be a perlocutionary act, one that brings about or achieves some other condition or effect by its utterance, for example, an act which convinces, amuses, deceives, encourages, bores, embarrasses, inspires, irritates, persuades, deters, surprises, or misleads someone. Any properly formed utterance is therefore a locutionary act. The difference between an illocutionary act and a perlocutionary act is that the second requires the first to be successful. The words *Stop that!* comprise a locutionary act because the utterance is well formed. *Stop that!* may also be an illocutionary act in the right circumstances, for example, if said by one person to another when something is being done that should not be done and the utterer has the right to insist it not be done and the person of whom the request is made is in a position, and under an obligation, to desist. If the illocutionary act is successful in bringing about an end to the activity, then that act plus its consequences constitute a perlocutionary act. Illocutionary acts are also locutionary acts, but perlocutionary acts do not require locutionary acts as their base: nonlinguistic acts can amuse, deceive, embarrass, irritate, and so on, but only words can be used to state, admit, request, welcome, and promise—or some conventional substitute for words.

Within the category of illocutionary acts there is in important division between constative utterances and performative utterances. Constatives are propositions which can be stated positively or negatively: *The sun will rise at seven tomorrow morning, I don't like cabbage, He's Fred's cousin, John denied the story, Angels guard my bed at night,* and so on. They are statements of "fact," sometimes the subject of agreement, other times the subject of dispute. At the center of any argument is the question of either the truth or the falsity of the statement (*No, the sun will rise at seven fifteen tomorrow morning*) or the impossibility of verification (*There aren't any angels*). On the other hand, performative utterances do not report on anything and cannot be said to be either true or false. It is the very uttering of a performative in the right circumstances that is the action or some part of the action: *I bet you a dollar* or *I promise I'll stop smoking.* The speaker does something by the act of saying something. A later report of the doing and saying is, of course, a constative utterance, that is, it is either a true report or not of a particular act.

Austin distinguishes five different kinds of performatives, each kind relying on certain characteristic verbs. The first type, verdictives, gives verdicts, findings, or judgments: the umpire's *Out* or *Safe*; the jury's *Guilty* or *Not guilty*; and the appraiser's *I estimate forty dollars.* The second type, exercitives, shows exercise of powers, rights, or influence: the lawyer's *I advise you to say nothing*; the judge's *I sentence you to five years*; the policeman's *Stop*; the employer's *You're fired!*; and the voter's *Aye* or *Nay.* The third type, commissives, indicates commitments or promises of different kinds, or the taking on of an obligation, or states an intention: anyone's *I promise . . . , I agree . . . , I swear . . . , I intend . . . , I guarantee . . . , I plan . . . ,* or *I bet . . . .* The fourth type, behavitives, comprises a miscellaneous group to do with expressions of attitudes and social behavior: verbs like *congratulate, compliment, welcome,* and *apologize*; statements like *I'm sorry*; expressions of approval like *Thank you*; and terms of abuse. The final type, expositives, keeps discussion and argument going by providing different kinds of clarification: *I assume . . . , I concede . . . ,* or *I hypothesize . . . .* The types are not clearcut since they overlap, but the general performative nature of individual utterances is usually quite clear.

So far as use of such verbs and expressions is concerned, while the subject *I* and the object *you* is often present they do not have to be. Generally, any performative can be recast to include *I* and *you* if one or both are absent. Likewise, the performative is in the present tense and the word *hereby* can be included: (*I hereby judge you*) *out*; *I* (*hereby*) *bet you five dollars*; or (*I hereby say to you*) *I'm sorry.* Of course, the performative utterance must occur in suitable circumstances. I must be in a position to judge the fact that you are either out or not; there must be a point in dispute on which a wager is possible, my wager must not be outrageous (*I bet you a million dollars*), and you must accept if it is to be on; and I must be aware that you have been injured in some way. That the utterance itself occurred in the proper circumstances is also sufficient to establish that an act occurred: that a particular call was made at first base; that a bet was made; or that an apology was offered.

So far as the various speech acts themselves are concerned, certain conditions must prevail if they are to be used correctly. For example, requests or commands must be reasonable: the speaker must genuinely want something done; it must also be possible for the person of whom the request is made to do that something, a condition that rules out *Be seven feet tall* and *Bring me all heaven for a throne* as genuine commands; the person would not otherwise do what is requested—being told to do something one is going to do without telling may well cause some ill-will; and the person making the request must be in a position to make the request of the person or persons to whom it is made. If the request is reasonable, that is, if it meets these conditions, it must be honored. Of course, the request may be disputed in different ways, but if the conditions have been met, failure to honor the request must be construed as an act of defiance of some kind. In like manner, statements must give an appearance of being true if they are to be believed to be true. Certain conventions serve to mark particular classes of statements as not to be believed from the start: *Once upon a time, Have you heard the one about . . . ?* and *Let us suppose that . . . .* Questions must be answerable or follow fixed patterns as in riddles (*Why is a Volkswagen like an elephant?*) or in rhetorical usages (*Are we going to stand for this?*). *Why aren't you going to wash the dishes?* said to someone who was going to wash the dishes is a challenge not a question, and *Why don't you love me anymore?* said to a spouse whose love is unchanged is hardly likely to produce anything but discord. Answers must be truthful not evasive, and promises sincere. Sincerity or genuineness of intent is frequently a matter of concern in conversations of all kinds.

This approach to language function through an attempt to understand speech acts is a useful one. It is obvious that utterances are intended to be understood in certain ways. Sometimes the intent is apparent from the form of the utterance itself, sometimes not. Generally both form and intent are also supported by the physical and social context. Lack of clarity in the relationships among form, intent, and context leads to ambiguity and possible misunderstanding. A superior's *wish* may be intended as a command, understood as a command, but later denied to be a command. When, in addition, each party to a particular language transaction brings different assumptions about what others know and do not know, different views of events that are under discussion, different perceptions of social relationships, and different agendas about the purposes of the discussion itself, still further complications are likely to arise. What is perhaps surprising is that so much understanding does seem to occur in such unlikely circumstances. Of course, survival requires no less.

People who know each other well are often quite sure about each other's intent. Strangers do not have those same assurances, particularly strangers who do not share a similar background. The less background that is shared the more explicit everything must be, even what is to be judged as this kind of act or that kind of act. Ceremonies which draw strangers together on an irregular basis make every act completely explicit: for example, weddings, trials, funerals, and initiations. At the other extreme, overfamiliarity can have its dangers. In eliminating many of the customary overt markers of the different kinds of acts, it can produce uncertainty about the status of a particular utterance, its form alone being insufficient to establish the kind of act it is. Again, a speech act does not occur in isolation but within a series of acts chained together. What was said, therefore, in any exchange is not just a few words which happen to be exchanged (though why these particular few are exchanged is of some interest) but the totality of meaning that the individual speech acts communicate in the context. Impressions of conversations usually last longer and are stronger than memories of the actual words—or all but a very few.

Verbal Exchanges

The actual words of any verbal exchange must be fitted into a wider physical, mental and social context. Actual communication can take place only in situations in which the participants share much in common: a physical location; a goal; an interest. In most cases communication does not involve ideas that are brand new, the conveyance of large masses of knowledge, or attempts to bring about complete changes of view or behavior. The goals are generally much more limited, and achieving them depends on processes of adjustment and accommodation. The participants assume that a shared body of knowledge and understandings provides the basis for the necessary exchange. Their activities must be coordinated in order to ensure that sharing occurs. One of the most important things shared is knowledge of language and its uses in communication.

When the participants have long shared much in common, an "ordinary" event may occasion very little verbal interaction. Even an extraordinary event may arouse little discussion. When there is a great commonality in background, assumptions, and interests, few words are needed, and what words that are used may not be very explicit. A heavy dependency will be placed on what is shared, and everything will be viewed and commented on within that common perspective. People who have enjoyed a long and intimate relationship with each other often need few words to communicate. Those few very adequately reveal to the other what is on the mind on most occasions. In the presence of an outsider they must expand what they say if they wish to include that outsider: the outsider is not privy to their common perspective. At any time though that outsider can be excluded through resort to that privately shared perspective. All of us at one time or another have had the experience of being excluded quite suddenly by others in this way: what was said and how it was said drew on resources beyond our knowledge and did so knowingly. Of course, after two people become attuned in this way and one later has reason to distrust the other or the relationship changes, the inexplicitness is potentially dangerous. No longer are assumptions shared, so the language may become ambiguous, the speech acts not clearly differentiated, and effective communication jeopardized.

When people are asked to explain what went on in a particular conversation, their answers indicate how inadequately the actual words themselves comprise a record of what happened. The participants are likely to agree that many things not mentioned directly were talked about or talked around. A particular word or sentence quickly opens up and closes a whole area and indicates how the issues in that area were resolved. But this process does not go on in a logical way. Different pieces are fitted together, something is checked, and the conversation continues. Ambiguity, unclarity, gaps are all tolerated in the expectation that there will be a later resolution if uncertainty remains. Each participant assumes that only really new information is important and that only the smallest quantity of old information necessary to set the scene is called for. The obvious need not be stated. Those who insist on stating what everyone knows are likely to be exhorted "to get on with it."

The actual record of any sequence of utterances almost certainly will provide an outsider with a poor idea of what happened. The outsider sees a collection of utterances which are hard to understand if nothing is known about the participants: their biographies, the nature of their relationships, the events talked about, the agendas (intents) of the participants, and so on. It may be possible to draw a few conclusions about these from the sequence, for it will have its own internal orderings, its own action and reaction; and it is about something and some of that something is likely to be known to the outsider. But verbatim recordings of conversations can be very misleading and leave open a variety of interpretations. Personal recollections of conversations are weak enough, and explanations of why something was said and what was meant by it may be even less accurate.

Participants must agree about a number of things if a conversation is to be effective. Such agreement is implicit rather than explicit. They must agree that certain kinds of knowledge are shared and do not have to be mentioned. Likewise, they must agree that certain rules of conduct apply during the course of the conversation: a conversation is a social event with its own conventions. There must be some kind of agenda, that is, some sharing of perspective on what the conversation is about. There must also be some recognition of who is and who is not party to the exchange, hence the abhorrence, on the one hand, for "bugging" and "eavesdropping" and the need, on the other, to speak "off the record," that is, to conceal a source to some extent. So far as what is said is concerned, each participant must tolerate a considerable inexplicitness on the part of the other. Vagueness rather than precision will prevail; words will be understood metaphorically as well as literally; exhaustiveness will be neither sought nor required; appeals to the obvious and what everyone knows will be made; items will not be sequenced linearly or logically, some may not be mentioned at all, and others never explained; and constant extrapolation, filling in, and checking out will be necessary. And all these will occur within a context which assumes that the conversation has a legitimacy of its own: interruptions must be excused and clearly marked as such, and someone's "hanging up on someone else" on the telephone or a negotiator's "breaking off of talks" may have serious consequences because of the severity of the violation of this convention.

Communication requires cooperative endeavor. Participants recognize that they should say only what they need to say, and that their contributions should be informative, relevant, and truthful. They should not say too little and they should not say too much. A question requires an answer. *Where are you going?* can be answered *Home, None of your business, I'm not telling, Why do you want to know?*, or *Ask him*, depending on circumstances. Answers like *Apples are red* or *Because it's raining* are quite unlikely. An answer like *It's noon* may be appropriate, but only if the answer can be related to the question through some understanding the speaker and listener share. If they are strangers to each other and have no such mutual understanding, then the answer is just as inappropriate as the others. Disruption is the antithesis of communication as well as a form of communication of its own.

There is an element of trust in a conversation. In order for any conversation to work the participants must take much of what is said to them at its face value. The participants must assume that they are being given only relevant, necessary, and truthful information. Someone who says *John tried to hit Fred* when John did indeed hit Fred has not told an untruth but only a partial truth. However, that partial truth will be regarded as an untruth in a conversation once it is discovered, for it will have misled any listeners. If three people were invited to a party and none came, but, in reporting this fact to someone who knew the circumstances of the invitation, a speaker merely said *John didn't come*, then the listener will assume that the other two came. We can note that the utterance implies something different from or something in addition to what it asserts. If we inquire over the telephone for someone and are told *He's not in* only to find out later that the person has been dismissed, we are justifiably aggrieved in our belief that *He doesn't work here anymore* would have been a more appropriate response. Children sometimes produce partial responses of this kind. In an answer to the question *Why is John crying?* a child may answer *Because he fell down*, which in fact he did, rather than *Because I pushed him down*, which was actually what happened. They may be telling the truth and nothing but the truth; however, the assumption on which conversation proceeds is that they are telling the whole truth. It is not surprising that we have a term *half truth* for failure to observe this requirement.

The philosopher Paul Grice calls these other meanings that are not asserted, conversational implicatures. Participants in a conversation must watch not only their words but also what their words imply. What is implied is sometimes quite different from what is asserted. It is sometimes the stuff of the "big lie" or the dirty insinuation rather than of the slanderable action, as in *I am not aware of any wrongdoing on the part of my opponent for office.* As has been pointed out, if two acquaintances are talking about a mutual friend now working in a bank and one asks the other how that friend is getting on and is told: *Oh, quite well, I think. He likes his colleagues, and he hasn't been to prison yet,* the final clause violates the maxims of not saying more than is required and not offering gratuitous information. The utterance may well be taken to assert that the mutual friend is a dishonest person because of these violations. The mutual friend has been victimized without being slandered. In like vein, a remark like *Oh, your wife is faithful!* introduced by one male haphazardly into a conversation with another is likely to prove to be far more unsettling than reassuring. At the very best the conversation is likely to undergo a profound change in topic and the agenda of the husband, if not that of both parties, will be considerably rearranged.

Some of the assumptions in conversations are actually built into the linguistic forms themselves. For example, *I saw John leave* can be true only if someone called John exists, he did leave, and the speaker saw it happen. Sentences have presuppositions: *I reported the burglary* presupposes that a burglary took place; *I bought another car* that the speaker had a car at some time; *John stopped shouting* that John was shouting (hence the unfairness of *Have you stopped beating your wife?* as a question if you indeed have never beaten her); *Jones has been here before* that Jones is alive, and in the word *before* asserting that he is expected to return; and *Our cat had kittens* that the cat is female. The presuppositions are not all of the same kind, nor are the examples intended to be exhaustive. However, the range illustrated shows how various kinds of linguistic information are also involved in the interpretation of sentences used in conversation.

Regulating Exchanges

Language transactions require that their participants agree not only on certain assumptions about what can and should be said, but also on how specific encounters are to be regulated. Every encounter occurs in a social setting, and there are rules to regulate what goes on, whether the occasion is a commencement address, a business gathering, a seminar, a cocktail party, or a late-night snack. There may also be sudden shifts of participants and setting, and each shift will be accompanied by changes in the rules. A complex setting such as a courtroom will see many shifts and changes: a dispute between counsel; a remark to the jury; the questioning and cross-examination of a witness; a ruling by the presiding judge; and so on. An elaborate system regulates turn-taking in a courtroom and determines who gets to speak, how topics are introduced, how accounts are developed, how questions are answered, and how certain things must be left unsaid and still others not even implied. A doctor-patient interview may be far less elaborate, but it too must have its own rituals: careful elicitation of symptoms; systems of checking and cross-checking information; uni-directional questioning with nearly all the answers and offers coming from the patient; and cautious diagnosis and prognosis. The doctor-patient relationship as it reveals itself through turn-taking and questioning is a particularly interesting one as the medical profession undergoes change. Good doctoring depends in part on good exchanges, but ideas about what a good exchange is differ widely among doctors and patients. One group of doctors, psychiatrists, even make a professional specialty of exchanges. A peculiar characteristic of certain psychiatrist-patient exchanges is that at any time the psychiatrist may bring up any remark made by the patient during the course of those exchanges and place it on the immediate agenda. Similar "dredging up" in ordinary conversations is not expected and scarcely tolerated when it occurs.

We must not forget that usually only one person speaks at a time and that silence is required of the other during that speaking. Talk is orchestrated in such a way that the floor tends to be given up voluntarily. Not allowing someone to talk is a deliberate act. To be commanded to be silent is sometimes too unnatural a command to obey. But silence can also be used effectively when the rules require speech. Silence itself can be a speech act, the consequence of a deliberate act not to speak. It may indicate agreement with the speaker or be understood as indicating assent, as it was when used in the phrase *the silent majority*; it may be regarded as a device for insuring that someone eventually gets heard, as in *We haven't heard from Jim. What do you have to say?*; it may be required as a sign of respect, as in *Children should be seen and not heard, No talking in church, Don't speak until you are spoken to,* and *Who asked you?* Self-imposed silence can have many uses: a sign of disrespect, reinforced perhaps by asides or side exchanges; a calculated snub bringing about a comment such as *He didn't even speak to me*; a refusal to venture an opinion when asked, as in *No comment*; and a refusal to answer a question in court. Knowing when to keep silent or refusing to talk is part of knowing when to talk, for the consequences are the same: each act reflects a person's knowledge of what is or is not acceptable in society and contributes to that person's success or failure in society.

As soon as any attempt is made to give a full and systematic account of how language is used in actual speaking, the complexity of such a task becomes apparent. The number of variables is considerable. Language exchanges can vary in many different ways. Characterizing what is going on in a particular exchange requires an understanding of the context in which the exchange occurs and of the relationship of the participants to each other and that context: strangers interact differently from familiars; familiar contexts bring about different reactions than do strange ones. An exchange between close friends in a familiar setting is likely to be very different in form and content from one between two strangers meeting in a setting unfamiliar to both. The agenda of the exchange is also important; what each participant hopes to accomplish through it. Likewise, constraints will regulate what occurs: a job interview is different from a blind date, and both are different from a legal hearing. But even so, it is still possible for the participants to vary the degree of formality they adopt, make subtle alterations in tone, or play with usually accepted norms. They may also vary what they do because of certain characteristics of the environment: a radio commentary on a sporting event is different from a television commentary on the same event, as anyone who has merely listened to (not both listened to and watched) such a commentary on television can testify. And, finally, there are the actual language devices that are used: the particular types of speech act; the specific words; the pauses; the devices which allow one to be heard; the sequence signals; the techniques by which beginnings, endings, and new topics are signaled; and so on.

Investigators who have actually attempted to state what happens in conversations, a large amorphous subset of exchanges, have necessarily limited themselves to very specific topics. They have investigated such topics as how certain conversations begin and end (for example, telephone calls and psychiatric interviews), how new topics are introduced and followed up in conversation, how others are addressed, how the whole issue of using names is avoided, how successive utterances are sequenced in relation to each other, how speakers assert their rights to be heard, how refusals are made, how individual utterances are understood in context, how particular places are referred to (for example, the layout of rooms within a house), and how strangers are given directions. They have also been concerned with the ways in which certain kinds of individuals use language to attain their ends: for example, teachers and students, doctors and patients, and mothers and children. Imparting knowledge, diagnosing illnesses and treating them, and controlling children lead to different kinds of language behavior.

It is possible to pick out various types of linguistic signals that correlate directly with what a speaker intends in a particular exchange. For example, expressions like *Yes, Uh huh, I see,* and *That's right!* signal some kind of agreement while another person is speaking. Those like *Oh!, Really!,* and *Is that so?* offer an additional comment on what is being said. Then there are prefacing expressions such as *anyway, say, well, here, why,* and *now* which serve to introduce a comment, offer, or reservation: *Well, I'll have to think about it; There, I'll do that;* and *Anyway, we have to leave.* Expressions like *I believe, I guess,* and *I think* used during a conversation or presentation serve to meliorate what is being said, making it less positive so that the speaker therefore appears less assertive. Certain situations require this lack of assertiveness, even though everyone present regards the qualifying expressions as empty, for example, situations in which one person is clearly the leader and the others the followers but in which leadership is being exercised covertly rather than overtly. Even intonation can be used by one person to offer some kind of comment on what someone else has said. A high-pitched repetition of something that has been said draws attention to what was said, whereas a low-pitched repetition tends to discount it, before any further comment is offered. An exact repetition, with only necessary pronoun changes, if any, also places whatever it was that was said immediately on the agenda.

Taking one particular kind of exchange as an example, telephone calls, we can show a few typical characteristics of language used in such calls. Telephone summonses have specific rules. In North America the person picking up the telephone must answer whereas in certain other cultures, Norway for example, the person calling must speak first when the connection has been established. In North America the ringing telephone is interpreted as a summons to be acknowledged by a spoken response not just by picking up the telephone. Once the initial response is made, the caller must initiate the substance of the conversation or indicate that a call is being returned. In those cases where the call is purely social it must be acknowledged as such straight away (*Oh, I just thought I'd call*) if the caller is not suddenly to be asked a question such as *Well, what's on your mind?* Telephone calls, like telegrams and unlike casual greetings in the street, are assumed to be about something. However, if at the beginning of a casual greeting in the street one party to the exchange breaks the bond of casualness, that person takes on an obligation to initiate some kind of follow-up by introducing a topic. When telephone companies began to encourage family members and friends to call each other long distance just to "keep in touch" rather than to convey messages, one of the difficulties they had to confront directly was the non-use of the telephone for this kind of phatic communion—the mother's inquiry of her son *Why are you calling, son? Are you in trouble?* was answered by the son protesting he was all right and was just calling to say *hello* in the telephone companies' promotion of this use of the telephone.

The telephone has another unusual characteristic for many people: it gives summonses which they generally feel unable to ignore; there appears to be a strong social obligation to answer the telephone. If there is no answer when the telephone rings, the caller assumes that nobody was there to answer, not that the summons was ignored. There is also often a feeling of considerable dissatisfaction if a telephone call is not later returned if the person summoned is not present and is asked to return the call. Of course, since summonses are a subclass of greetings, therefore of offerings, ignoring a particular summons is a snub, threat, or rebuke involving primal feelings. It is understandable, therefore, that there should be rituals which cover this class of events even in the special circumstances of telephoning. Another ritual is the pretense that you do not listen in on another's telephone conversation when that person must answer the telephone in your presence. You can make a comment on the conversation only if you are invited to do so. Otherwise, it is bad manners even to pretend the conversation occurred. This rule accounts for some of the reprehensibility felt for the practice of bugging: telephone conversations are as private as letters.

If we approach exchanges from the point of view of asking how a particular kind of activity—the use of questions—is involved, we can take the example of the classroom to show some issues. Questioning in the classroom is very different from questioning in most other circumstances. For example, most of the questions go in one direction, from the teacher to the students. Students are allowed to ask questions, but the teacher may choose not to answer them at all or to answer them immediately or at some other time determined by the teacher. But students are expected to answer immediately. The teacher's questions are quite often given to a group of students with an instruction that those students who are prepared to answer should indicate their preparedness in some way, generally by one kind of gesture or another. The teacher then chooses one student to answer. The typical pattern of interaction is that the teacher confirms or disconfirms that answer. The teacher decides the overall agenda. Any questions the students ask must fall within that agenda or be classified as diversionary acts. The teacher also knows the answer to any question asked by the teacher. It is the students' job to find out that answer, the one the teacher wants, to a particular question. In other circumstances questions of this kind are regarded as insincere. If the person asking the question knows, or is discovered to know, the answer already, comments such as *You know, so don't ask me* and *Why, you knew all the time!* are legitimate. The first comment is socially unacceptable in a classroom, and the second is assumed to be redundant: everyone knows the teacher knows. Children must learn how questions are used in classrooms when they go to school. If they do not learn or refuse to go along with the questioning convention, their behavior will be regarded as disruptive in one respect or another as they provide repeated inappropriate answers, refuse to wait until an answerer is designated, ask too many questions, thereby usurping the teacher's function, or reject the teacher's answers.

The examples in the preceding paragraphs show how difficult it is to make statements about language exchanges. Extended pieces of language—long conversations, discussions, texts, both formal and informal (for example, oral narrative or casual correspondence)—serve to compound the difficulties. Not only must every individual locution be examined closely, but it also must be examined for its illocutionary or perlocutionary force in the context in which it occurs. The locutions are also parts of exchanges and sequences which are often themselves constituent parts of some still more general exchange or sequence. Finally, each exchange takes place against a background of all that the participants know, or believe that they know, about the world, themselves, and the place of that particular exchange in the further development of that knowledge and their relationship to one another.

General Functions of Language

Still another way of looking at how language is used in social relationships is to attempt a broad classification of the basic functions of language. Roman Jakobson, a linguist thoroughly familiar with just about every aspect of modern linguistics, both European and North American, has offered a six-fold classification of language functions. According to Jakobson, language must serve the following functions: cognitive or referential to convey messages and information; conative to persuade and influence others through commands and entreaties; emotive to express attitudes, feelings, and emotions; phatic to establish communion with others; metalingual to clear up difficulties about intentions, words, and meanings; and poetic to indulge in language for its own sake. Another classification, proposed by the British linguist Michael Halliday, refers to seven different categories of language function: instrumental, regulatory, representational, interactional, personal, heuristic, and imaginative. Still other classifications employ different categories and use different terms, but all cover essentially the same data. Halliday's classification provides the basis for the comments which follow.

The instrumental function refers to the fact that language allows speakers to get things done. It allows them to manipulate the environment. People can ask for things and cause things to be done and happen through the use of words alone. An immediate contrast here is with the animal world in which sounds are hardly ever used in this way, and, when they are, they are used in an extremely limited fashion. The instrumental function can be "primitive" too in human interaction; quite often the intent of a speaker is judged on the basis of an intrinsically deficient utterance, one possibly complemented by gesture, but the intent is unequivocal nonetheless. Performative utterances have instrumental functions of their own if the right circumstances exist; they *are* acts: *I name this ship* Liberty Bell; *I pronounce you man and wife;* and *I bet you a dollar.* But the instrumental function may be served by other utterances than performatives, by suggestion and by persuasion as well as by direction: *I suggest you stop; It's going to rain (so take your umbrella);* and *You'll get hurt (so stop).*

The regulatory function refers to language used to control events once they happen. Those events may involve the self as well as others. People do control themselves through language: *Why did I say that?; Steady;* and *Let me think about that again.* But more conspicuous is the fact that language regulates encounters among people; it helps to mark roles, provides devices for regulating encounters, and affords a vocabulary for approving and disapproving, and controlling and disrupting the behavior of others. Language allows complex patterns of organization to be established to regulate behavior, from game playing to political organization, from answering the telephone to addressing the nation on television. It is this function of language which allows people to exercise deliberate control over events that happen.

The representational function refers to the use of language to communicate knowledge about the world, to report events, make statements, give accounts, explain relationships, relay messages, and so on. In general, an exchange of information occurs. Sometimes misinformation is given; telling lies is an example of this same function. As we mentioned earlier, certain rules exist to regulate language behavior when an exchange of information is involved: the truth must be whole not partial; assumptions must be made about what the listener knows; the information supplied must be neither inadequate nor gratuitous; and, if the intent is honest, any kind of misrepresentation and ambiguity must be avoided. In circumstances in which a speaker has a highly idiosyncratic view of what the world is like, utterances which claim to represent the world will be treated as peculiar by others. Certain types of peculiarity will lead to the speaker being classified as either a genious or a fool; others as a visionary or a madman; still others as a sinner or a saint; and some perhaps even as a revolutionary or a savior. The precise designation of an individual may shift from time to time as the consensus which forms the basis for judging various representations of the world shifts: the earth as flat; atoms as particles; God as dead; sex as dirty; language as speech; and so on.

The interactional function refers to language used to ensure social maintenance. Phatic communion is part of it: those small "meaningless" exchanges which indicate that a channel of communication is open should it be needed. In a wider sense this function refers to all uses of language which help to define and maintain groups: teenage slang; family jokes; professional jargon; ritualistic exchanges; social and regional dialects; and so on. People must learn a wide variety of such different kinds of language usages if they are to interact comfortably with many others. Successful interaction requires good "manners," saying things appropriately whatever they are, and doing things in the prescribed way. Breaches of manners are easily observed, whether they are "dirty" words in the wrong setting or refusing to stand on certain occasions. They are likely to be punished far out of proportion to any misdemeanor that was actually committed.

The personal function refers to language that is used to express the individual's personality. Each individual is conscious of the fact that language comprises part of that individuality. Individuals have a "voice" in what happens to them. They are also free to speak or not to speak, to say as much or as little as they wish, and to choose how to say what they say. Language also provides the individual with a means to express feelings, whether outright in the form of exclamations, endorsements, or curses or much more subtly through careful choice of words. There may even be a cathartic effect in *letting it all hang out* or *in getting it off one's chest.*

The heuristic function refers to language used as an instrument itself in order to acquire knowledge and understanding. Language may be used to learn things about the world. Questions can lead to answers; argumentation to conclusions; hypothesis testing to new discoveries; and so on. This heuristic function is the basis of the structure of knowledge in the various disciplines. Language allows people to ask questions about the nature of the world in which they live and to construct possible answers. Formal education is partly a means for introducing the young into this heuristic function. The product is often an abstract system devised to explain something. So symbolism is an essential corollary. Insofar as the inquiry is into language itself, a necessary result is the creation of a meta-language: a language used to refer to language containing terms such as *sound, syllable, structure, transformation, function,* and so on.

Finally, the imaginative function refers to language used to create imaginary systems whether these are literary works, philosophical systems, or utopian visions on the one hand or daydreams and idle musings on the other. It is also language used for the sheer joy of using language as sound: a baby's babbling; a chanter's chanting; a crooner's crooning; and sometimes a poet's pleasuring. Pig Latin, punning, verbal games, playing the dozens, telling tall stories are just a few other instances of the imaginative use of language to entertain oneself and others. The imaginative function also allows people to consider not just the real world but all possible worlds—and many impossible ones besides. It enables life to be lived vicariously and helps satisfy numerous deep esthetic and artistic urges.

Much of the everyday use of language has a representational function, but instrumental and interactional functions are also well represented. Channels are also constantly tested to see that they remain open. The imaginative function is prized when it leads to artistic creation but for most people seems to be more of a safety valve than anything else in the opportunities for creativity and escapism that it allows. The heuristic function has tended to become institutionalized in educational settings and the knowledge industry, but the possible ways of knowing through language and without language still continue to fascinate different investigators. How knowledge itself is structured, reordered, and developed is also a matter of concern. Language plays an important role in the changes which occur in the rhetoric of the various disciplines. The personal function undoubtedly exists but is possibly the most difficult of all to describe with any exactness. In that function, language, thought, culture, and personality come together to interact in ways that are still quite mysterious, as we saw in the previous chapter. The various functions are also not discrete. They overlap. Speaking is a complex activity which proceeds on more than one plane at a time: a single brief exchange can be made to serve more than one function.

Language in Communication

Language has many different functions and is put to many different uses in society. An important part of the knowledge that every speaker has of the language is how to use that language in different circumstances. Speakers must learn not only the sounds and grammatical forms of the language, but they must also learn how to use these sounds and forms appropriately. They must learn who speaks when to whom for what reason about what things and in what way. Children acquiring a language must learn the complexities of this ethnography of speaking; they must learn how to use sentences appropriately concurrently with how to form them correctly.

We can easily recognize that such an ethnography of speaking does exist because of our ability to detect violations of the codes of linguistic behavior. Contradictions, half truths, inadequacies, and irrelevancies are often easy to detect because some of the requirements mentioned earlier are ignored. We are also sensitive to linguistic discourtesy and rudeness, as when there is a failure to observe accepted patterns of exchange or when a particular language encounter is wrenched out of shape. We may even know people with whom any kind of language encounter is scarcely possible or extremely painful because they apparently have never learned the rules that govern encounters, or they deliberately violate the rules, or they fail to obey them because of some psychological impairment. People may be considered "crazy," "disruptive," "smooth," or "brilliant" partly on the basis of their control of such rules, or their lack of control. And control seems quite independent of control of the rules of syntax and phonology or of control of the written form of language. As the actor David Garrick remarked of the poet Oliver Goldsmith, he "wrote like an angel, but talk'd like poor Poll."

Language, of course, is just one of the codes that must be handled in general social interaction. There are also behavioral codes and moral codes to be observed, the products of law or custom. There is a code that regulates distance and one that regulates permissible physical contact. And there is a general code that regulates the trust each person places in others to observe all the other codes. Violations of this last code apparently produce the gravest kinds of psychological damage as when, for example, captives who undergo brainwashing procedures can never be sure what is going to happen to them next. In such circumstances this fundamental trust that certain types of behavior will regularly prevail is broken, a break often considered quite necessary before any kind of "re-education" can begin, such re-education being mainly concerned with building an alternative system of trust. The particular trust that people place in words is also, unfortunately, the source of considerable harm: lying and deception depend on that trust for their success.

In dealing with others, we must assume a great deal of shared understanding about the world. We must assume that the stage on which we are to perform the particular dance of a language encounter is set very much alike in the minds of the participants in that encounter. We must then proceed to choreograph or direct the actions and events on that stage jointly with the other participants so that at any time all can agree where everything is and what everyone is doing. But the language we use and the rules for using the language require that at any one time only certain things can be said and usually that only one participant can be speaking. There are therefore numerous ways in which a participant can quickly get out of step in the dance. Consequently, constant checking back, reviewing the present moment, and projecting forward are necessary. The total pace of the dance must also be controlled as must its relationship to the dances which preceded and those which are to follow. Any knowledgeable choreographer or director will assure us that that is not the best way to put together a successful show. But it is the best we can do with language, and the results are often surprisingly good.

References

Four collections of papers by Giglioli (1972), Laver and Hutcheson (1972), Pride and Holmes (1972), and Sudnow (1972), at least the first three sections of Fishman (1970), and a book by Robinson (1972) provide a wide range of materials on some of the issues discussed in this chapter. Labov (1972b) discusses the paradoxical sources of linguistic data at the beginning of his eighth chapter. "Phatic communion" comes from Malinowski (1923). See Argyle and Dean (1965) for eye contact.

Austin (1962) and Searle (1969, 1972) both write on speech acts. Cicourel (1973), Gordon and Lakoff (1971), and Grice (1971) deal with different aspects of what is understood, said, and not said in various kinds of exchanges. The different kinds of presuppositions are discussed by Keenan (1971). Brown and Ford (1961), Brown and Gilman (1960), and Ervin-Tripp (1969) discuss pronominal usage. Ervin-Tripp (1969) discusses conversational openings, Jefferson (1972) asides in conversation, and Duncan (1972) the taking of turns. Goffman (1955, 1957, 1971) is concerned with various kinds of rituals and exchanges, and Frake (1964) with one particular ritual, asking for a drink. Schegloff (1972) describes how places are referred to and Labov (1972a, 1972b) how ritual insults are exchanged. Basso's subject (1972) is silence, Turner's (1972) therapy talk, and Pittenger, Hockett, and Danehy's (1960) the first few moments of a psychiatric interview. Classroom interactions are described by Barnes, Britton, and Rosen (1971), Boggs (1972), and Mishler (1972). Lakoff (1972) makes a number of interesting comments on a variety of issues concerned with the use of language in context.

For their views on language function see Jakobson (1960) and Halliday (1973). Hymes (1962, 1964, 1972, 1974) discusses many aspects of the ethnography of communication.

6

The
Social
Context

Language and Dialect

Considerable variation exists within a language not only in how people use sounds, words, and structures but also in the actual choices which they make on different occasions. Of interest to us are the extent of such variation and the possibility that discrete, identifiable subvarieties of the language exist. The existence of the terms *dialect* and *idiolect* suggests that investigators have found it useful to acknowledge the presence of subsystems in languages. They have considered a dialect to be a regional, less often a social, variety of a language and an idiolect to be a variety spoken by a specific individual. A dialect is also sometimes distinguished from a standard variety of the language (when one exists), the standard variety being the one favored by the "establishment"—social, political, religious, or whatever—and supported by the major social institutions. However, attempts to give more exact definitions to *dialect* and *idiolect* and even to *language* itself have proved rather unsuccessful. Once more the problems are complex, with the major source of difficulty this time being the pervasiveness of variation in language.

It has been said that not too long ago a person could journey from the north of France to the south of Italy and, if the journey were slow enough, the traveler would never be conscious of crossing a language boundary and hardly be conscious that the language was changing during the course of the journey. Yet speakers living in some of the different regions through which the traveler passed would be quite incomprehensible to one another. They could not be said to speak either the same language or even very different dialects of the same language. Yet how many languages and how many different dialects of these languages did the traveler come into contact with during the course of the journey? This last question can be answered only if there exist clear definitions of the terms *language* and *dialect*. Linguists generally agree that a language is a linguistic system which a number of speakers share when different, but mutually intelligible varieties of that system exist; these varieties are dialects. Sometimes, too, one dialect may have more prestige than the others as a result of the prestige of the people who speak it. This dialect may then come to be regarded as the standard form of the language, even to the extent of being considered *the language*. In that case the other dialects may appear to be inferior variants of this standard form. *Dialect* will then come to take on a certain pejorative sense.

However, such definitions do not help us a great deal in making decisions as to where to place the boundaries for the language and dialect areas traversed by our fictitious traveler. They are much too broad and inexact to be very helpful in that task. Even today there are parts of the world (for example, India) with characteristics not unlike those which were mentioned for France and Italy, as well as areas in which speakers communicate with each other even though they claim to speak "different" languages (for example, Scandinavia) and fail to communicate even though they claim to speak the "same" language (for example, China).

Today, what is or is not regarded as a language is often related to what is or is not regarded as a nation. We live in an era of national languages, and dialects are quite often defined as subvarieties of those languages. As one observer of the results noted: "A language is a dialect that has an army and a navy." Numerous anomalies result. Norway, Denmark, and Sweden are three nations but Norwegian, Danish, and Swedish are not really three different languages in the same way that Norwegian, English, and French are. They are much closer, even closer than certain dialects of a single language are in some cases, for example, dialects of some of the languages of India. Spanish and Portuguese blend into each other in the Spanish province of Galicia, and Dutch and German blend in the same way in the border area. Hindu and Urdu are basically the same language with different written scripts (Devanagari and Arabic-Persian), different borrowing traditions (Sanskrit and Persian), and different religious affiliations (Hinduism-Buddhism and Moslem). Chinese is not one language but at least six which are not mutually intelligible: Mandarin, Cantonese, Wu, North Min, South Min, and Hakka. They do share a common writing system which brings speakers of the different varieties together through its codification of meanings rather than of sounds. English, a language with a very wide distribution in the world, exists only in distinctive dialects, socially within regions, regionally within nations, and nationally within its international distribution. A Scottish crofter from the Highlands may find it difficult to communicate with a Texas oilman from Houston and a student from Calcutta with a teacher from Liverpool.

Linguists have generally assumed that it is worthwhile to examine the geographic, that is, regional, distribution of anything they consider to be a language. They have also considered regional differences to have been brought about by the same kinds of processes that account for linguistic change in general. Dialect study has always been an important part of work in historical linguistics, and over the years a considerable amount of linguistic effort has gone into devising ways for distinguishing among dialects and accounting for dialect differences using procedures which were first employed nearly a century ago. The last decade or so has seen considerable questioning of the continued usefulness of such procedures.

Regional Variation

The most obvious way to describe the regional characteristics of a language is to conduct some kind of geographical survey. However, surveys generally are not easy to make. Even the ten-yearly census which seeks only the simplest demographic information in a population creates major problems. Sampling of some kind is almost always necessary when a large population must be surveyed. But, as everyone knows who has engaged in survey work, finding a good representative sample and then eliciting from that sample the information which is sought are troublesome tasks. In a language survey who are truly representative speakers or informants, what are truly representative linguistic tasks, and what do the results really indicate? The history of dialect study is also a history of attempts to answer such questions.

In the late nineteenth and early twentieth centuries, investigators such as Wenker and Wrede for German, Gilliéron for French, and Jaberg and Jud for Italian used a variety of sampling techniques. In the study of German the principal technique was use of a questionnaire sent to every German-speaking village in Europe. The questionnaire was to be completed, generally by the local schoolmaster, and returned. It asked the schoolmaster to translate forty-four sentences given in standard German into the local dialect equivalents. Comprehensiveness was the goal in that forty-four thousand villages were surveyed. However, there was obviously no guarantee of the quality of individual responses. All there was was a certain safety in numbers which would tend to make truly aberrant responses rather conspicuous. In his study of French, Gilliéron employed a single person, or fieldworker, Edmont, to collect the data he sought in visits to over six hundred villages in France and neighboring countries. Edmont also collected only a narrow range of phonological data. The Italian study, which covered the southern part of Switzerland as well as Italy, saw further refinements in the selection of informants, the training of a number of fieldworkers, and the addition of towns and cities to the survey. Parts of the general survey were also followed up by studies of particular regions or of particular linguistic items.

One of the most sophisticated approaches in this paradigm was initiated by the American Council of Learned Societies in the 1920s as the first part of a projected linguistic atlas of the United States and Canada. The initial investigation covered the regional distribution of speech forms in New England and was conducted between 1931 and 1933 under the direction of Hans Kurath. It required systematic selection of those speech communities which were likely to produce the kinds of information that were being sought. This selection was carried out with the help of social historians and anthropologists. Three or four speakers of certain kinds were chosen in each of the selected communities to provide the information sought by a relatively short, well-organized questionnaire. Only highly skilled fieldworkers were used. More recent surveys, for example, the one conducted in Great Britain, have been concerned with refining the techniques rather than with questioning the major underlying assumptions of this approach to dialect study.

The basic outcome in each case is an atlas containing a series of maps: the *Deutscher Sprachatlas,* the *Atlas Linguistique de la France,* the *Sprach- und Sachatlas Italiens und der Südschweiz,* and the *Linguistic Atlas of New England.* These maps record the data so that it is possible to see just which words are actually used, how these words are pronounced, and so on, in the various regions shown on the map. Because map making itself has proved to be extremely expensive, lists of forms by place and informant are often supplied instead. Numerous derivative studies often follow from the information which the maps and lists provide. The distributions of forms on the maps also allow investigators to determine possible "dialect areas."

A dialect area is an area which possesses unique linguistic characteristics; no other area has quite the same distribution of linguistic forms. The distribution of forms can be determined by inspection of the data recorded on the maps. The maps allow lines, called *isoglosses,* to be drawn. An isogloss is a line which indicates that a particular linguistic form occurs on one side and not on the other. When several isoglosses for different forms run together, or form a bundle, this convergence is often interpreted to indicate a dialect boundary. One famous set of isoglosses in Europe is the "Rhenish Fan," the boundary between Low German and High German. The *ik-ich* isogloss crosses the Rhine at Ürdingen, the *maken-machen* isogloss crosses it between Düsseldorf and Cologne, the *Dorp-Dorf* isogloss south of Bonn, and the *dat-das* isogloss south of Coblenz. These iso-glosses converge to the east. As we have just noted, when several isoglosses for different forms converge, we can interpret the information to indicate the bor-der between two dialect areas, in this case between Low German to the north and High German to the south.

However, the existence of the "fan" effect requires an immediate word of caution. As we shall see in Chapter Nine, an important assumption of much work in historical linguistics is that sound change is quite regular. There probably should have been no such "fan" effect, for the same change is involved in each case, a change from fricative to stop: High German fricatives have changed to Low German stops in the north. Apparently each word has its own history, but *within* an overall pattern of fricatives becoming stops. Other forces than geographical ones must have been involved in the change or it would have been uniform for all the words. While isoglosses often do follow natural geographic boundaries, they also frequently coincide with other kinds of boundaries as well: for example, political, social, and religious boundaries. This kind of relationship is not easily demonstrat-ed, certainly not on the conventional linguistic atlas maps. Moreover, the data re-quired to establish the relationships are not always available because the assump-tion behind the data which were collected was that the most important factor in variation would be geographical rather than social or cultural distribution.

The conclusions that result from this method of collecting and processing data are therefore, not surprisingly, in large part predetermined by the under-lying assumptions. Some of those assumptions may be stated as follows: One is that distinctive regional varieties of a language exist and that it is possible to distinguish among them through plotting the distributions of a relatively small set of linguistic forms. Moreover, the differences in the distributions of those forms can be accounted for through well-known processes of change. Most of the exceptions will result from borrowing. A second is that fieldworkers can un-cover the different forms by gathering data from a very restricted, carefully chosen sample of informants, the data being responses elicited in interviews of predetermined form and content. A third is that the best source of data lies in "folk speech," although "cultured" and "educated" speech is of some interest too. The fourth is that the results are most revealing when they are presented in the form of a set of maps and derivative studies. Such maps allow the distri-bution of linguistic forms to be related to geographical features, trade routes, settlement patterns, political and other boundaries, and so on. The derivative studies deal with any interesting characteristics which the maps reveal: distinc-tive dialect areas and specific linguistic forms such as the distribution of certain pronunciations, grammatical constructions, and words.

As a result of this interest, much of the discussion in dialect geography cen-ters on the regional distribution of forms. In the United States the interest focuses on such matters as whether or not *r*'s are pronounced after vowels, whether *pin* and *pen* and *cot* and *caught* are distinguished, whether or not *easy* and *greasy* rhyme, what the quality of the vowel is in *pass* and *aunt*, and whether *Tess* and *test* and *den* and *then* are homophonous. Those are phonological items. In syntax the issues concern such matters as past tense formation (*dived* or *dove*), the distribution of particles, for example, *for* in *He asked for me to do it*, the formation of verb phrases (for example, *might could*), and the peculiarities, if any, of verbs like *be, do,* and *have*. Vocabulary provides a very fertile area: Do you say *skillet, spider,* or *frying pan*? Do you say *polecat* or *skunk*? Do you address your father as *Dad, Pa,* or *Daddy*? Do you buy *gas* or *petrol* for your *car* or *automobile*? And so on. Dialect geographers then proceed to distinguish among dialects spoken in the United States on the basis of responses to inquiries such as these. The division of the United States into North, Midland, and South dialect areas is one result, but not one that is universally accepted as valid. The distinctions are broad ones, and the need for a separate Midland dialect area has been much debated.

The result is that a linguist can talk about different dialects using the distributions of specific linguistic forms to define each dialect. As we have said, a dialect area is a region which possesses unique linguistic characteristics: for example, it alone is characterized through the presence of a particular vowel quality in a certain set of words, the absence of a particular expected phoneme in still another set, the use of certain names for objects, and the particular extension of a syntactic feature. The uniqueness of this distribution of linguistic forms defines the dialect area. Other unique distributions define other areas.

However, even a cursory inspection of this way of thinking about dialect and language shows that the dialect areas overlap. A real language is not composed like a jigsaw from discrete parts as this kind of approach suggests. A real language is more like a sea made up of waves which have no clear boundaries and which shift constantly.

Some Difficulties in Interpretation

What we have just said suggests that still more is involved in dialect differentiation than the kinds of factors accounted for in the atlas-type studies. Dialect differences are more subtle and pervasive than such studies tend to indicate. The studies imply that fairly sharp dialect boundaries exist and that speakers in different dialect areas often use quite different phonemic systems. They also have different distributions of phonemes in words and make noticeably different word choices. But these differences are mainly an artifact of the methods used to gather the data. The sampling and mapping techniques, the use of restricted questionnaires, and sometimes the selection of older, untraveled, and poorly educated informants all guarantee that only certain kinds of data will be recorded.

Although there may well be certain characteristics of speech which have an exclusive regional distribution, the majority of the characteristics which mark off Bostonians, New Yorkers, and Virginians from one another are too subtle to describe merely by using the techniques employed in linguistic atlas work. Whether *r*'s after vowels are or are not pronounced and the quality of the vowels in *aunt* and *half, law* and *order*, and *down* and *out* may be very noticeable differences perhaps, but alone they make up only a small part of the total set of differences among the speakers. An emphasis on such gross differences can offer little more than stereotyped descriptions. For example, it can hardly come to grips with the subtlety of the pronunciations of monosyllabic words containing *a* in Philadelphia in which tensing of the vowel occurs in words like *mad, man* and *mass*, but not in *sad*. Such subtleties require more refined methods of exploration and description.

One way of assessing the results that emerge from dialect studies is to ask what help they provide in understanding what happens when speakers of different dialects talk to each other. The atlas-type approach suggests that in such circumstances speakers communicate by means of a matching process: they match individual sounds, linguistic forms, and classes of forms in the speech of others with equivalents in their own speech. So *spider* would be matched with *skillet* and *r*-less words with *r*-ful words, and so on. We must assume that a similar matching process occurs for all those items not covered by the original questionnaire on which the atlas was based. Such a model for interdialect communication is a very improbable one: a language is more than an inventory or collection of items, no matter how systematically arranged, and such a matching process, either item by item or class by class, is just too cumbersome to account for what happens when people who speak "differently" succeed in communicating with one another.

An alternative approach requires shifts of a different kind to be postulated. It requires the listener to make very general shifts to accommodate what is heard: a set of simple general rules equates the system employed by the speaker to that of the listener. This equation or conversion process is similar to the one people use even when gross dialect differences are not involved: we continually adjust to the personal characteristics of other speakers' voices without being aware of the fact. The kind of shift involved in listening to another dialect has nothing special about it. The process is also a lot easier to understand if language ability is assumed to be an abstract ability that requires realization rules to allow for self-expression and processing rules to allow for others to be understood. There may, of course, be individual differences in the ability to use some of the realization and processing rules: such abilities as being able to mimic others and speakers of other dialects and even of being able to understand speakers of other dialects do not seem to be equally distributed to all.

Only a few of the problems that arise in the study of regional dialect have been mentioned. These problems are important enough to demonstrate that even though regional differences in language do exist, it is very difficult either to characterize them in the most revealing fashion or to explain how individual speakers adjust to the differences. But there is an even more serious problem. To a considerable extent the concept of regional dialect requires an assumption that groups of speakers exhibit considerable linguistic homogeneity within themselves. The linguist must assume that the speech forms of a particular community are essentially uniform, invariant, and fixed. The sampling techniques used to gather data for the various atlases embodied that assumption. The static presentations of data on maps further reinforced it. The exclusion of urban speech communities, younger educated informants, and complex social distinctions did nothing to undermine its apparent validity. Perhaps heterogeneity is more typical than homogeneity and variation than uniformity, and perhaps other distributions than regional ones are important. Such a possiblity was not seriously considered until very recently, and it is to that possibility we must now turn.

Social Variation

Social variation is as much a fact of human life as regional variation. No society is without it: only the extent appears to be different. The variation may be manifested in any number of ways, some of them largely symbolic: "blue blood," for example, or descent from ancestors who came over on the Mayflower. But usually the manifestations are more overt: money, possessions, clothes, manners, that is, artifacts and other characteristics associated with a particular job, age, sex, or some other group designation. Almost any artifact or characteristic can be used as an indicator of social difference: possession of a particular type of automobile, a huge piece of stone "money," a caste mark, a club membership, a trophy, an "Oxford" accent and so on.

In every society people must learn what characteristics are used to make social distinctions. They must also learn how particular characteristics can or cannot be acquired and lost, that is, what freedom exists to change social position. Sometimes there is little or no freedom, so change can occur only through some kind of revolutionary upheaval; sometimes there may bee too much freedom and change becomes synonymous with anarchy. Sometimes the change is bestowed: a knighthood or an earldom or an appointment to an ambassadorship or a judgeship; and sometimes it is mandated: a loss of certain rights on conviction for a felony. The important point in all these examples is the pervasiveness—sometimes very subtle—of social variation. The subtlety itself is very important. The indicators of social variation are many times below conscious awareness, and they are often all the more powerful for that reason. But just because they are below conscious awareness does not mean that people are insensitive to them. As we shall see, people are quite sensitive to linguistic indicators of social differences, even though they may be quite unable to explain exactly what it is that they are sensitive to.

Each individual exists in a variety of social settings and relationships; hermits and prisoners kept in solitary confinement may be some of the rare exceptions. There is not just a single social system in a society: rather there is an overall social system composed of myriads of interrelated subsystems. Each person must learn to adjust to the demands of that variety and to seek fulfillment through mastery of the intricacies of the individual subsystems. Each linguistic community exhibits complex patterns of social organization and is composed of numerous subsystems. It is not, therefore, homogeneous in this one important respect at least.

There is no reason either to assume that any one individual consistently uses the same linguistic forms in every situation. There appear to be few, if any, single-style speakers, that is, speakers whose language never varies no matter what the circumstances. Speech usually varies according to the social context in which it occurs. Some contexts demand certain styles of speaking because of their physical characteristics, for example, speech-making in a large auditorium without a microphone, but the most usual cause of variation is the social relationships that exist among the participants in any exchange. These relationships account for the degree of formality each speaker adopts and for the amount of conscious attention which is devoted to the act of speaking itself. A speaker can speak differently on the same occasion to different listeners, for example, to make an aside during a formal presentation, and to the same listeners, for example, to clarify a point. Moreover, a speaker can repeat the same kinds of behavior on other similar occasions, thus indicating that the shifts are systematic and part of a total repertoire of language knowledge and behavior.

The Linguistic Variable

It is systematic ability to shift from one kind of speech to another that is at the center of any study of social variation in language use. Two questions arise immediately. What kinds of shifts occur? What occasions the shifts? To answer the first question the linguist must isolate a particular linguistic phenomenon to see what happens in a variety of circumstances. Such a phenomenon is called a linguistic variable. It may be the exact pronunciation of the ends of words like *hunting* and *going* (alternatively *huntin'* and *goin'*), or the pronunciation of the middle consonant in *water, better,* and *sitting,* or whether a word such as *bath* is pronounced as though it were *baff* or *then* as though it were *den*, or the quality of a particular vowel, as in *now* or *bag*, or the distribution of a particular tense or aspectual form, as in *He is here, He here*, and *He be here*, or a negation system, as in *He doesn't have any, He hasn't any*, and *He ain't got none*. The linguist looks for instances of the use of the variable and for the particular realizations which occur. The different realizations are then related to quantifiable characteristics of the social contexts in which they occurred. The linguist answers the second question about what occasions the shifts in use by relating the distribution of the variable to identifiable parameters in these social contexts, such as regional origin, social class, age, ethnicity, occupation, and so on. The conclusion is a statement of the distribution of the variable in a population rather than a description of the linguistic behavior of any specific individual.

Two variables may be used as examples: final *-ing* and word-final *t*. Words of more than one syllable which end with an *-ing* spelling are given varied pronunciations. In informal speech *-in'* is likely to replace *-ing*, and boys are more likely to behave in this way than girls. Cutting across this distribution, however, is the fact that "common" verbs like *chew, punch*, and *swim* are more likely to be given *-in'* endings than "learned" verbs like *correct, criticize*, and *read* in otherwise identical situations. The sexes are alike in this regard. In addition, *Cushing* and *Flushing* are nearly always pronounced with *-ing* in any circumstance. So far as final *t* is concerned, it is most likely to be dropped when it represents a past tense in front of a word beginning with a vowel, as in *He passed Ann* (*He pass Ann*), and least likely when it is part of a word (not a past tense marker) and the following word begins with a consonant, as in *the past week*. *Passed* followed by a consonant, and *past* followed by a vowel show intermediate degrees of loss of the final *t*. Again the amount of loss is correlated with the degree of formality being attempted: less formal situations show a greater incidence of loss in all four forms than more formal situations.

One considerable difficulty arises in trying to define context exactly. Social class is notoriously difficult to define as are levels of formality. Data collection procedures which depend on sampling are laborious and expensive. Everyday social settings cannot easily be classified. Even so, considerable success has been achieved in each area. Linguists and psychologists have also been able to relate certain styles of speaking to people's perceptions of social relationships and the actual techniques for eliciting data have likewise been considerably refined. It is generally agreed, for example, that reading a passage aloud produces a very careful, formal type of speech: it puts people on their "best" linguistic behavior. Reading word lists aloud, answering a fixed set of questions, participating in informal talk with the investigator, talking casually with associates in the presence of the investigator, and finally, but possibly unattainable, talking casually without any awareness of being observed successively take people further and further away from that best behavior. William Labov, the linguist who has undoubtedly done more work on variation than any other, has even argued that this last kind of talk, this casual unobserved language behavior, would be the most informative of all to observe if it were possible, in that it would be more consistent than any other behavior. However, the "vernacular style" is certainly no more representative of a speaker's total linguistic behavior than any other style and, studied exclusively, it would offer little or no help in understanding variation and change. The study of variation requires that attention be given to all the styles of speech.

The central issue in work with linguistic variables is that of relating particular manifestations of a linguistic variable to the situations in which they occur. This particular problem did not arise in the linguistics of the 1940s and 1950s which was concerned with categorial differences alone, that is, whether a particular linguistic form was significantly different from, therefore contrastive to, other linguistic forms. Any other kind of variation was free, or nonsignificant, variation. Work which employs the concept of the linguistic variable requires considerable modification of these concepts of difference and significance. The concept of categorial differences is recognized, but specific differences are maintained only according to circumstances. A distinction made in one set of circumstances is missing in another set. The principle of "once a phoneme, always a phoneme" no longer applies. Consequently, as circumstances change so do the nature and extent of the differences that are maintained. The change, or variation, that results in the language is not free; it is correlated with events external to language. Moreover, as people either consciously or unconsciously modify their linguistic behavior in relation to external events, the language itself changes as particular distributions of variants change. As we shall see, many different kinds of external factors affect the linguistic choices which speakers make.

Choice of Forms

A speaker's choice of linguistic forms will be partly influenced by how society as a whole regards certain types of language. Choice is related to function in this very general way. For example, how closely an Indian conforms to a standard variety of Hindi will depend on family background, regional origin, educational level, political and social beliefs, the topic under discussion, and so on. The different varieties that result are socially acceptable only so long as they are appropriate. So, too, it is appropriate for the speaker to use Sanskrit in other circumstances. Like Latin in medieval Europe and Classical Arabic in the Near East, the use of Sanskrit is deemed appropriate in very definite formal and religious circumstances. Coming nearer home, we need only recollect that it took a fairly recent papal fiat to allow the mass to be celebrated in vernacular languages rather than in Latin. The choice of language varieties is therefore socially controlled to a considerable extent.

A good example of this control is the situation that exists in Northern Norway with regard to the local dialect form *Ranamaal* and one of the two national forms *Bokmaal* (formerly *Riksmaal*)—the other being *Nynorsk* (formerly *Landsmaal*). Ranamaal forms are appropriate to show intimacy, informality, and identification between speaker and addressee. Bokmaal forms signal distance, formality, and difference. Bokmaal is the language of formal instruction, officialdom, business affairs, and of politeness to strangers, but Ranamaal is the language of local identification, social interchange, and personal friendship, for example, between teacher and student or government official and laborer. A particular conversation may employ both varieties as the topics change. The topic decides the variety used.

On occasion people decide the variety of the language they wish to use regardless of topic. Sometimes speakers employ certain linguistic forms for no other purpose than trying to identify with a particular group. When that group is regarded as socially superior, the dangers of hypercorrection are great and the result can be the use of expressions like *between you and I* and *He felt badly about it*, inappropriate word usages, euphemisms, and even malapropisms. The imitation of social superiors appears to be one of the basic causes of language change. Deliberately using forms known to be characteristic of social inferiors, for example, the double negation and form of *be* used in *I ain't got none*, indicates a different kind of group identification and therefore different motives.

The various social groups in society have ways of marking their members so that each member may easily identify other members and detect strangers. This marking operates in language through the linguistic choices which the speakers of a particular group customarily make. Adolescent slang is one example; professional jargon is another; an "Oxford" or "Harvard" accent is a third. Preferences for particular words, grammatical forms, and pronunciations help characterize the different social groups. But any individual is always free to some extent to accept or reject some of the consciously recognized norms in accord with that individual's feelings concerning the group. Since what actually constitutes the total set of norms is not always very clear to those who wish to observe them or break them, a fertile opportunity is created for distinguishing between members and nonmembers on the one hand and for change to occur on the other as people strive to gain or lose membership in a group.

According to Labov, the feelings that speakers have about their social mobility have a very profound influence on the linguistic forms they choose. Upwardly mobile people tend to adopt the speech norms of a higher social group, generally the next highest group in society with whom they have contact. Social stability is marked by relatively little style shifting and stable norms. In contrast, downward mobility leads to a rejection of some of the stable norms as well as any norms from an obviously higher social group. In his study on Martha's Vineyard of the centralizations of the diphthongs in words like *right, ride, my, about,* and *down,* Labov found interesting examples of each kind of mobility. The increase in centralization which the older Yankees on the island exhibited had been accompanied by a downward mobility of that group. Mobile younger Yankees exhibited least centralization: they were the ones who moved to the mainland or intended to do so. Interestingly enough, those who had returned to the island not having "made it" on the outside exhibited very strong centralization. The older Portuguese and Gay Head Indians on the island, who were regarded by the Yankees as socially inferior and who tended to regard themselves in the same light, showed almost no centralization. However, the younger Portuguese and Gay Head Indians no longer felt any inferiority to the Yankees and displayed on the whole more centralization than the Yankee Islanders: they were quite happy to identify, even to the extent of overidentification, with the next superior group of permanent residents on the island.

The Individual and the Group

While it is certainly interesting to describe the language of subgroups in society and to demonstrate how "idealized" members of such groups typically behave, we must still remember that we are not looking at how specific individuals behave. This point is extremely important. All of this kind of evidence about language and social behavior has been acquired from responses gained from large numbers of informants. Then the responses are counted, plotted, averaged, graphed, and so on. We are told that in one set of circumstances we find that eighty per cent of the speakers who were observed used "Form X," but that in another set of circumstances only fifty per cent did so. Or that sixty-five per cent of the speakers used "Form Y," thirty per cent "Form Z," and five per cent did not seem to have anything equivalent to "Y" or "Z." What we have are group norms, not descriptions of individual behavior, and they are group norms stated within broad categories. Linguists usually show the distributions of the variants on graphs of one kind or another. They do not, except in very rare cases, employ statistics to test for the significance of differences, attempt to describe linguistic profiles for individuals, or predict the actual linguistic behavior of an individual in a specific social situation. They exchange the idealizations of the regional stereotype and of the ideal speaker-listener in a completely homogeneous speech community for characteristics of speakers which can be expressed in a few numbers and on simple graphs.

What we can still say with some confidence is that individual speakers are aware of some of the language differences that exist among the subgroups in society. As a result, their speech tends to shift in certain of its characteristics depending on the listener, the situation, and the topic. Individual speakers often demonstrate considerable variation in their speech. They do not have anything that can usefully be called a single idiolect at their disposal. They do not produce the same linguistic forms with absolute consistency. Instead variation abounds. Certain circumstances will lead particular speakers to pronounce more final consonants or more postvocalic r's than other circumstances. The raising, centering, or tensing of vowels may also vary according to circumstances, as will choices of words and grammatical constructions. A formal speech situation—for example, reading aloud—will produce many of the most prestigious forms a speaker knows, even to the extent of overcorrection. A relaxed peer-oriented setting will produce an entirely different kind of linguistic behavior.

Individual speakers generally know which linguistic forms are preferred in society. They are aware that some forms are associated with certain kinds of social prestige and others with the lack of it. They are also aware that certain kinds of language are favored by powerful agencies in society, particularly formal educational institutions, government, and the mass media. Individuals then must make choices in speaking as to how they will present themselves to others and what roles they are prepared to play. Ultimately, by playing certain roles very well, an individual may be permanently cast in certain parts and come to possess all the requisite attributes and artifacts, even those of speech. The putative actor in the most difficult position is the one who cannot find a clearly defined role or who must make do with one which no one else wants to play. If the actor has ambition, his task is to learn new and desirable roles with as little delay and faltering as possible. But, of course, the opportunity must be there. Lacking opportunity and ambition, he is unlikely to learn roles preferred by the wider society and may settle instead for ones that are rejected rather than preferred.

Language plays an essential part in the process of social adjustment and self-realization. It may even be a very potent indicator of just where an actor is at particular stages in his development or lack of development: nearly thirty years ago the eminent dialect geographer Raven McDavid suggested that recruiters for police agencies in the southern states might well consider whether a southern applicant pronounced r's after vowels in arriving at a decision as to the applicant's suitability for police work. Labov has also expressed the hope that linguistic variables may also come to serve as indices to measure other forms of social behavior, mentioning specifically social aspirations, social mobility and insecurity, and changes in social stratification and segregation. Desirable though such outcomes might be, linguists are still quite far from achieving them with the methods they currently employ. Much work remains to be done if linguists are to be able to extrapolate from linguistic findings to social and psychological matters. In particular, prediction will have to supersede observation as a major goal in linguistic research.

Age-Grading

Speech varies according to the age of the speaker and the listener. For example, as we shall see in the following chapter, children go through a process of language learning which results in different kinds of speech at different ages: babbling for a while during part of the first year; speaking in single-word utterances at some time early in the second year; and gradually building up to using extremely complicated utterances by the end of the third year. Parents and older children also often speak to very young children using linguistic forms specially adapted for the occasion. "Baby talk" is something very young children learn from their elders. Some of the forms used in baby talk may be helpful to very young children: reduplications like *bow wow, bye bye*, and *choo choo*; simplifications like *tummy* for *stomach*; marking of nouns with a *-y* ending as in *kitty* and *doggy*; and referring to oneself as *Daddy* or *Mommy*. However, some are probably not very helpful, particularly phonological distortions such as substitutions of *w* for *r* in *wabbit* for *rabbit* or those of pitch and vowel quality.

We assume that children of five or six have learned enough language to be able to begin some kind of formal education. However, their speech continues to change. In particular, school-age children continue to refine their grammatical knowledge, exchanging the influence of parents for that of peers. The language of early adolescence is particularly likely to show considerable peer-group influence. The whole of the childhood-early adolescent period is also the period during which children acquire much of the folklore of their culture and become aware of, and eventually master, many of the rituals on which successful human relationships depend. The later part of the period is also characterized by the adoption of special vocabularies of slang terms whose function it is to identify the members of particular groups. Specific slang words rarely find their way into regular use, but slang as a phenomenon persists relatively unchanged over the centuries. Early adulthood sees the elimination, or fossilization, of much of this slang as more emphasis is given to acquiring the language necessary for work and leisure-time activities.

Because language use varies quite predictably with the age of its user we can say that certain language usages are age-graded. Each individual seems to pass through a sequence of "age grades" on the way to linguistic "maturity." Violations of age-grading are readily noticed when they occur: a forty-year old talking like a teenager; a ten-year old talking like an old man; a six-year old talking like a baby; a thirteen-year old attempting to talk like a nineteen-year old; and so on. Sometimes the result is embarrassment or discomfort to listeners because of the false note that is struck. However, since the grades in age-grading are not discrete the possibility exists for variation to occur. It may not always be possible to know exactly what is required to "be your age" so far as language is concerned.

And when a considerable part of society devotes itself to cultivating the appearance—and, to some extent, the habits—of youth, it is not surprising that linguistic habits are aped as well. Forty-year olds talking like teenagers are no longer as rare as they once were.

Sex Differences

Sex differences in language usage also exist. Differences associated with sex should be easier to detect than those associated with age because there are only two sexes (more or less) in contrast to the continuum with which any consideration of age differences must deal. Certain differences have been observed between the characteristic language uses of men and women. On the whole women have higher pitched voices than men because of anatomical reasons. They also tend to be more precise and "careful" in speaking: for example, they are more likely than men to pronounce the final -*ing* forms with a *g*, to say *fighting* rather than *fightin'*. In general, they take more "care" in articulation. This behavior accords with other findings that women tend to be less innovative than men in their use of language and to be more conscious of preferred usages. They are also more likely than men to use "appeal tags" such as *isn't it?* or *don't you think?*, and they employ a wider range of intonation patterns.

Women also tend to use some words that men do not use or to use certain words in different ways from men. Women use more different names for colors than men: *mauve, lavender, turquoise, lilac,* and *beige* are good examples. Men either do not use such color words or, if they do, tend to use them with great caution. Intensifiers such as *so, such,* and *quite,* as in *He's so cute, He's such a dear,* and *We had a quite marvelous time* comprise a set of words used in a way which most men avoid; emotive adjectives such as *adorable, lovely,* and *divine* are hardly used at all by men.

Recently, it has been asserted that a language can have a bias against women built right into it, and English has been cited as an example. English speakers talk of *mankind* not *womankind* or *personkind* and use *him* to refer to *person,* thus, it is said, giving a preference to men rather than to women in the species as a whole. *He's a professional* and *She's a professional* have very different meanings, as have the words *master* and *mistress.* Differences such as these are said to indicate quite clearly that language is used to downgrade women in society. Words like *lady* and *girl* are also said to demean their referents in many usages, for example, *a lady doctor* and *She's gone out with the girls.* Men may sometimes be addressed by last name alone (*Smith* or *Jones*), but this practice is generally avoided completely with women who tend instead to be addressed by a term which refers to their marital status and sex (*Mrs Smith* or *Miss Jones*) or is patronizing (*Mary* or *Jane*). (The fact that many men find this naming practice distasteful seems to have been overlooked by those who regard its unavailability for use with women as a slight.) The adoption of *Ms.* in writing has been a deliberate attempt to right a perceived imbalance in the system of formal written address: a single (or married) *Mr.* but the two-fold *Mrs* and *Miss*. Likewise, *woman* is preferred to either *lady* or *girl*, even though historically its meaning is something like "man's woman."

That English has a sex bias remains unproved. It does have sex classification as do many other languages, but the kinds of correlations that have been declared to exist do not prove anything. Correlation must never be confused with causation. That speakers of English, men or women, may have sex biases is a topic which is much more readily researchable. What does seem certain is that there are sex differences in the actual use of language and that people do react to the different usages in predictable ways. We might feel it unfortunate that a male worker on an assembly line cannot easily say *What a marvelous idea!* to a co-worker without having his masculinity questioned or that a woman's profanity is sometimes much differently regarded than a man's. The important issue so far as language itself is concerned is how particular linguistic forms are regarded at different times and why they are so regarded. To say that they should be differently regarded is to adopt the role of the social engineer not that of the linguistic scientist. It may be important to adopt that role, but it should be clear that a role change occurred.

Ethnic Differences

Ethnicity also plays some part in language variation: we can identify certain styles of speaking with certain ethnic groups. In particular, the Pennsylvania Dutch and the Jewish groups in the United States have provided popularizers with numerous examples of ethnic pronunciations, grammatical structures, occasional morphological patterns, and vocabulary items. Yiddish, for example, has provided a particularly fruitful source: *You should live so long, Beautiful she isn't, I need it like a hole in the head, He asked me for it yet, Jerk schmerk!*, and so on.

Most recently black Americans have occasioned the same interest as a search has been undertaken to find any special characteristics that might be distinctive of the English spoken by this group. Various characteristics have been proposed as defining typical examples of "Black English." For example, in words like *pin* and *pen* the vowels will be nasalized and the final consonants may be dropped. These two words will also become homophones, that is, they will be pronounced alike, through the resulting neutralization of the vowel contrast. Such neutralization of vowels also occurs before *r* or *l*, which often vocalize in addition. Final clusters often are simplified so that *test* sounds like *Tess* and *mask* like *mass*.

Then and *den* seem to be interchangeable pronunciations of *then,* and *three* and *tree* seem to be interchangeable pronunciations of *three.* Final *-ing* is pronounced *-in'*; in general unstressed initial syllables are lost: *'bout* and *'cept*; and stress is often shifted forward: *Détroit, pólice,* and *hótel.*

In syntax the use of *do* is very different from the use of *do* in standard English, as in *I done baked a cake.* Likewise, the use, or non-use of *be* is different, as in *He be waitin' for me every night* and *He waitin' for me now.* The *be* in the first example shows a customary, recurring activity, that is, it marks a durative aspect, whereas the absence of *be* in the second example shows a momentary nonrecurring state. Labov has pointed out, however, that *be* can be deleted only in those places in which contraction is possible: *I don't care what you are* resists deletion of the *be* (*are*). Agreement of subject and verb is also different: *He have done it* and *He walk there every day*; multiple negation is very frequent; *ain't* abounds; and quite different statement forms from Standard English are sometimes found: *I asked Tom do he want to go, I want to know did he do it,* and *Didn't nobody see it.*

Rhetorical, that is, stylistic, usages are also likely to be quite different. Black English employs considerable exaggeration and hyperbole, a wide intonation range, use of the falsetto voice on occasion, and audience or listener participation and encouragement (*Amen, Right on*). Many different kinds of verbal displays are also found in which an emphasis is placed on the quality of the performance: toasting, rapping, signifying, sounding, playing the dozens, and so on. Good performances are *cool*; to be unable to participate is to mark oneself as a *lame.*

There has been considerable discussion of whether Black English is a variety of southern states English, therefore ultimately of British origin, or a creolized form of English derived from West African and Caribbean sources. The question of its ultimate origin is still a matter of dispute and controversy within linguistics. It has been argued that Black English is just a variant of the Southern dialect or that it is just one of the dialects of American English. In either case any differences between it and other dialects are quite superficial. For example, Labov's point about the impossibility of deletion of *be* in certain circumstances is an argument in favor of treating Black English as being really little different from other varieties of English: the differences are only slight differences in what certain rules cover or how they are ordered in relation to each other. The creolist view though is that the differences are fundamental, being differences in "deep" features of the dialect rather than in "surface" features: superficial similarities disguise the differences. It is still too early yet to be sure how the dispute will be resolved; the first position seems to have more support than the second, but we must remember that it accords more with current linguistic thinking than the second and may be biased on that account.

Various experiments have shown that people are able to distinguish between blacks and whites on the telephone, with about an eighty per cent accuracy, in general failing only to pick out atypical individuals. Studies denying this fact have always used a disproportionate number of atypical individuals; the results are therefore useless so far as making generalizations to the total population is concerned. Stereotyping, that is, using only one or a very few features for the purposes of classification, is clearly demonstrable in black-white relationships in general and in speech in particular. The particular combination of linguistic difference between blacks and whites and the social changes which are occurring in race relationships in society are likely to lead to linguistic change. The setting seems almost ideal. The one factor that makes the situation less than ideal is the pervasiveness of the black-white color issue: if linguistic variation and change are closely related to social variation and change, any barrier to the latter must also affect the former in some way.

Stylistic Differences

Occupational and role differences can also be associated with language differences. Occupations tend to have their own jargons, that is, technical linguistic usages, including their own ways of using otherwise familiar words. Linguistics is full of special words: *phoneme, morpheme, uvular,* and *tagmeme.* It also uses familiar words in unfamiliar ways: *generate, transformation, role,* and *construction.* Doctors, preachers, and pimps obviously use different words, and they use them in different ways for different effects. Successful doctoring, preaching, and pimping require mastery of the different kinds of language each vocation requires, and the professional fairly readily distinguishes the imposter through failures in usage.

An individual, of course, must choose among jargons according to circumstances. Language must be varied according to the role that is being played: father, son, consultant, drinking companion, and so on. Speaking requires a choice of register. A doctor discussing a medical problem with colleagues will use one register, flowers with a nursery employee another, bicycles with a daughter still another, and car insurance with an insurance agent a fourth. But if a register offers choices which depend on topic and listener, it also offers stylistic choice too. A medical problem can be discussed at various levels. The anthropologist Clifford Geertz has pointed out that Javanese, for example, provides its speakers with a rich system for making choices in both register and style. Considerations of age, sex, kinship, occupation, wealth, education, religion, and family are among those that determine exactly what form a particular linguistic act will take, even a simple statement or question. On the other hand, Indonesian is a neutral "democratic" language in that it does not have this elaborate system. Consequently, it is often used in Java when uncertainty exists as to what Javanese forms would be appropriate.

The linguist Martin Joos has distinguished five styles of speaking: frozen, formal, consultative, casual, and intimate. Frozen style uses highly formalized and ritualistic language. In a sense the listener is completely ignored, being unable to influence what is said in any significant way. Pledges are pledged; prayers are intoned; proclamations are proclaimed; and set pieces such as poems, plays, and often speeches are delivered. Interruptions rarely occur. When they do occur, they stop or violate the performance rather than change it. The speaker or speakers try to go back to where they were before the interruption and begin again at that point as though nothing had happened, or they ignore the interruption entirely. In frozen style the performance is often as important, sometimes more important, than the message itself. This style is also the style of much published writing.

Formal style also allows for little participation by the listener. It is speech that is carefully planned and deliberately delivered, sometimes to a large audience. Between individuals formal style indicates social distance, reproof, or deference. It is the mother's *John Smith, what are you doing?* to her son. Consultative style, on the other hand, does involve the listener. Information gets communicated, and feedback occurs. There is no excessive planning, and set pieces are avoided. Ellipses, contractions, and interruptions are possible. This is the style that Queen Victoria expected when her prime ministers consulted her. Unfortunately, William Gladstone tended to use a formal style which led Victoria to observe that: "He speaks to Me as if I was a public meeting."

Casual style is the style which friends use with each other, or which people who are intimately acquainted with a topic adopt for discussion of that topic. Casual style indicates a sharing of considerable background information and many assumptions. Ellipses, contractions, interruptions, jargon, and slang occur frequently. The sharing of so much enables many comments and decisions to be made quickly: *'s good movie; Can't go—homework; O.K.* Intimate style is even more terse, often just consisting of rather infrequent single-word utterances and nonverbal communication. Its function tends to be different from the functions of other styles. It is used to express feelings rather than to make statements or to work through to decisions. It is therefore the language of people who know each other extremely well and is often very private: it is the language of the long married, of lovers, and sometimes of people engaged in very intricate and well-practiced work: for example, a team playing basketball, performing surgery, or drilling an oil well.

Register and style are intimately related if only for the fact that neither can be clearly separated from the other, for both address themselves to many of the same issues. People do have a wide range of choices available to them when they speak: they can be technical or nontechnical, formal or informal, conscious of their role or unconscious of it, familiar with the listener or distant; and so on. The consequences will show in the language they use: the amount of technical terminology employed; the care taken in articulation; the speed of delivery of utterances; the kinds of omissions made and tolerated; the types and complexity of grammatical constructions; the standards of grammatical "accuracy" observed; the use of phrases like *You know* and *You see* and colloquialisms in general; and even the use of the pronoun *I*.

The Importance of Variation

Language variation may seem as regrettable a fact about language as language change. A single language used by speakers throughout the world with no variation may appear to many people to be a perfect state of affairs. The development and spread of major world languages, the rise of literacy, and the potency of the mass media might be interpreted as indicating that the fulfillment of such a wish cannot be too far distant. At such time people would not have to worry about their speech "giving them away" in their personal relationships, and the processes of change might be slowed down and even stopped. At last, conscious, deliberate regulation of language would be achieved, and the academicians would have their endless day. But how realistic and desirable is such a situation?

Very likely linguistic imperialism will continue, and languages spoken by small numbers of people will die out. There is likely to be continual pressure to give up a minor language for one of the major languages. Minor languages will be maintained only for special reasons, but this maintenance will, of course, serve to emphasize their dysfunctionality rather than their utility. Ultimately, it may not really matter whether there will be one or more major languages so far as the question of change is concerned, for change will continue as long as the users of that language or those languages remain heterogeneous in belief, occupation, religion, training, and so on. That is, so long as widely different life-styles, career patterns, and social opportunities are available there is likely to be variation and change in language. In the absence of these differences there is likely to be little variation and there may also be considerable success in attempts to "fix" the language, that is, to resist change.

The question about the desirability of such an occurrence is obviously not a linguistic one alone. Linguistic change and variation are associated with cultural change and variation, and possibly more fundamentally with human change and variation. It may even be argued that this kind of variation, cultural, linguistic, and biological, is a necessity for the very survival of the human species. The diversity encourages types of evolutionary development that sustain the viability of the species. A species which cannot change and adapt becomes at best a living fossil, out of place in the times it finds itself in and at worst extinct. Fernando Nottebohm's investigations of the songs of chaffinches and white-crowned sparrows have led him to speculate that the "dialect" differences he found in such songs have a survival value for the birds. The differences create just enough distance to keep groups of birds apart but not enough to stop cross-breeding. The result is a healthy, varied, gene pool. A single catastrophic blow would not wipe out a whole species because the variation in the pool would ensure the survival of some members. Adaptation would be possible to a new set of circumstances.

In considering the ultimate course of linguistic change and variation, we should be sure not to confuse cause and effect. Linguistic change and variation result from factors in the world, mainly regional and social differences. If these differences are eliminated, then linguistic change and variation may also be eliminated. If the removal of all differences ultimately eliminates humankind as a species, the species will not have been eliminated by interfering with language. Of course, such a gloomy future is unlikely to come about. Language and mind offer humans considerable possibilities for controlling their evolution, a control already exercised through the cultural evolution that has come to dominate genetic evolution in so many ways. Humans may eventually be able to remake themselves genetically and linguistically as they choose, without having to worry about either the catastrophic collapse of the species on the one hand or certain inabilities to communicate with fellow humans on the other.

References

The collections of papers in Allen and Underwood (1971), Bailey and Robinson (1973), Fishman (1968), Giglioli (1972), Pride and Holmes (1972), and Williamson and Burke (1971) are all very useful, as are Burling (1970) and Gumperz (1971). Haugen (1966) discusses the problem of defining language and dialect. Pickford (1957) offers a sociolinguistic appraisal of American dialect geography. Wolfram and Fasold (1974) provide an introduction to social dialectology.

The best book-length treatment of variation is Labov (1972c). Bailey (1973a, 1973b) expresses somewhat different views on the same topic. The discussion of *-ing* and *-in'* is based on Fischer (1958) and that of final *t* on Labov, Cohen, Robins, and Lewis (1968). See Chapter Five of Wolfram and Fasold (1974) for a discussion of the linguistic variable. Lambert (1972) describes many of the factors which affect people's reaction to different varieties of language. Gumperz and Blom (1971) is the source of the data on the situation in Norway. Social mobility as a subject is frequently mentioned by Labov, particularly in his (1972c). His Martha's Vineyard study is reported there as well as in his (1966). McDavid's comment on postvocalic *r* is in his (1949), and Labov's hope is expressed in his (1972c), p. 120.

Key (1972), Lakoff (1973), and Miller and Swift (1973) make a number of observations about language differences between the sexes. Rosten (1968) is a popular source of information on the influence of Yiddish on English. There is an extensive literature of Black English; four recent book-length treatments are those of Burling (1973), Dillard (1972), and Labov (1970, 1972a). Both Dillard (1972) and Stewart (1967, 1968) discuss the creole-origin hypothesis in some detail. Labov's views on *be* are expressed in his (1969). Geertz (1960) is the source of the data on Javanese. Joos (1962) is a stylish entertaining account of differences in style, and Turner (1973) a broader-based account. Queen Victoria's remark is recorded in Russell (1898), and Nottebohm's observations on "dialects" in birds in his (1970).

7

The Developmental Context

Some Basic Issues

There is a long history of interest in questions concerning the course of language development in children. A considerable amount has been written on the topic. Some of the writing must be judged to be quite speculative, but much is sound reporting of the results of conscientious observation. There are even records of simple experiments involving bringing up young children in isolation to discover what language they would "naturally" speak. In the last half century much of the investigative work has been taxonomic and normative in nature: records of the appearance of first words; lists showing the order in which specific sounds are acquired; inventories displaying the growth of inflectional control; catalogues of the sentence types used at different ages; and so on. Such work became considerably more revealing following the development of modern linguistics. That development led researchers to pose various interesting questions about such matters as the course of phonemic development, the progressive differentiation and control of linguistic categories, the increasing awareness of semantic relationships, and the acquisition of complex performance skills. Issues to be resolved rather than inventories to be compiled became the matter of studies of language acquisition in children.

At the same time investigators were forced to confront the issue of what language itself is and how that something—whatever it is—could be acquired so uniformly, so easily, and so quickly by naive children. Is language development a natural kind of development like physical growth itself? Are human beings endowed with a specific capacity for language? Is language therefore innate in some sense? Or is language an entirely learned phenomenon, learned in much the same way as many skills are learned? What, therefore, are the relative influences of nature and nurture on language acquisition? One aspect or another of this last issue is behind just about every controversy in language acquisition today.

Investigators were also forced to consider the actual process of language acquisition. Linguists have never been well equipped to handle dynamic, changing systems and the variability that exists in large quantities of data. The result is that there still continues to be an emphasis in the studies on "stages" of development and a noticeable tendency to draw evidence not from large numbers of children but usually from one, two, or three children studied periodically at fixed intervals. Of course, this concept of stages of development fits quite well within the usual linguistic emphasis on categorial differences, that is, whether two characteristics are contrastive or not, and on whether a particular distinction exists or not in a body of data.

Another consideration which has come to the fore from time to time has been the need to make explicit the assumptions behind any theory of acquisition. Something must be innate if language is to be acquired. It could be a specific capacity to acquire language, but it could also be a capacity to do certain kinds of things with phenomena which the developing organism encounters, that is, an innate general capacity to learn in carefully regulated ways or a general cognitive capacity which increases through and with experience. But there are other issues too that are specifically concerned with the acquisition of language. Language is "doubly articulated" in that it employs two systems, one of sounds and the other of meanings. Do children "know" that fact about language in advance of learning, or must they discover it for themselves? What kind of knowledge would such knowledge be? Or what kind of discovery? Where do the primitive concepts of "sense" and "sentencehood" come from? Sentences make sense, but how do children know that? Does this knowledge come from inside children, because they know the world must make sense, or does it come through reinforcement, because people make sense of the world for children? If the latter, how do processes of reinforcement and generalization work with essentially the abstract set of relationships that any language is? Why should young children talk anyway, since almost every need that they have is met almost immediately? Yet all children do eventually talk unless sorely afflicted. And, finally, if ontogeny recapitulates phylogeny—as many believe—can anything be learned of the possible origins of language in the species by looking at the origins of language in children?

As we shall see, as soon as researchers begin to delve into issues related to language acquisition in children, they must consider just about every important issue in linguistics. Partly for this reason language acquisition has become one of the most interesting and controversial topics in linguistic research in recent years. It is impossible to proceed very far in such research without asking important questions or taking sides in disputes. And it is hardly possible to discover something that does not also have important consequences for linguistic theory itself.

The Course of Language Development

Most of the studies of language acquisition have concentrated on the first half dozen years of life with the preponderance of emphasis directed to the second through fourth years, these appearing to investigators to be the most interesting years. Children, even children of mute parents, babble for a considerable time during their first year. This babbling ranges over the whole inventory of possible human sounds but in one view gradually "drifts" toward the phonetic characteristics of the environment, possibly as a result of reinforcement. According to this view, there is adequate evidence that children have begun to acquire the sound system of the particular language spoken in their environment well before the period of babbling ends.

A second theory of the development of sounds systems in children maintains that such development proceeds according to a set of universal principles. Babbling actually ceases altogether near the end of the first year of life, and children learn to make certain basic distinctions in a fixed order. They learn to make a consonant-vowel distinction, with a *p* (or *b*) the first consonant and an *a* the first vowel in an open syllable of the *pa* kind. *P* is the optimal consonant because of the closure of the vocal tract at its furthest point and because of its low energy level. *A* is the optimal vowel, the one which is widest at the front and narrowest at the back. It is also a continuant with a very high energy level. In *pa*, therefore, a basic and very obvious labial closure comes to contrast with the simplest of all vowels, the low central vowel. Then children learn to differentiate labial nasals from stops, *m* from *p* or *b*. (In this view *papa* therefore precedes *mama* in a child's speech.) Afterwards they differentiate labials from dentals (*b, p,* and *m* from *d, t,* and *n*), contrast *i* with *a* and then *u* with *i*, and add velars such as *k*.

According to Roman Jakobson, the linguist who proposed this theory, the operative principle is one of "maximal" contrast at each successive differentiation. This principle applies to every language through laws of "irreversible solidarity." No language can have back consonants unless it has front consonants, or fricatives unless it has stops, because front consonants are more basic than back consonants and stops are more basic than fricatives. They are more basic to language itself, to language learning in children, and to language impairment in certain kinds of aphasia in which the more basic contrasts are retained and the less basic lost. Although Jakobson's theory has not been well tested, it continues to intrigue linguists because of its widespread implications for all kinds of investigations: linguistic ontogeny; historical linguistics; language universals; and language dissolution. Regardless of the actual course the process of phonological acquisition takes, it is just about complete in children by the age of six, with all the major characteristics having been learned much earlier.

So far as control of the system of meaning is concerned, the first meaningful units are sometimes considered to be holophrastic in nature, that is, to be whole words possessing some kind of "sentencehood" of their own. Such holophrases are found late in the first year or early in the second year. They appear to express commands to others or to self, as in *go*, or to refer to objects, as in *Dada* or *milk*, or to express emotions sometimes in highly idiosyncratic ways. They can also refer to locations, name objects, assert properties of those objects, and indicate agents. Of course, single-word utterances are heavily context-dependent for their success in communication. Each word overtly expresses only a single concept, so if "sentencehood" is defined as the overt expression of a relationship between two or more concepts, single words would not qualify as sentences. Such words would then have to be considered the building blocks out of which children proceed to form sentences in the next stage of their development.

Two-word utterances characterize the last half of the second year of life: *Allgone milk, Allgone shoe, There chair, More juice, More cookie, More read, No baby*, and so on. Such utterances must be regarded as sentences but have been described as "telegraphic" in nature. They consist almost entirely of "content" words such as nouns and verbs together with "function" words such as articles, particles, prepositions, and conjunctions. The verb *be* and inflections have no place in such utterances. However, the utterances themselves are still quite comprehensible to those who hear them. Adults react to the utterances and even expand them in ways quite acceptable to the children who utter them. The words in the utterances often seem to fall into fixed patterns: for example, *allgone, there, more,* and *no* in the above examples appear to operate as a small set of "pivot" words always used before members of a much larger set of "open" words: *milk, shoe, chair, juice, cookie, read, baby,* and so on. There appears to be a definite principle at work.

At this stage too the words which children use are perceptually salient in that they are the words which carry the heaviest stress as well as the most meaning. Function words, unstressed and contracted *be*, and inflections lack salience; consequently, they are almost always absent from utterances. When children repeat long adult words, they generally say only the stressed parts, for example, *'raff* for *giraffe* and *'pression* for *expression*. At this stage children are also quite capable of using stress and intonation for effect, for example, to distinguish *Christy room* ("Christy's room") from *Christy róom* ("Christy is in the room"). The word-order patterns are also apparently fairly fixed for children, even though the language that is being acquired may have a rather free word order, as have languages such as Finnish, Russian, and Korean. Since the words are uninflected in children's speech, children apparently substitute a fixed word order for the lack of inflection. It is of no small interest that the uninflected word itself is quite distinguishable even at this stage: it possesses some kind of reality for children.

After the two-word stage, children slowly begin to develop control of the inflections of words and to use function words. There is good evidence that three-year olds are aware of all the major form classes in the language. Children learn the irregular forms along with regular forms and often exhibit a pattern in which the learning of a general rule for dealing with regularities leads to the elimination for a while of already learned irregular forms. *Goed* may replace *went* for a while. These irregular forms must later be relearned. Six-year olds have mastered most of the inflectional system of even a complex language.

Syntactic development proceeds concurrently with the learning of inflections. A three-word stage appears briefly after the two-word stage. Three-word utterances appear to be hierarchically ordered rather than linearily ordered, that is, to be combinations of two two-word patterns rather than to be entirely new three-word patterns. However, the pace of development is so fast with noun phrases, verb phrases, and systems of modification all developing such complexity that some organizing principle other than hierarchical arrangement must soon operate in the acquisition process. Using negation as an example, we can observe the emergence of different kinds of complexity. First of all, the negative element is attached in the form of *no* or *don't* to some kind of sentence nucleus to produce utterances such as *No flag, No go back,* and *Don't wear shirt.* Then, at a later stage negation appears in still more forms (*not* and *can't* for example) and is used internally in utterances as well as attached to them, as in *Why not he go?* and *He can't go.* In the next stage the negation appears much as it appears in adult language but on occasion without a complete mastery of all the details, as in *You don't want some supper* and *That not go in here.* Still later there are the special complexities with negation involving quantifiers, double negatives, and tag questions, which children must eventually master.

As we have indicated, utterance length and syntactic complexity increase quickly, the limits appearing to be cognitive in nature rather than linguistic, that is, limits associated with general intellectual development, available memory span, and increasing knowledge of the world. One view of what happens in language acquisition is that *all* the groundwork has effectively been laid by the time children complete their fourth year of life. A lot of details remain and these take a considerable time to master, but the major task is over by the fourth birthday. Carol Chomsky's work has shown that between the ages of five and ten English-speaking children learn to use sentences like *The doll is easy to see* later than sentences like *The doll is eager to see,* the second sentence being syntactically less complex than the first in that *doll* is subject of both *eager* and *see,* whereas it is subject of neither *easy* nor *see* in the first sentence. Likewise, they find *ask* more difficult to use properly than *tell* because it can take different kinds of objects. *Promise* is also difficult in much the same way as *ask,* but since it is consistently difficult, it causes children fewer problems than *ask.* Chomsky also found that pronominal reference created difficulties: a sentence like *He knew that John was going to win the race* is often interpreted as though it were equivalent to *John knew that he (himself) was going to win the race.* As we saw in an earlier chapter in discussing people's ability to paraphrase noun compounds, language development is probably a life-long process so far as the control of details and the development of intuitions are concerned. It does not stop at five, ten, or any other age. However, all the groundwork has been laid before children begin their formal schooling.

A Behaviorist View of Language Acquisition

Why do children all learn to speak, and why do they all follow much the same pattern of language development? Several different answers have been proposed to this question, two of which are diametrically opposed to each other. The first is a behavioristic or empiricist answer which holds that language is learned in much the same way as anything else is learned and that it is the essential similarity among environments in which general laws of learning operate which accounts for the observed samenesses. The second is a nativist, rationalist, or mentalist answer which holds that children are born with an innate ability to acquire languages of a specific type, in this case human languages, and that they go about that learning using principles unique to language learning.

The chief exponent of the behaviorist view has been the psychologist B. F. Skinner. Skinner's principal interest is in the prediction and control of functional units of behavior. He argues that language is of special interest because language behavior is behavior which human beings alone can reinforce and which reinforces only through its effects on others. In his book *Verbal Behavior* Skinner attempts to specify the functional stimuli for utterance types, the functional response classes, and the various kinds of reinforcement which relate the two. He describes two important categories of verbal behavior: mands (from *commands* and *demands*) and tacts (from *contacts*). Mands are words or groups of words which bring reinforcement in the form of rewards which satisfy needs that the speaker has: *Please pass the sugar, Stop, Got a cigarette?* Tacts, on the other hand, are comments about the world: *It's raining, I'm tired, I saw him yesterday.*

They receive no direct reinforcement, but, according to Skinner, by a process of generalized reinforcement, through a listener's smiles, nods, praise, and attention, the speaker is encouraged to say things. Minor categories of verbal behavior include echoic responses (imitative responses), textual responses (responses involved in reading), intraverbal responses (knowledge of word associations), and autoclitics (verbal behavior about one's own verbal behavior, as in the use of expressions like *I think* and *I guess*). Functional considerations, that is, the uses made of language, are obviously in the forefront of Skinner's concern. He believes that reinforcement of selected responses is the key to understanding language development. Gradually, by a process of successive approximation, children learn the linguistic norms of the community.

In this behaviorist view a language is a sophisiticated response system which humans acquire through processes of conditioning. For example, only certain sounds out of the vast array of sounds used during babbling are reinforced. This reinforcement causes children's sounds to "drift" toward those of their parents. In syntactic development, the process involves generalization from one situation to another as particular linguistic patterns are reinforced. Discriminations and generalizations which effectively produce results are therefore encouraged. On the other hand, those which fail are not reinforced and are eventually extinguished. Each child is a *tabula rasa* at the beginning of the process of language acquisition. What is universal are the principles of learning that all children apply to the raw data of their experiences. Society rewards them for evidence of linguistic conformity and either ignores or punishes aberrations.

When we examine some of the data cited in the previous section in the light of such principles, we can understand how it is possible to entertain a proposal that syntactic development is largely built up through a process of contextual generalization using two-word utterances of the pivot-open variety as the "building blocks." According to this proposal, children observe that certain sets of items occur in certain positions and then proceed to make generalizations about the abstract characteristics of positions rather than about the sets of words which occupy the positions. The positions themselves are not simply linear; they are also hierarchical in that utterances longer than two words may be considered to be composed of hierarchies of two-word patterns. This generalization process may also be extended to cover the learning of the complex syntactic relationships that exist among sentences, those relationships that have sometimes been called transformational: affirmatives to corresponding negatives, actives to passives, statements to questions, and so on. Another rather similar view of what happens is that children learn the frames of a phrase structure grammar and how to substitute items within these frames. In this case the proposal is that children at first simply imitate utterances. Later they extrapolate or generalize to form open-ended classes of responses which they use within patterns which they have abstracted from the data.

The use of the term *generalization* to account for what happens in language learning has been severely criticized. Noam Chomsky has argued that its use effectively eliminates from consideration just about everything that is of real interest in learning, leaving only superficial issues behind. He also criticizes the overemphasis on reinforcing contingencies. While acknowledging that reinforcement, casual observation of data, natural inquisitiveness, generalization, and hypothesis formation all have their place in language acquisition, Chomsky claims that neither one separately nor all together can account for what actually happens. Children cannot possibly generalize from word-order patterns because no dominant patterns of word order exist for them to generalize from, even in a language like English. They also apparently produce similar fixed patterns even when the language they are learning has a very free word order, so neither reinforcement nor generalization can account for what happens in those cases. The counterclaim is that children must learn abstract structures for which no overt word-order patterns exist in the data to which they are exposed: a language is a system of abstractions, not of word-order patterns.

Imitation must play a role in any behaviorist view of language acquisition. However, the evidence for the importance of imitation is not very convincing. While there is evidence that children do practice some of the language they hear and do repeat some of the utterances of persons around them, they do not imitate them indiscriminately. Babies do not attempt to imitate all the sounds in their environment but only human sounds: they seem to be "predisposed" toward human sounds. The prelinguistic vocalizations of deaf infants are also apparently indistinguishable from those of normal infants; consequently, imitation is of little or no importance for some types of language-related behavior. A close analysis of one very young child's pre-sleep monologues revealed numerous examples of repetitions and imitations of utterances encountered during the day but also many original variations on those utterances. Congenital speech defects can also prevent speech activity, but children with such defects can nevertheless learn to respond quite normally in other ways to the spoken language around them.

Children are not very good imitators if perfect reproduction of imitated utterances is taken as the criterion measure. Imitation often involves reduction: *Daddy's briefcase* becomes *Daddy briefcase, Fraser will be unhappy* becomes *Fraser unhappy,* and *I am drawing a dog* becomes *I draw dog* when children repeat parental utterances. They offer telegraphic versions of the parental utterances and eliminate inflections, function words, and the non-salient elements. Children produce in imitation only what they would say in spontaneous speech. They reduce adult-provided utterances to the kinds of utterances they are currently using. If they are asked to imitate types they are not yet using, they fail badly (*The boy the book hit was crying* is imitated as *Boy the book was crying*), or they change what they hear to conform to what they can say (*The man who I saw yesterday got wet* becomes *I saw the man and he got wet*). Imitation does not seem to be grammatically progressive, that is, it seems to be used only to give practice in what has already been learned and not to try out new forms encountered in the environment. Children reduce the language around them to their level; they do not try to achieve a match with the language that surrounds them. Even deliberate and apparently simple requests made to children to imitate certain examples are likely to be quite unsuccessful. One child asked ten times in succession by the child's mother to repeat *Nobody likes me* could finally do no better than *Nobody don't likes me*: the child's grammar was quite unaffected by the mother's repeated model.

The greatest difficulty with relying on imitation in any theory of language acquisition is the fact that much of the speech to which children are exposed is fragmentary, and what they must do, and quickly succeed in doing, is respond to and produce entirely novel utterances, not repeat fixed examples. Indeed, not a few examples must be entirely discarded because of their intrinsic deficiencies as models. An ability to reject poor examples is as difficult to explain as the ability to understand more difficult sentences than those which can be produced. Children actually prefer to be told *Throw me the ball* rather than *Throw ball* or just *Ball*, even when they themselves can produce only the last two utterances and cannot even repeat the first. Imitation can account for neither ability. Children soon use forms and expressions they have never heard: *goed* instead of *went*, *sleeps* instead of *sleep*, and utterances such as *Allgone shoe, Allgone lettuce, All-gone milk*, and *Why not can you go?* This creative aspect of language use cannot be explained by appeal to imitation, analogy, or generalization. In each case the central issue is skirted, that of explaining how an organism, in this case a very young child, can on the basis of a small corpus of data—and sometimes not very "clean" data either—soon extrapolate a system which allows anything at all to be said.

Not only do children imitate their parents and older children to some extent, but parents and older children imitate young children. Conversations sometimes resemble exchanges of telegrams between two parties with each party trying to figure out exactly what the other meant by a particular message. Even so parents and older children use utterances in such exchanges which tend to be longer than those the younger children use. They also quite often expand the utterances of young children. A child's *Baby highchair* will lead to an older child's or adult's *Baby is in the highchair* and *Eve lunch* to *Eve is having lunch*. The words and structures are imitated and expanded, and the expanded utterance serves as a kind of check on what the child said ("Is that what you meant?"). It also acts as a fully formed model even though an uncomplicated one.

Some agreement exists that middle-class mothers expand their very young children's speech about thirty per cent of the time and that such expansion is a normal part of the mother-child relationship. These mothers therefore understand their own children's speech quite well. One study tested the hypothesis that expansions of children's utterances would encourage language development more than would comments on their utterances and that either would produce better results than using neither expansions nor comments. Twelve two-year olds were divided into three groups: the first group received intensive and deliberate expansions of their utterances, so that an utterance like *Doggie bite* would be expanded to *Yes, the dog's biting*; the second group received an equal exposure to well-formed sentences that were comments on their utterances but not expansions, so that the same utterance would be commented on, possibly with *Yes, he's mad at the kitten*; and the third group received no special treatment at all. The experiment, which lasted twelve weeks, did not show quite the expected differences: commenting, not expanding, was the more effective treatment. That is, semantically enriched responses of different syntactic form were more effective than syntactically enriched responses, even ones which closely followed the children's own language, in encouraging language development.

Two further studies examined how adults responded to syntactic deviance in their children. One, based on an analysis of conversations between mothers and children aged one to four years, reported that the syntactic correctness or incorrectness of a child's speech does not control the mother's approval or disapproval. Rather, the truth or falsity of the utterance does. A child's *There's the animal farmhouse* was corrected because the object was a lighthouse not a farmhouse. Parents tend to reward true statements (*That's right, Very good, Yes*) and punish false ones (*That's wrong, No*); however, the result is that children eventually produce syntactically correct sentences but, paradoxically, not always truthful ones. The second study confirmed these findings. In general, parents pay little or no attention to deviant utterances. The truth value of utterances concerns them more than does their syntactic correctness. A child's *What you was having on you nose?* may even be repeated by a parent as *What I was having on my nose?* before being answered *Nothing, I was rubbing my eyes.* What correction is done is of occasional mispronunciations, irregular word forms such as *goed* for *went*, and use of socially disapproved words. Deviant utterances like *Why not can you go?* seem to pass unnoticed on most occasions.

Children do imitate, parents do expand, some words and expressions are more frequent than others, analogies are made, and generalizations are tested. There is evidence to support some of the claims of the behaviorist view of language acquisition. However, no one disputes the fact that data are important, that children must have access to the language they are to learn, and that adults and older children provide help in that learning. The basic issue is whether what has to be learned in language learning can be learned entirely through the principles described in behaviorist theories of learning. The evidence suggests not. It suggests that parts only can be explained, but that the central issues of the essential creativity and abstractness of language are either ignored or skirted.

A Nativist View of Language Acquisition

The nativist view of language acquisition has several exponents, one of the principal ones being the psycholinguist Eric Lenneberg. Lenneberg relies heavily on biological evidence of various kinds and stresses the importance of human cognition as the basis for language. However, that cognition is itself based on the specific combination of biological peculiarities which defines the human species. He emphasizes the development of the various capacities of the human organism and demonstrates how these mature according to a fairly fixed schedule. Language emerges in children during the course of this maturational process when anatomical, physiological, motor, neural, and, above all, cognitive development allow it to emerge. At about six months children can usually sit up alone and stand upright with support; these developments coincide with the onset of babbling. At about one year children can walk if held by one hand, and they can understand and speak a few words. When they can creep downstairs backwards at the age of one and a half, they are ready to begin the really rapid development of language. The ability to walk up and down stairs at about two is correlated with the ability to use sentences of two or three words in length. Tricycle riding at three is accompanied by still more grammatical complexity and the ability to talk intelligibly to strangers. When children can readily catch a ball, or jump over a rope, or hop on one foot at four, they also exhibit considerable language competency. Children must learn the specific details of the languages of their communities, but language learning ability itself is innate and part of the human organism's biological endowment. It is a species-specific ability which enables humans to learn languages of a certain type. The learning mechanisms, such as certain modes of perception, abilities in categorization, and capacities for transformation, are biologically given. According to Lenneberg, children "resonate" to the language of their environment during the acquisition process: they react automatically to various kinds of language stimuli. One of his most interesting observations is that there is a critical, biologically determined period for language acquisition between the ages of two and twelve.

Since Lenneberg is interested in the biological bases of language, he says little about the learning of particular linguistic forms, but he does deny the importance of statistical probability and imitation in that learning. His basic claim is that language acquisition is a natural activity, much as learning to walk is a natural activity. Both activities occur universally unless a pathological condition exists. They exhibit a regular developmental sequence, are relatively unaffected by the environment, are not particularly useful when they first occur, and are initially quite clumsy but do not lose that clumsiness through practice alone. Learning, as this term is traditionally defined by learning psychologists, is not involved. Instead, Lenneberg carefully locks language development into the general biological development of the human organism. A corollary is that no other species is capable of learning a human language because of the extreme specificity of language in the human species.

Another major exponent of the nativist, or rationalist, view is the psychologist David McNeill, who has attempted to explore the implications of Noam Chomsky's views on language for language acquisition. Chomsky himself has been one of Skinner's severest critics. He regards language acquisition as a process of theory construction from limited data. Moreover, it is theory construction carried out in a very short time, independently of intelligence, and in a like way by all children. Chomsky concludes that children must be specifically endowed with a data handling or hypothesis formulating ability. McNeill argues likewise that anyone who wishes to study language acquisition must first be concerned with the problem of determining exactly what it is children must acquire. In his opinion they must acquire a generative-transformational grammar. Furthermore, in order to acquire such a grammar children must possess certain kinds of innate knowledge of what is to be acquired and abilities to use that knowledge. Children must possess such innate knowledge and abilities, for otherwise it is impossible to explain how the random, finite, sometimes degenerate, linguistic input the environment provides is converted into the linguistic competence which allows children eventually to say what they please.

According to McNeill one kind of innate knowledge that children have is the concept of "sentence." McNeill argues that children "know" what sentences are from the very beginning of their language learning. Another kind of knowledge is an awareness that only a certain kind of linguistic system is possible and that other kinds are not. Therefore, children need entertain only certain kinds of hypotheses about data. McNeill claims in effect that children are born with an innate knowledge of linguistic universals, both "weak" linguistic universals, that is, reflections in language of universal cognitive or perceptual abilities, and "strong" linguistic universals, that is, reflections in language of specific linguistic abilities. He is more interested in the latter and rather skeptical about the importance of the former. One innate ability that children have enables them to distinguish speech sounds from other sounds in the environment: they are "pretuned" to human language. A second ability allows them to organize linguistic events into various classes and categories which they can later refine. This ability allows for the eventual development of both the phonological and syntactic systems out of the various classes and categories. A final ability children have allows them to engage in constant evaluation of the developing linguistic system in order to construct the simplest possible system out of the linguistic data they encounter: they have a built-in evaluation procedure.

McNeill buttresses his arguments by attacking behaviorist views of language acquisition. He claims that behaviorists actually go so far as to redefine language to make phenomena fit their theories. He insists strongly on the abstractness of linguistic knowledge, the validity of the generative-transformational model of language, and the necessity of an innate structure in humans which determines what can be learned and how it can be learned. According to McNeill, children have an innate capacity to learn and generalize, but they must realize this capacity within certain innate constraints that a particular linguistic theory suggests.

The behaviorist and nativist views of language acquisition are almost diametrically opposed. However, neither view alone seems adequate for explaining all that must be explained. The behaviorists tend to make the data fit their theories even to the extent of redefining language so that it becomes nothing like what linguists believe it to be. Having redefined language, they can then use processes such as association formation and generalization to "explain" acquisition. Children themselves are assumed to make no active contribution to the total process: they learn language in much the same way as they learn anything else. It is the principles of learning which are important, not the learners and not language. However, there is a healthy insistence in behaviorism that the environment in which the learning occurs is important and that general principles applicable to all learning should be sought before special principles applicable to only a very narrow range of tasks are postulated.

The nativists, on the other hand, tend to adopt a linguistic theory and say that a theory of language acquisition must be developed to fit the requirements of the linguistic theory. Giving a particular linguistic theory a central place in language acquisition immediately leads to the postulation of innate predispositions toward the acquisition of very specific linguistic facts: children are assumed to "know" much about language in general before they learn any specific details. Such an approach deliberately minimizes the importance of environmental factors. It also shows no real concern for considering why children should say anything at all: acquisition of the uses of language is almost totally neglected in favor of considering only acquisition of the forms of language.

A "middle" view recognizes that children must bring some general principles to their task of acquiring language: some kind of learning principles, or some information or knowledge about what is to be learned, or both. A child's mind is not a *tabula rasa*. Certain principles of learning do operate, and certain limitations are apparent in how children react to different kinds of data. The most parsimonious account of language acquisition requires an attempt to relate the principles children use in such acquisition to those that they use in acquiring other kinds of skills and knowledge. It is to just such a parsimonious view that we now turn.

A Cognitive View of Language Acquisition

A third view of language acquisition may be associated with the psychologist Dan Slobin. Slobin says that children are born possessing sets of procedures and inference rules rather than knowledge of a set of universal linguistic categories. These procedures and inference rules enable children to process linguistic data. The acquisition process itself is an active process controlled at each stage by the various abilities of children, particularly the cognitive ability to deal with the world and the mental ability to retain items in short-term memory, to store items in long-term memory, and to process information increasingly well with age. The development of these abilities controls the pace of language acquisition. Other abilities are important too, for example, the ability to segment utterances into sounds and meanings and then to combine and recombine these segments, the ability to isolate meaning units, and the ability to make wide generalizations before attempting to accommodate exceptions. However, according to Slobin, general cognitive and mental development is the critical determinant of language acquisition. Children do "know" something about both the structure and function of language and actively seek to develop means for expressing what they know within the limitations imposed by their knowledge of the world, their processing skills, their abilities to remember, and the perceptual strategies which are available to them. Slobin also maintains that strictly linguistic acquisition may be completed by the age of three or so and that continued language development may reflect no more than further lifting of performance restrictions and general cognitive growth.

Two-word and three-word utterances may be used to show how children's language develops so as to allow them to express more and more complicated meanings and relationships far beyond those of simple naming, referring, requesting, or questioning. Two-word utterances from a variety of languages including English, German, Russian, Finnish, Turkish, Samoan, and Luo show that the combinations express many different semantic relationships if the data are given a "rich" interpretation. A rich interpretation is one that seeks to establish the intent of an utterance as well as its form. Intent is not easy to establish in young children. For example, what does a child who says *Daddy* in the absence of the child's father intend? However, it certain patterns appear consistently in certain situations, we can speak with considerable assurance about intent. That is the assumption behind the classification of utterances which follows.

In two-word utterances the most frequently expressed intended relationships are agent-action (*Mommy push*) and action-object (*Bite finger*). But object-location (*Cow there*), possessor-possession (*Dolly hat*), and attribute-object (*Big bed*) also occur. Later in development occur agent-object (*Mommy cup*), action-location (*Sit chair*), and demonstrative-object (*That book*). Simple negatives (*Not daddy*) and questions (*Where daddy?*) also occur as well as minor patterns such as identification (*Mommy lady*) and conjunction (*Dog cat*). The order of the parts is often reversible without a change in meaning: *Finger bite* as well as *Bite finger* and *Chair sit* as well as *Sit chair*.

Three-word utterances are built up by omitting the redundant item in two two-word utterances which share a common item: *Mummy sit* and *Sit chair* can become *Mummy sit chair,* and *Eat lunch* and *Eve lunch* can become *Eat Eve lunch.* But apparently for a while *Mummy drink coffee* and *Drink hot coffee* cannot be combined to form *Mummy drink hot coffee.* Children do not yet have the cognitive capacity to deal with such complex utterances. If at this stage children wish to express a complicated idea, they must string together a long sequence of short utterances. As Lois Bloom has pointed out, young children say things like *Raisin there* / *Buy more grocery store* / *Raisins* / *Buy more grocery store* / *Grocery store* / *Raisin a grocery store* instead of a single sentence about buying more raisins at the grocery store.

Bloom has also investigated the negations children use in their two-word sentences. She found that an utterance such as *No truck* could have various meanings and that these meanings showed a definite order of emergence: non-existence ("There's no truck here") precedes rejection ("I don't want a truck") which in turn precedes denial ("It's not a truck; it's something else"). She concludes that children's underlying semantic competence is much more differentiated than the surface forms of their utterances; children are aware of more types of meaning relationships than they can reveal through the linguistic devices they control. They must use the forms they have acquired to express any new or complex meaning relationships they wish to express.

Both Slobin and Roger Brown, another psycholinguist who has conducted extensive research into child language, have been interested in the connections between linguistic forms and language functions. Slobin has observed that new forms first express old functions and that new functions are first expressed by old forms. Brown examined how three children came to use verb inflections. Before they used any inflections at all, the children used uninflected verbs like *break, come, drink,* and *fall* to express one of four possible functions: indicating something of temporary duration; referring to the immediate past; stating a wish or intention; and commanding. Then inflections emerged to provide new forms for these functions: the *-ing* inflection for duration; the *-ed* inflection for past; the verbs *hafta, gonna,* and *wanna* for wish or intention; and the word *please* to serve as a clear indicator of commands since the command form of a verb is itself uninflected. The development of a system of negatives would be a further example of new forms being acquired to express the various functions of the negative that Bloom discusses. Likewise, the genitive *'s* eventually serves as a clear marking of the possession indicated initially as *Dolly hat* but later as *Dolly's hat*. Slobin also cites evidence of new functions being served by old forms. Children first attach words such as *now* and *yet* to statements about the past to indicate the perfect aspect: *I didn't make the bed yet* and *Now I closed it*. Later they use *I haven't made the bed* and *I've closed it*.

The new forms and the new functions themselves both result from the increase in cognitive ability that accompanies age. For example, as children get older they can increasingly free themselves from the immediate situation and the actual order of events in the world, and they can imagine themselves to be at other points in time and space and view events from that different perspective. This increase in cognitive ability enables children to express new meanings; they therefore acquire the syntactic apparatus which allows them to express these new meanings after they try for a while to get by with the apparatus that is already available. The new apparatus has always been available, for there is nothing inherently difficult about the forms themselves: for example, past tenses are both frequent and salient. However, cognitive limitations, which are gradually set aside, lead to particular forms or combinations of forms being almost completely neglected for a time.

So far as the acquisition of linguistic forms themselves is concerned, Slobin suggests that the order of emergence of various syntactic categories depends in general on their relative semantic complexity rather than on their grammatical complexity. The first grammatical distinctions to appear are those like the singular-plural distinction which make reference to readily observable situations in the outside world. Later to emerge are the diminutive suffixes of nouns, imperatives, and categories based on relational criteria, such as the case, tense, and person markings of the verbs. Conditional forms of the *if-then* variety are not learned until near the end of the third year. They express abstract relationships. Still other abstract categories of quality and action continue to be added until the age of seven. Slobin points out that Russian children find grammatical gender the most difficult of all categories to master since it has almost no semantic correlates. No easily discoverable rules exist to make the learning easier, so Russian children spend considerable time learning the correct gender assignments of words.

However, when a rather simple semantic category requires the use of extremely complicated grammatical marking, this principle may not apply. Finnish questions requiring either *Yes* or *No* for an answer are formed by attaching a question marker to the word questioned and moving that word to the beginning of the sentence. Finnish children do not ask formally marked *yes-no* questions at the same age as children who speak other languages use such questions. Arabic children find the inflectional system of noun plurals difficult to master, even plurals of very familiar nouns, and this difficulty can last well into adolescence. English tag questions, that is, those questions that employ tags such as *aren't you?* in *You're going, aren't you?* or *didn't he?* in *John left, didn't he?* are extremely difficult to learn. They are syntactically complex, requiring a mastery of interrogative, negative, pronominal, and ellipsis-producing systems. So children tend to use *right?* and *huh?* as substitutes and even adults cannot agree what the "correct" tags are for certain questions: *Neither Fred nor John stayed, did he?/did they? Each of us is leaving, isn't he/aren't we? Few people like me, do they?/don't they?* Both linguistic complexity and semantic-cognitive complexity are important in the process of acquisition. However, since the two kinds of complexity are intimately related, as they are in the constructions and their associated meanings which Carol Chomsky investigated, it may be difficult to decide exactly which is more important on a specific occasion.

Because of their cognitive limitations, young children do not attend to and perceive linguistic stimuli in the same way as adults. They attend to language in different ways and adopt different processing strategies at different times. For example, children between eighteen and thirty months pay more attention to utterances like their own than they do to the expanded utterances of older children and adults. We recognize this intuitively when we "telegraph" our own speech in talking to very young children. But children must have the fuller adult utterances available if they are to learn to speak properly. Children also for a time try to relate words which occur closely together in terms of specific syntactic patterns with which they are familiar. They are likely to interpret a passive sentence such as *The car is pushed by the truck* as though it were the active sentence *The car pushed the truck.* Since most sentences are active rather than passive, a strategy which seeks to interpret noun-verb-noun sequences as agent-action-object sequences usually "pays off" in that it provides the correct interpretation without delay on most occasions. It may be that it is children's adoption of particular strategies which causes them the difficulty that Carol Chomsky noted they experience for a while in understanding the verbs *tell, promise,* and *ask* in sentences such as *I told John to go, I promised John to go, I asked John to go,* and *I asked John where to go.*

One consequence of adopting this view of language acquisition is that the evidence from investigations of the acquisition of different languages should indicate that semantic ability develops in a fairly consistent way across those languages and that the same kinds of cognitive limitations appear on the expressibility of concepts. Such appears to be the case. Everywhere children seem to be actively pursuing the expression of more and more complicated meanings, relying as they do so on certain innate abilities to guide them in knowing what to look for and how to go about looking. There appears to be a universality about the process, just as there appear to be universal patterns of general human development.

Piaget and Language Acquisition

The Swiss psychologist Jean Piaget has long been interested in universal patterns of growth and development in children. Trained as a biologist—his doctoral thesis was on mollusks—and experienced as a researcher in human intelligence in the laboratory of Théodore Simon, he turned his attention while still young to how children experience the world and come eventually to fit into the world of adults. Piaget postulates that the child is an active organism innately structured to develop according to a fixed pattern. During the course of development nature and nurture interact with each other in a principled way. Piaget set out to explain these principles. Recently, he has been concerned specifically with the development of scientific thinking in the various disciplines and in children—and the relationships between the two—at his Center for Genetic Epistomology in Geneva. He even goes so far as to claim that the development of scientific thinking in children recapitulates to a large extent the same development in the history of the species.

Piaget's early work, done forty years or more ago, is far ranging. In a series of books published between 1924 and 1937 he laid out many of his basic ideas in a way that was never intended to be definitive; hence his use of small samples, the sketchy reporting of procedures, the reliance on metaphor and analogy in explanation, and the individualistic and sometimes opaque style of presentation. Recent years have seen more and more attention given to his ideas. Structuralism has become fashionable; taking a "whole" view of children is seen as necessary in understanding how they develop; the need for an integration rather than a fragmentation of knowledge is stressed by an increasing number of thinkers; and lastly, and specifically, Piaget's ideas seem to be confirmed rather than refuted when they are put to the test.

So far as cognitive development is concerned, Piaget postulates the existence of three separate, sequentially arranged, and qualitatively different stages through which all normal children proceed: a sensorimotor stage from birth to eighteen months; a stage of concrete operations from eighteen months to eleven years; and a stage of formal operations from eleven to about fifteen years. In each stage children explore their world and discover inconsistencies between their beliefs about that world and how it actually works. In each stage children are forced to make the adjustments which are necessary to accommodate the inconsistencies so as to achieve the necessary homeostasis that continued existence requires.

During the sensorimotor stage children learn that objects in the environment have a permanent existence. Objects do not cease to exist when children no longer look at them: they appear and reappear because they have an independent existence of their own. At this same time children also acquire basic notions of space, time, and causality. Sensorimotor intelligence itself is limited to the very simple operations which affect this small, concrete world. The stage of concrete operations may be subdivided into a stage of preoperational thought lasting until about the age of seven and one of concrete operational thought lasting until eleven. In the first of these substages children are able to manipulate symbols and signs but only in a very limited way in operations which are concrete, immediate, and irreversible. In this substage children are still heavily involved in what they are doing: they can see things only from their own perspective because of a pervasive egocentricity. In the second substage children are able to manage classes and relationships of a complicated kind: they can reverse operations, make compensatory adjustments, grasp the principle of conservation, and adopt another's perspective. The final stage of formal operations is the stage of deduction, of manipulation of discrete variables, of hypothesis testing, of seeing implications, and of handling many different kinds of abstractions and systems of abstractions.

If we look at the kinds of language children use during the course of their linguistic development and the kinds of meanings they express in that language, we can see how both are limited by the particular Piaget-type stage the children are in. In the sensorimotor stage, for example, children learn names for things and events in the world. They also learn that the same name may be applied to obviously different things and events and that the names may be used both in the presence and absence of whatever is named. In the first substage of concrete operations they learn to analyze events, for example, into agents, actions, and objects, or into objects and locations, or into existence versus non-existence, as in negation. At first children do not have the capacity to express more than two aspects of any event but later develop this capacity and can mention three or more aspects. The result of this cognitive limitation is, of course, "telegraphic" speech if we consider only the syntactic form of what is said.

Piaget believes that cognitive development controls language development. He points to a specific test of this hypothesis as proof. A number of children were divided into three groups on the basis of how well they made judgments about the sameness or difference of quantities in different circumstances. Children who understand the principle of conservation realize that when a quantity of liquid is poured from a glass of one shape into a glass of another shape, the quantity of the liquid does not change even though it may appear to. In the test, children who could not do the conservation task were almost always unable to describe two objects, for example, a short thick pencil and a long thin one, using comparatives. They were able to comprehend an instruction to find a pencil that was longer and thinner than another, but they could not say *This pencil is longer and thinner* or *That pencil is shorter but fatter*. Instead they used pairs of sentences such as *This pencil is long* and *That pencil is short*, that is, independent sentences without comparatives. It also proved to be very difficult to teach the non-conservers the terms used by the conservers. Specific linguistic training resulted in only ten per cent of the non-conservers exhibiting a grasp of conversation when the initial conservation task was repeated. The results led Piaget to conclude that intellectual operations give rise to linguistic progress, not vice versa. Language training pursued to encourage cognitive growth may therefore be quite ineffective.

Language Functions

The discussion so far has concentrated on how children develop control of linguistic forms to express various meanings and the reasons hypothesized for particular developments. From time to time remarks have been made about the development of the functional control of language. It is time now to take a closer look at that development. However, as was indicated in an earlier chapter, linguists have given much less attention to language function than they have to linguistic form, so it is very likely that the findings will be fewer.

The very first observation to make therefore is that we know much less than we would like to know about *how* children use language. We know much more about *what* language they use. Studies of the language use of young children have usually focused on how parents and older children use language in the presence of young children and how they in turn respond to that language. Parents and older children both imitate the telegraphic style they hear and "expand" the utterances they hear in a random way. Expansions, like corrections, are not at all systematic. Moreover, the systematic expansion of children's utterances has no significant effect on consequent utterances. Evidently too, children prefer that parents to not use telegraphic speech to them—they recognize it as deviant in some way—but find it quite functional themselves in the familiar contexts in which it is used. One interesting fact about telegraphic speech is that children find that it works in the vast majority of cases, yet they very soon abandon it for more complicated systems requiring the mastery of articles, inflections, and involved syntactic arrangements. One possible explanation is that the developing cognitive capacities of children require them to construct more and more inclusive systems for the linguistic data they encounter; another is that the social pressures to communicate require more and more explicit statements about the world and children can make these statements only by adopting the necessary linguistic devices. In other words, children soon become aware that their listeners do not know everything they know and that they can communicate what they know only by expanding their linguistic system.

So far as children's use of different kinds of "speech acts" is concerned, again we have less evidence than we would like. Children do state things, ask questions, make requests, and give commands. They also learn to react to the variety of subtle ways in which different kinds of social control are exercised through language. Their behavior in play provides ample evidence that such learning is occurring as they manipulate each other and act out their versions of events and roles. But just how such learning occurs is not clear. As was indicated earlier, language is used for a variety of purposes for self-control, for controlling others, for imaginative purposes, and so on. But neither a complete inventory of usage types nor a theory of use exists. Consequently, it is not surprising that we know much less about how children learn to use questions and answers, to make requests, to employ performative utterances, to state hypotheses, and so on, than we do about adult use in each case.

Evidence from several sources does suggest, however, that the cumulative effect of being in certain kinds of environment influences children's use of language for thinking and self-expression. "Telegraphic" speech, for example, arises from speakers assuming that listeners share the speaker's knowledge. It contains much less than the usual amount of redundancy, and speakers assume that listeners share the same reference points in space and time and possibly even the same attitudes toward the subject matter. The British sociologist Basil Bernstein has argued that many children retain something like these same assumptions about language long after the stage of "telegraphic" speech.

Bernstein contends that two different kinds of language codes can be observed in British life: restricted codes and elaborated codes. A restricted code is characterized by short, simple, often unfinished sentences; simple and repetitive use of conjunctions such as *so, then,* and *because*; little use of subordination; dislocated presentation of information; rigid and limited use of modifiers; categorical statements often confusing cause and effect; and a large reliance on physical context, for example, in pronoun usage, and on the sympathy of the listener to get a particular message across. On the other hand, an elaborated code is characterized by accurate and full syntactic usage; grammatical complexity; frequent and extensive use of subordination and modification; and qualification of statements. Restricted codes are used by familiars and help achieve solidarity, but they are necessarily very severely limited in their functions. Elaborated codes are unrestricted in comparison.

Restricted and elaborated codes, however, are correlated directly with social class in British life according to Bernstein. On the whole working-class members control only restricted codes but middle-class members control both types and move freely between them according to circumstances. Bernstein regards the conditions that prevail in working-class life as responsible for the limitation: strong communal bonds; monotonous work; lack of opportunities for decision making; feelings of collective rather than individual responsiblity; a preponderance of physical rather than mental work; overcrowded authoritarian home life; and little intellectual stimulation for children. Restricted codes reflect therefore the communal rather than the individual, the concrete rather than the abstract, substance rather than process, the immediate and the real rather than the hypothetical, action rather than motive, and authority rather than persuasion.

Bernstein's ideas have been much debated in Britain and largely rejected in North America on the grounds that correlation is not causation, that his data do not support his claims, and that the British social situation is quite different from the situation which exists in North America. However, until more is known about language function it would be well to withhold categorical acceptance or rejection of Bernstein's ideas, particularly a rejection that stems from the belief that all languages and dialects are as good or as efficient as all others, a belief as little likely to be true or as testable as its opposite. As objects of study all languages and dialects may be of equal interest, just as all kinds of animals may be to biologists, but to say that they are all equal in all respects is to make a human being as interesting, or as uninteresting, as a laboratory white rat—which, of course, has also happened.

That different parents do behave differently in the way they use language with their children is not in dispute. Some parents encourage questions, enjoy discussion, indulge in verbal play, and value tentativeness in the formulation of ideas and conclusions. They deliberately try to encourage the development of their children's intellects and personalities. They are person-oriented. Other parents have little such interest and tend to view children as objects to be controlled. They are position-oriented. Studies of mother-child interaction in a variety of settings—for example, while sorting blocks, working together on a sketching task, and waiting in a doctor's waiting room—show that parents of the first kind are likely to try to answer questions prefaced with *why* with real reasons whereas parents of the second kind are more likely to assert their own authority and respond with an answer like *Because I said so.* The one group is likely to be concerned that children understand what they are to do and why they are to do it, and with seeking verbal responses and providing positive verbal reinforcement. The other group is likely to rely more on actions than on words and in the use of words provide negative verbal reinforcement. Different children, through such reinforcements, acquire different kinds of cognitive styles in dealing with the world: a tentative person-oriented style at the one extreme and an authoritarian position-oriented one at the other.

Learning to Read

One crucially important language function with which all children must become familiar is that of the written language. There is ample evidence, however, that many children experience a great deal of difficulty in developing a useful control of the writing system. Whereas the spoken language is acquired gradually and the process of language acquisition has no conscious beginning and ending for children learning to read and write often has a sudden onset, although some children are fortunate enough to avoid this kind of introduction. Even though some of the cognitive and motor skills necessary for reading and writing have been developed for other activities, children are often required to put them all together quite abruptly in new ways in a formal school setting in which language itself suddenly becomes the major topic of attention.

The level of anxiety in this setting may also be quite high: the anxiety of parents, teachers, and children. Little such anxiety is present during the process of learning to speak. There is also often a concomitant assignment of blame for any failure which occurs in the acquisition of the skills of reading and writing. Children are not blamed when they fail to acquire language; rather, they are given special help. Instruction in reading and writing also tends to be very formal and deliberate. Language, however, is learned informally and unconsciously from a wide range of stimuli. No deliberate instruction is necessary. Language is not learned from programmed stimuli, from making conscious distinctions among stimuli, from learning *about* language, and from acquiring control of a variety of analytic and synthetic techniques. While controversy does exist concerning the precise function of linguistic stimuli in language acquisition, there is agreement that such stimuli vary in both form and content in ways which are not well understood, but which children are well able to handle. Speech is reinforced. In contrast the usual reinforcements experienced by literate adults are irrelevant to most children: to young children the benefits of literacy are quite abstract, distant, and meaningless, and the efforts to be expended for such a remote end may seem to be quite wasteful and unpleasant. On the other hand, the benefits of learning to speak are too obvious to mention.

Learning to read and write and learning to listen and speak are also different in certain other ways. Reading and writing depend on the visual modality. The kinds of redundancies found in the speech code and in the written code are different. Different kinds of content are conveyed in the two codes. Writing is not simply speech written down: it is more abstract than speech in content; it usually employs carefully edited and controlled language for purposes different from speech; and it functions differently in the lives of the recipients of the message. The Russian psychologist Vygotsky pointed out that writing involves a very high level of abstraction. It is speech without a well-defined listener. The recipient exercises little or no control over what is said in writing, so there may be little motivation either to write or to read what someone else has written. Reading and writing are abstract, intellectual, and remote in their motivation unlike speech which serves immediate needs. They also require deliberate, analytic responses. In speaking, children are hardly conscious of the sounds they use and quite unconscious of the mental operations they perform. In writing, however, they must become aware of the sound structure of each word, and be able to dissect it and reproduce it according to conventions that must be learned. Numerous investigators have pointed out that many children do not really understand what reading and writing are all about, what they are supposed to be doing when they read and write, and what the terms mean that are used in the instructional process, terms like *letter, sound, syllable,* and *word.*

These last remarks on how children often have difficulty with the terminology used in language instruction raise the issue of how conscious knowledge of language develops. It is, of course, difficult to test such knowledge in very young children: to ask a child if something is grammatical, nonsensical, or acceptable. Even questions about whether something is "good" or "silly" produce widely varying answers. Children's responses about language are far less orderly than those of adults, and they exhibit almost no pattern at all in the pre-school years. However, children even as young as two are willing to attempt such tasks, a finding which indicates either that some kind of knowledge is available to be tapped, or that children usually cooperate with adults.

Generative grammarians have long stressed the need to tap intuitions to arrive at notions of competence. So far, children's intuitions have proved to be largely unreachable; that fact provides a necessary caution about any claims made concerning the kinds of linguistic competence young children of different ages *must* have. As we saw in an earlier chapter, adults are quite willing to make grammatical judgments, so a developmental pattern most certainly exists and could be investigated. Whether it is worth investigating is another matter, given the kinds of variation in responses which adults exhibit. We should not forget that linguists make their observations following many years of study of language as an object: few others have either that opportunity or the inclination. And even after many years of such study linguists can still disagree widely about what the facts are!

Language Acquisition and Linguistics

Language acquisition is one of the most fascinating areas of linguistic investigation. Just about every issue in linguistics is involved: an understanding of what grammars are; the "reality" of grammatical rules; language change; related biological, intellectual, and social factors; language functions; linguistic universals; and so on. It provides an excellent testing ground for theory. Any linguistic theory which describes language in such a way that it could not be learned by a human being must be inadequate. Likewise inadequate must be any learning theory that cannot possibly explain language use. Finally, language acquisition cannot most profitably be studied in isolation from the acquisition of other kinds of knowledge and abilities. The process of language acquisition must be studied in conjunction with the processes of biological, intellectual, and social development.

There is a strong biological component in language acquisition, both physically and cognitively. Language, in the sense of a predisposition to communicate symbolically, possibly even within a very narrow range of means, is innate in the human species: the congenitally deaf, dumb, and blind provide the necessary evidence. The environment offers the opportunity for realization. It is very likely that such concepts as response generalization and reinforcement are useful in explaining what happens in the environment, just as it is almost certain that other predispositions than the one to symbolize exist: for example, those that control other aspects of attention, perception, and cognition. The particular language that is acquired is extraordinarily complex, but no more complex than the system acquiring it. The pace of acquisition itself is controlled by the developing complexity of the children who are doing the acquiring. Their cognitive capacities are the controlling factors at all stages of acquisition.

References

The best book on child language acquisition is Brown (1973). Other useful sources are Cazden (1972), Dale (1972), and Slobin (1971a, 1971b). Bar-Adon and Leopold (1971) is a comprehensive collection of readings.

Jakobson (1968, 1971) provides a theory of the development of sound systems. Brown and Bellugi (1964) discuss "telegraphic" speech. Braine (1963b) is a good source for material on "pivot-open" patterns, and Slobin (1968) offers data from several languages concerning the development of inflectional control in children. Klima and Bellugi (1966) is the source of the data on negation. C. S. Chomsky (1969) is an account of development of certain syntactic abilities between the ages of five and ten.

Skinner's views are presented in his (1957) and attacked by N. Chomsky (1959). For a full discussion of "contextual generalization" see Braine (1963a, 1965) and Bever, Fodor, and Weksel (1963, 1965). Brown and Bellugi (1964) is a useful source for material on imitation and expansion, and Weir (1962) offers the account of pre-sleep monologs. The *Nobody don't likes me* example is from McNeill (1966), p. 69. Shipley, Smith, and Gleitman (1969) describe various command   forms and children's responses to them, and Cazden (1972) different types of expansions. The two studies concerned with syntactic deviance are those of Brown, Cazden, and Bellugi (1967) and Brown and Hanlon (1970).

Lenneberg's views are most fully expressed in his (1967), McNeill's in his (1970), and Slobin's most succinctly in his (1971a). The fullest discussions of the meanings of one-, two-, and three-word utterances are contained in Bloom (1970, 1973) and Brown (1973). The relationship between linguistic form and language function is discussed in Brown (1973) and Slobin (1971a). Brown and Hanlon

(1970) is the source of the data on tag questions. Ervin-Tripp (1973) discusses possible learning strategies used in the first two years of life.

See Evans (1973), Flavell (1963), and Gardner (1973) for overviews of Piaget's work. See also Sinclair (1971) and Sinclair-de Zwart (1969, 1973) for further details and for the experiment involving conservation. Bernstein's writings are numerous; he presents an overview of them in his (1971). The details concerning the codes are from Bernstein (1961). Adult-child and child-child language relationships are discussed in J. B. Gleason (1973), Hess and Shipman (1967), Robinson (1971), and Robinson and Rackstraw (1972). Vygotsky's views on the abstractness of writing are contained in his (1962). Downing (1970), Meltzer and Herse (1969), and Reid (1966) all report on the difficulties children experience with the language terms used in teaching them to read.

8

The
Biological
Context

The Evolutionary Perspective

Language is possessed by humans alone, but humans themselves are part of the animal world. The interest which linguists have in language must be pursued within the wider context of the general study of humans within that world. This study involves consideration of humans as physical, social, and intellectual beings. But other species may be said to share some of these same characteristics. Any physical, social, and intellectual characteristics that humans share with other species should be recognized if those characteristics impinge in any way upon language. To do otherwise is to give human language a unique position in that world merely by asserting that it is unique rather than by presenting a strongly buttressed case which also takes into account any evidence from the animal world which might be relevant.

One requirement of such a study is to view language in an evolutionary perspective. Immediately, we must recognize that language poses a serious problem within such a perspective, for humans are the only animals possessing the ability to speak. How therefore can the origin of speech be explained within the history of human development? In what ways are human language and the various communication systems of other species the same? In what ways different? Are those differences which exist between human language and the communication systems employed by animals quantitative or qualitative? But then how is it possible to distinguish between a quantitative difference and a qualitative difference?

According to the theory of evolution new species arise when, through processes of change and differentiation, adaptive variations lead to survival. Charles Darwin himself saw no problem in explaining how language fitted into evolution: it was a successful adaptation made by humans. He maintained that there was no fundamental difference between humans and the higher mammals in their mental faculties. Humans differed solely in the infinitely larger power they possessed to associate the most diversified sounds and ideas. Any differences between humans and animals were quantitative not qualitative. An examination of the history of nineteenth-century linguistics with its focus on historical linguistics and language change reveals how mutually supportive evolutionary theory and historical linguistics were. Of course, some linguists raised their voices in objection: Max Mueller for one objected that language was a serious obstacle to Darwin's theory.

In this chapter we will be concerned with examining the kinds of evidence that might be brought to bear on the issue of the relatedness of human language to systems of animal communication. We shall also attempt to examine various claims that have been made concerning what is unique about human language. Is it the human articulatory apparatus? Is it greater brain size? Is it the design feature of language which has been called duality, the fact that language employs two subsystems, one of sounds and the other of meanings? Is it the ability to symbolize? Is it greater cognitive ability, or cognitive ability of a quite different order? There is no doubt that language use does involve a skill or skills of which other species are incapable, or they would have spoken long ago. But there is also no question that among the many different species of animals a number can be found which exhibit some of the characteristics of human language, even though they do so in an extremely primitive way.

The Ethological Perspective

In recent years a serious interest has developed in ethology, the study of animal behavior in its natural setting rather than the study of animal behavior in the laboratory, the kind of behavior which has long interested certain psychologists and numerous other researchers. The natural behavior which is studied can be of various kinds: behavior brought about by "releasers" or "triggers" in the environment; the use of gestures, displays, and other kinds of communicative behavior and organization; bonding; dominance; the assignment of space, or "territoriality"; the use of "tools"; and so on. In particular, the behavior of primates, our closest "relatives" in nature, has come under very close study by ethologists.

It has even become somewhat fashionable to see humans as sophisticated primates or "naked apes." There are certainly many anatomical and physiological parallels between humans and primates. However, the psychological and sociocultural parallels are much more tenuous, even though many kinds of human and primate behavior can be shown to exhibit common characteristics. Humans and primates both yawn, bare their teeth, cough, scratch, cry out in pain, bristle with fear or anger, gesture, and menace one another. Both differentiate sex roles, bring up their young in systematic ways, tend to know their "place" in groups, and are conscious of the various spaces they occupy. We know too that both humans and some primates, in this case chimpanzees, are meat-eaters and tool-users, the zoologist Jane Goodall having witnessed chimpanzees eating a variety of meats (young monkeys, bush pigs, and baboons) and using sticks and chewed leaves as simple tools to collect termites and sponge up water. Some ethologists see the primitive animal in just about everything people do, "civilization" in this view being but the shallowest and frailest of veneers over an unchanged and possibly unchangeable "animal" nature. Freudian psychiatry with its emphasis on instinctual patterns and deep-seated wishes is another older variation on the same theme.

There are several difficulties with accepting this kind of biological determinism uncritically. The first concerns the vocabulary used to discuss both human and animal behavior. It may be just as inappropriate to apply terms used for describing animal behavior to human behavior as vice versa. Certainly, extreme caution is necessary in talking about an animal's "intent," or about anything presumed to be going on in its mind, or about its intelligence. It is possible to talk with a high degree of certainty about fixed instinctual patterns of behavior in some animals because such patterns are clearly demonstrable. However, humans can transcend instinct because of their cognitive and linguistic resources. Humans are products of culture as well as of nature. To say that nature nearly always gets the better of the two when there is a conflict or that its "laws" are immutable is either to deny that humans can change their lot through "intelligent" behavior and the resource which language provides, or to refuse to refine evolutionary theory to accommodate what humans have actually done. Another danger in the use of the same vocabulary is that of anthropomorphism. In this case animal behavior is seen in human terms from the human perspective, and semi-popular accounts of animals have long suffered from anthropomorphism. Animals have long figured in many of the stories people have told. Dolphins and chimpanzees have been the most recent beneficiaries—or victims!

Still another difficulty concerns any definition of natural behavior that is attempted. As we make more and more observations of the behavior of any species we notice more and more variations. Behavior becomes more intricate rather than less intricate. For example, bee, dolphin, and chimpanzee behavior becomes more complicated to explain as we make more and more observations.

But the greatest variation of all is in the patterns of behavior that humans evince. "Natural" human behavior must be behavior which is characteristic of all humans, but the weight of evidence from anthropological investigations is that few, if any, universal characteristics exist. We need cite only the example of movement and gesture for which basic universal patterns have been assumed to exist among all humans. Evidently there are no universal facial expressions, gestures, stances, or movements. People do move, manipulate, and position their bodies and body parts in different ways, but no single movement or gesture has the same communicative intent everywhere. Movements and gestures vary in their meanings according to the culture in which they are found. They are learned behaviors.

A final difficulty concerns the level of generality at which the investigator may attempt to state relationships between humans and animals. It is in some ways of little interest that both consume oxygen; it may be of more interest that there are certain anatomical and physiological relationships between humans and primates, as, for example, in brain organization and blood chemistry. We know that medical researchers have long used rats, dogs, and monkeys in their work because of their many resemblances to humans. But most psychologists have denied that these animals also share psychological characteristics with humans other than the very few which have been their concern in the laboratory. It would be of some interest so far as language is concerned if the properties that characterize human language could be shown to exist in activities elsewhere in the animal world. But, if, as Noam Chomsky has pointed out, the level of connection which is established between human language and animal behavior allows one to say no more than that animal walking is like speech in showing some purpose and internal principles of organization, such an observation is almost vacuous. In Chomsky's opinion it is not any resemblance which language shows to other communication systems that is important, but rather what specially characterizes language itself: what language really is, not what language is really like. To use another example, walking, swimming, and flying are all forms of locomotion, but little can be learned about any one from stressing only what all have in common as forms of locomotion. Walking is neither swimming nor flying, because it is walking. The real issue concerns what walking itself is.

Communication in Other Species

Before beginning a consideration of communication within other species, we must indicate that our concern is focused on patterns of innate behavior, the kinds of collective memory that the species hands on genetically from one generation to the next, and on variations of these patterns. Numerous investigations have shown that most communicative behavior in animals is genetic in origin and that almost no local variation exists within that behavior. They leave us free therefore to concentrate on the characteristics of a few of the more interesting systems.

no local variation exists within that behavior. They leave us free therefore to concentrate on the characteristics of a few of the more interesting systems.

Innate patterns of behavior, of course, are not activated at random. They are essentially functional and highly specific. Many must even be triggered in some very narrowly prescribed way. If a particular species has an instinct to flee from danger, cues as to what is dangerous must be available if flight is to occur in the proper circumstances. If mating is to be successful, cues to partners and rivals must exist to set off the appropriate response: possession of the partner or aggression against the rival. Very specific cues often act as triggers to behaviors in certain species. Female silkworm moths attract males by exuding minute traces of a chemical compound bombykol. The scent of blood produces deliberate searching movements in sharks. The blue strip on the belly of a male fence lizard arouses fighting behavior in other males. The cheeping of turkey chicks arouses brooding behavior in turkey hens, even when the noise comes from a tape recording inside a stuffed skunk, a natural enemy of the turkey. The red belly of the male stickleback arouses aggressive behavior in other males. A small stick painted red underneath will induce the same behavior in a male stickleback but a small stick painted red on top will not. The same red belly attracts female sticklebacks to the male's nest.

Many different instances of such kinds of behavior have been recorded. They show that often an animal's behavior can be predicted with almost complete certainty from knowing certain things about the environment because the animal instinctively must react in fixed ways in particular circumstances, that is, it must peck, fight, try to mate, or do something equally specific. To some extent humans too act in this fashion: human babies exhibit sucking and grasping movements when objects are presented to mouths and hands; and all humans prefer animals with large eyes, high domed heads, and a general roundness or chubbiness to those that are small and beady- or slit-eyed. In the vast majority of cases though human behavior seems to be under voluntary control rather than under instinctual control.

Turning to communication systems themselves, we can note that various systems have been examined. We will mention two briefly, those of jackdaws and dolphins, and then discuss a third at more length, that of bees. One of the great pioneers of ethology Konrad Lorenz studied the system of calls used by jackdaws as part of his overall study of those birds. Evidently jackdaws have a very limited number of calls at their disposal. These holistic calls may be described as a "food" call, a "danger" call, a "let's go" call, and so on. A "food" call brings other birds to a source of food, a "danger" call alerts them to the presence of a possible predator, and a sufficient number of similar responses to a "let's go" call leads a whole flock of birds to change location. No conversation is possible, and there is no important variation. Like some of the other kinds of behavior exhibited by the birds, the calls are instinctive to the species: the birds do not have to learn them; every jackdaw "knows" the proper calls because it is a jackdaw.

Dolphins have been of interest to people for a number of years, particularly the Atlantic bottlenose dolphin, and a considerable body of knowledge and a still more considerable body of folklore have gathered around them. Highly trainable, social, and playful, dolphins make a wide variety of calls, clicks, whistles, and yelps which seem to be communicative in function. However, investigations have shown that the total range of calls is very limited and that they are probably not used for "conversation" but rather so that the animals can monitor each others' positions, locate other objects in the water, and express a limited range of emotions. In one interesting experiment two Atlantic bottlenose dolphins, a male and a female, were taught to press one of two paddles for fish after a light was switched on to provide either a continuous signal or an intermittent signal. A continuous signal required the dolphins to press one paddle in order to be rewarded with fish; an intermittent signal the other. After this training the dolphins were separated in the tank by an opaque screen so that both had a pair of paddles but only the female dolphin could see the light. Fish were then fed to the dolphins only after *both* dolphins pressed the proper paddles. The female dolphin therefore had to "tell" the male dolphin which paddle to press. A success rate of better than ninety per cent was achieved in several thousand attempts during which the male dolphin could hear the female. Her calls were observed to differ as the light signal differed, that is, according to how the light was flashed. Consequently, communication was achieved between the two dolphins in these circumstances. However, the female continued in her behavior when the opaque partition was removed and she could see the male dolphin. She even continued in her behavior when she saw the male dolphin taken out of the tank. The results would seem to indicate how effective conditioning can be with an "intelligent" animal rather than that the dolphins had access to a communication system which they proceeded to employ.

The communication system of the bees is perhaps the best-known system of animal communication. Bees use both nonsymbolic and symbolic forms of communication. The bees in a hive can smell food clinging to the bodies of returning bees and judge its kind and quality directly. The temperature of the hive is also regulated by the direct transmission of water in a complex system of exchange. The symbolic system of communication allows bees to communicate about the exact location of food and the location of possible new homes when a swarm leaves the hive. Karl von Frisch and Martin Lindauer have offered explanations of how bees "dance" in order to convey information to each other.

A returning foraging bee performs a dance either on the vertical inside of the hive or on the horizontal platform outside to tell the bees in the hive where a source of food is located. A long and vigorous dance indicates a good supply of food; a short and weak dance indicates a poor supply. The dance itself has two variant forms: if the food is within a hundred yards or so of the hive, the bee performs a round or circular dance; if the food is beyond that distance, then the bee performs a wagging dance in the form of a figure eight. More precise distances are conveyed by the tempo of the dance itself, that is, the speed at which the figures are made: the quicker the tempo the shorter the distance to the food source. The direction of the food supply is indicated by lining up the axis of the dance with the food source. The bee apparently uses the location of the sun as a reference point even on overcast days. Outside the hive this procedure presents no problem. Inside the hive, if the axis of the dance is vertically up, the food is located in the direction of the sun, vertically down directly away from the sun, and at an angle from the vertical at that angle from the sun either toward or away from it as the case may be. Gravitational direction substitutes for the sun's direction.

All bees basically share the same system. In some bees the dance is more developed than others and interesting "dialect" differences have been observed. Italian and Austrian bees can live and breed together but misinterpret each other's communications about food locations. Italian bees never go far enough to look for food in response to Austrian bees' messages; Austrian bees consistently overfly food reported by Italian bee foragers. The Italian bees also have a sickle dance in the shape of an arc for intermediate distances which Austrian bees do not have and do not respond to.

One serious problem in emphasizing the importance of the bee dance as a form of communication is that hives are dark inside. Bees usually cannot see each other dance. However, they can feel each other dance and it may be that they acquire the necessary information that way about the food source. In that case the communication would be achieved by tactile means rather than by visual means. An alternative hypothesis is that the actual communication is not achieved through the dance at all, but through either the sounds which the bee makes during the dance or the odors which it brings back to the hive. It has been observed that bees which remain mute during a dance gain no response from other bees and also that the sounds made by returning bees correlate in certain ways with the dance. More recently, it has been argued that even though an observer of bee dances can "read" them for the distance and direction of food sources, bees themselves do not interpret dances in that way. The claim is that the dance is actually redundant: bees rely on the odors of the returning forager (locality odors, food odors, hive odors, and so on) both in identifying bees from their own hive and in locating food sources. However, von Frisch continues to claim that the dance is central to communication.

The communication systems of many other species have been examined but almost without exception in nowhere near the detail of those just mentioned.

The range of the species examined is large: crickets, grasshoppers, doves, finches, mynah birds, prairie dogs, whales, and various primates to name but a few. None has more than three dozen fixed holistic signs at the most (vervet monkey and Japanese monkey), and most have less than a dozen. It now seems appropriate therefore to examine some of the essential characteristics of human language to see how these extremely limited systems of animal communication measure up against those characteristics. Quantitative differences appear immediately. And some differences are so conspicuous that it is difficult not to call them differences of kind rather than of degree.

Language Design Features

The linguist Charles Hockett has specified a number of characteristics of human language which he has called design features. Since all human languages evidence such features, it is useful to compare any system of animal communication against the set of design features to see which features it shares and which it lacks. In one sense the design features define human language. Insofar as any animal communication system fails to exhibit one or more of the named features it is at least that much different from human language.

Human language makes use of the vocal-auditory channel: language is speech. It is produced by the mouth and received by the ear. The vocal-auditory channel is used by numerous other species, or just the auditory channel alone, as in crickets. Still other species use quite different channels: visual (sticklebacks); tactile (bees?); and chemical (certain insects). Other channels are also used by humans to supplement what they communicate: people react to gesture, touch, smell, and taste as well as sound. But language is speech.

Human language is broadcast at large but allows the speaker to be located. It is neither narrowly beamed on the one hand to a specific receiver nor broadcast in such a way that the source is completely unclear. Anyone within earshot can hear what is said and can usually tell exactly who is speaking. Hockett calls this feature broadcast transmission and directional reception. Speech itself is also rapidly fading. The channel does not get cluttered up: it remains open for use and reuse. A system which used smells would quickly be unserviceable. Smells stay around and mingle with one another. A system which used concrete objects would also create problems of storage and manipulation to keep the channel clear: it would be extremely cumbersome. However, rapid fading also means that different kinds of memory must be available to store and process the evanescent signals in the system. Humans have such memories.

A fourth feature is interchangeability. Any human being can be both sender and receiver of messages once linguistic maturity has been achieved. In the animal world communication is often sex-linked (for example, only male crickets chirp) or restricted in some other way (for example, only worker bees dance). Senders also have total feedback in that speakers can hear what they say. The result of these last two features is that people can talk to themselves. Just how much feedback bees get from their dancing is quite unclear. As we indicated in an earlier chapter, humans deprived of feedback (through listening to themselves speak and through the accompanying bone conduction) soon begin to sound strange to themselves and to others.

Specialization is a sixth design feature. Speech has no other biological function than communication. However, many animal communication systems are also just as specialized or even more so. Semanticity refers to the meaning content of the system: the system allows its users to say something. Language allows speakers to say anything they wish to say. On the other hand, the chirping of crickets probably lacks semanticity entirely, and the bee dance has a very limited semantic content: information about food sources. Openness refers to the novelty of the messages that can be conveyed. Bee dancing is open within a very limited set of topics: food sources and new home locations. Human language, on the other hand, is infinitely open, for new topics can be invented and the means for discussing these topics are always available. The signals used also possess the feature of arbitrariness. They bear no resemblance to the things they stand for and are almost completely noniconic. The word *cat* has an entirely arbitrary relationship to the animal named. In contrast, a bee dance to a considerable extent directly represents the quantity, distance, and direction of the food source in the movements of the dance.

The feature of discreteness refers to the fact that the system is made up of elements which are clearly distinguishable from each other. For example, *bin* and *pin* are clearly differentiated in their initial sounds. There is no sound intermediate between the initial sounds of *bin* and *pin* in English and no gradations that have to be recognized. Language is digital rather than analogical in its workings. Bee dancing lacks discreteness as any partially iconic system must. Another feature, displacement, allows for messages about the past, present and future, and also about both the real and the imaginary worlds. Gibbon calls are always about something present in the environment. Bee dances are always about something in the past. One is never displaced; the other always. Human language may be either.

Human language is also handed on by traditional transmission. It is learned anew by each generation. The specific language a child learns depends on the culture into which the child is born. No one is genetically programmed to learn any specific language. But bees are programmed to dance; even an Italian bee raised in an Austrian hive will dance the Italian dance not the Austrian one. Human languages are also learnable in that any human can learn any language and all languages are equally learnable so far as children are concerned. Even second, third, and still other languages can be learned. Animals, perhaps with some rare exceptions shortly to be discussed, do not learn new systems additional to the ones they were born with.

Duality of patterning is often said to be the most important design feature of human language. Every human language has two largely independent subsystems, one of sounds and the other of meanings. The feature of duality of patterning enables a small number of elements of one subsystem (the phonemes) to be combined and recombined into units and patterns of meaning (the morphemes and the syntax) in the other subsystem so as to create an infinite set of messages. No other species has a communication system with this feature.

The two final design features are reflexiveness and prevarication. Again, these features may be unique to human language. The first refers to the use of language to talk about language, that is, the system can be used to say something about the uses and the characteristics of the system. In contrast, dogs do not bark about barking and bees do not dance about dancing. The second refers to the possible use of the system to mislead others deliberately. Human beings tell lies, but bees do not lie about food sources or new home locations. There are occasional reports about animals using deceptive communications, Lorenz himself citing the example of his own dog who mistook him for a stranger and then "pretended" that a stranger had been present. However, the evidence is not at all strong.

These design features are not all independent. Some could not exist without others. For example, it would be impossible to lie if the system did not already possess the features of semanticity, displacement, and openness. Lies depend on meaning, in this case falsity of meaning. They are usually about things that cannot be verified in the immediate context unless they are completely barefaced. An open system is also required since closed systems seem to employ limited sets of calls which are entirely functional and honest. Of course, prevarication is not all bad. In one sense a hypothesis is a lie. It is a particular claim which may be true or false, but it is clearly marked as such in contrast to most ordinary lies.

The features may also be interpreted to have an all-or-none quality about them. A system is either open or not, either arbitrary or not. Bee dancing is open, but its openness is very different from that of human language. The design features have recently been recast to recognize this inadequacy and to make the list more coherent, orderly, and sensitive to degrees of difference. But the centrality of certain features is still maintained: the importance of the channel; the setting and purpose of the speech acts; and the internal structure of the communication system itself—its duality, arbitrariness, and openness.

It is, of course, quite possible to define language in many different ways. The approach using design features is just one of many possibilities. The features are stated at the level of generality which encourages investigators to find shared features among quite different systems because each feature allows for an enormous range of instances; one instance of duality or prevarication is as important as a pervasive duality throughout a total system of many instances of lying. It is just this kind of generality that Chomsky warns about. What really is needed in studying possible connections between human language and animal communication is some way of navigating between the Scylla of an extreme generality of statement which conceals differences and the Charybdis of an extreme special pleading which conceals similarities.

Communication with Other Species

Still another approach to the problem of studying communication systems is possible through investigations of communication between species rather than within species. Specifically, we can look at attempts to teach a human language to animals rather than at attempts to explain how members of other species communicate with each other. The issue then becomes one of finding out what other species are capable of doing rather than what they naturally do. The literature teems with examples of attempts to establish communication with animals of all kinds, all remarkably unsuccessful. Even the celebrated performing horse Hans in nineteenth-century Germany turned out to know nothing more than how to respond to cues his master and others gave him. The cues gave him the appearance of knowing all kinds of things and of being able to respond in his own way to German, but unfortunately he really knew nothing except how to respond to cues. In recent years there has been a resurgence of interest in communicating with animals, particularly in teaching them various bits and pieces of human language, mainly as a result of some very interesting experiments with chimpanzees.

Since primates are our nearest "relatives" in the animal world, it is not surprising that from time to time attempts have been made to teach an occasional captive primate parts of human language. The chimpanzee has been the usual primate chosen. Either the chimpanzee or the gorilla is the nearest ape to human kind, but gorillas are not readily available and are also too dangerous for the kind of close work involved in language experiments. Even a mature chimpanzee has to be treated carefully, for it is many times stronger than an adult human. Both chimpanzee and human share many anatomical and physiological characteristics. They have certain similarities in blood chemistry that are found nowhere else in nature, and they carry some of the same parasites. Social and sociable creatures, chimpanzees are also the only animals which recognize themselves in mirrors, pictures, and movies. They have excellent color vision too. There is, however, no resemblance at all between the communication systems which wild chimpanzees employ and human language. The captive chimpanzee must be taught everything she—the experiments have nearly all used females—is to learn. The two best documented earliest attempts were those by the Kellogs and the Hayes.

In 1931 the Kellogs "adopted" a seven-month-old female chimpanzee, Gua, as a companion to their ten-month-old son, Donald. They treated Gua like a typical middle-class baby, giving her her own bed and highchair, dressing and undressing her, and establishing household routines for her. The chimpanzee and the boy were brought up together, and the Kellogs kept a record of the joint development of each over a nine-month span. Gua was the more agile of the two, Donald the more imitative. The boy's imitating the chimpanzee was one of the main causes for the eventual abandonment of the experiment: the presence of the chimpanzee appeared to be retarding the boy's development. At the end of the experiment the Kellogs reported that Gua understood 95 words and Donald 107 words. The chimpanzee would, for example, extend her arm in response to the request to *Shake hands*, sit on *Sit down*, point to her nose when told *Show me your nose*, and emit a food bark when asked *Want some milk?* or *Want some orange?* She never learned to say anything though, an attempt to teach her the word *papa* failing utterly. But she was extremely responsive to tactile communication, reacting promptly and correctly to even the slightest touch. On the other hand, Donald much preferred to react to words: he had an obvious preference for language.

Nearly twenty years later the Hayes brought another chimpanzee, Viki, into their childless house when she was only a few days old to see if they could teach her to speak. But teaching Viki to speak was not at all easy. At eighteen months Viki could say *mama*; a few months later she added *papa*, and later *cup*. A fourth word *up* was a still later addition. Viki's pronunciation was always very poor. Nor did she use these words with their specific referents: they were attention getters in the first two cases and a request for water in the third. Simple psychological tests requiring the sorting of pictures given to Viki when she was five years old showed she apparently could make a few basic distinctions among categories such as animate and inanimate, red and green, large and small, and so on. But she never made much progress in responding to language. Most people who met her apparently regarded her not so much as a retarded child but as a chimpanzee who had learned a few interesting bits of human-like behavior as a result of a long period of intimate contact with human beings. It is of some interest to note that during the picture-sorting tasks Viki unhesitatingly placed a picture of herself with humans not animals. A picture of her chimpanzee father, however, went into the animal pile. The "socializing" experience had not been without its effects on her! However, there was no real bridging of the language gap that existed between human beings and animals in her case, just as there was none with Gua.

Washoe

The next major development in such studies came as a result of a deliberate shift in emphasis. The Kellogs and Hayes had tried to treat chimpanzees as though they were the investigators' natural infants. In such circumstances chimpanzees must learn to behave like children and cannot capitalize on some of their peculiar characteristics. They cannot profit from their agility and dexterity and are not encouraged to imitate gestures, something which they do well. Instead attempts are made to teach them to speak something which they do not do very well. There is now some reason to believe that speaking is a task which is probably impossible for them to accomplish both anatomically and cognitively. Apes do vocalize in the wild when they are excited. Human vocalizations are generally "unemotional" in contrast—they are usually content-oriented not expression-oriented.

When Allan and Beatrice Gardner, two comparative psychologists, adopted Washoe in June, 1966 she was approximately ten months old. They decided to teach her the sign language of the deaf and rear her in an environment optimal to her not them. Washoe was taught American Sign Language, not the finger spelling form in which words are spelled out letter by letter, but the form which uses holistic signs for concepts and relationships. While American Sign Language is only partially based on English, it can apparently be used to "say" anything one can say in English. Some of the signs are highly iconic, some completely arbitrary. The sign for *drink* is the thumb extended from the fist to touch the mouth; for *smell* it is the palm held in front of the nose and moved slightly upwards several times; for *cat* it is the thumb and index finger moved outward from the corner of the mouth; and for *up* it is the arms, and possibly the index fingers as well, pointed upwards. Washoe learned her signs in various ways: through instrumental conditioning, her reward being tickling which she enjoyed immensely; molding of her "hands"; repeated prompting; and deliberate imitation. She also learned her signs in a rich environment. Kept in a trailer in the Gardners' back yard, Washoe had few restraints, continual human companionship during her waking hours, lots of games and activities, and a constant flow of signs in her presence. No human language was employed, but expressive sounds were permitted. She lived in a rich, altogether naturalistic environment not unlike that of the human infant in many ways.

In such circumstances Washoe made remarkable progress. After less than two years she had learned to use 38 signs correctly. She did not use a particular sign for a particular object only. The sign *dog* could be used for a dog, a picture of a dog, a drawing of a dog, or even the barking of a dog. She therefore applied signs to classes of objects and events rather than to individual objects and events. Washoe's signs were not always as they are made by the human deaf, because

Washoe is not human, nor were her trainers completely proficient in American Sign Language. Her signs were also often immature or "babified" just as are signs of deaf children. Deaf people who have seen films of Washoe understand her signs quite easily, and deaf children are particularly captivated.

In three years Washoe's repertoire had increased to 85 signs, each sign having been confirmed through rigorous testing procedures devised to ensure that the investigators were actually testing what they claimed to be testing. Washoe used not only single signs; she also used signs together, combining as many as four or five signs at a time. The Gardners report combinations of signs such as the following: two signs like *hurry open, more sweet, listen eat, listen dog, you drink,* and *Roger come*; and three or more signs like *key open food, Roger Washoe tickle, key open please blanket,* and *you me go in*. These combinations are not unlike the telegraphic speech that young children use for a while. An examination of how Washoe used specific signs shows that a sign such as that for *open* rapidly extended from use with a particular closed door, to closed doors in general, and then to closed containers such as cupboards, refrigerators, boxes, jars, and briefcases. Eventually, it was extended to water faucets and even pop bottles. Likewise, the sign for *more,* initially a request for more tickling, was later extended to anything enjoyable, for example, to swinging and grooming, to favorite foods and extra helpings of these, and still later to requests for repetitions of events. Such semantic development is not unlike that which occurs in young children, as we saw in the previous chapter.

But what of Washoe's syntactic development? Are the signs ordered in any way which indicates that Washoe has a grasp of syntactic relationships and processes? The example *Roger Washoe tickle* is of interest. Who is to do the tickling, Roger or Washoe? Would the signs for *Washoe Roger tickle* be interchangeable with the first set in describing the same event or would there be a contrastive difference in the use of the two sets? Linguists have asked such questions about Washoe's performance since they regard language not merely as a set of signs, or names, but as a set of signs subject to certain syntactic arrangements which contrast with each other. There is no doubt that Washoe exhibits considerable ability to name, even in complex situations. But the naming in such situations appears to be unordered. On different occasions Washoe used the following combinations of signs at a locked door: *gimme key, more key, gimme key more, open key, key open, open more, more open, key in, open key please, open gimme key, in open help, help key in,* and *open key help hurry*. Syntactic ordering of any kind seems to be absent: the signs seem to be combined at random. Washoe also does not apparently initiate questions, even though questioning forms a large part of her environment—questioning appears to be something that humans do, not chimpanzees.

The Gardners themselves are not vitally interested in the issues which have just been mentioned, preferring to let each investigator define language as the investigator sees fit. Their hypothesis is that communicative behavior that is at least continuous with human language can be found in other species, and their search is for similarities. They recognize the possibility that animal communication and human language may be two distinct and noncomparable types of phenomena but insist that such a possibility should not foreclose efforts to see if their hypothesis is correct. They prefer their results to be judged for what they are—an initial attempt, remarkably successful, at two-way language-like communication with an animal of another species. Two-way is important, for Washoe obviously initiated communication in considerable quantities during the course of the Gardners' investigation.

Sarah

A second experiment of almost equal importance involves another chimpanzee, Sarah, and the attempt of another psychologist, David Premack, whose primary interest is the nature of intelligence, to teach her to communicate. Premack's interest is in finding out what Sarah *can* do, not what she *cannot* do. Sarah was an almost mature six-year-old caged chimpanzee at the beginning of the experiment. Premack deliberately attempted to shape her language-like behavior through using strict training procedures which limited the possibility of occurrence of other kinds of behavior. Sarah has been taught to place well over a hundred metal-backed plastic tokens of various sizes, shapes, and colors onto a magnetized board mounted on a wall. She "writes her sentences" vertically top-to-bottom by arranging the tokens in specified orders. Each token represents a word (*Sarah, green, banana,* and so on) or is a "syntactic operator" (*is the same as, is different from, goes on,* and so on).

Like the Gardners, Premack avoids the problems inherent in trying to teach his chimpanzee to speak. He goes so far as to claim that though speech may be a property of human language it is not necessary to language. This position is in agreement with his general approach to language, an approach which allows him to define it for his own purposes. For example, he does not consider duality to be important. Instead, he asks what kinds of operations does language typically allow, and then he devises schedules for teaching Sarah to perform those operations with plastic tokens on the magnetized board. The teaching is carried out using sophisticated reinforcement to shape behavior by successive approximation. Sarah's rewards are foods of various kinds. Once the desired behavior has been achieved it is tested and is apparently manifested correctly on about eighty per cent of occasions, regardless of the complexity of the behavior called for.

The operations Sarah is asked to perform are of various kinds. There is a naming operation which requires her to place on the board the plastic token which correctly names an object: *Mary, apple, Sarah,* and so on. An increasingly complicated set of operations requires the use of several plastic tokens in sequence to indicate   certain conditions in the real world: *Mary give apple Sarah.* A four-sign sequence such as this is built up through the use of previously mastered two- and three-sign sequences. Both *yes-no* and *wh-* questions are also built up using real objects: the former as "X" *is (not) the same as* "Y" *question* (where "X" and "Y" are actual objects, and *is (not) the same as* and *questions* are tokens), with the answer either *yes* or *no*; the latter either as "X" *is (not) the same as question*, with the answer a choice between objects available to Sarah, or as "X" *question* "Y," with the answer *is the same as* or *is not the same as.* Other operations involve an *if-then* pairing, a metalinguistic task which requires responding with an appropriate token to *name of* in the presence of an object, and an identification task which requires classification of objects according to their color, shape, and size.

One particularly interesting task involves both compounding and deleting, therefore mastery of some kind of hierarchical ordering among structures. First of all Sarah learned to construct arrangements of tokens to represent *Sarah insert banana pail* to describe her placing a banana into a pail and *Sarah insert apple dish* to describe her placing an apple in a dish. Then she learned *Sarah insert banana pail Sarah insert apple dish* followed by *Sarah insert banana pail insert apple dish* with *Sarah* as subject of both occurrences of *insert.* Finally, she learned *Sarah insert banana pail apple dish.* Further work with the verb *withdraw* substituting for *insert* showed that Sarah was able to transfer or generalize what she had learned: a principle of hierarchical constituent structure relationships.

Premack's results are considerably more controversial than those of the Gardners. It is not easy to explain why Sarah should be equally successful, or unsuccessful, in scoring at about the eighty per cent level of success on all tasks regardless of complexity. It would be much easier to explain either almost perfect learning, or complete failure, or some kind of gradation in difficulty according to task. Secondly, Sarah almost never initiates communication or gives any kind of response which is not required. But all her learning occurred in very controlled situations keyed to specific tasks. The free construction of "sentences" was never encouraged. Sarah almost never played with her "language" as Washoe did when she was alone. Of course, the circumstances under which the two chimpanzees lived and the methods of training they experienced were very different. Sarah lived in a wire cage with a cement block wall, few toys, very little exposure to human beings, and no opportunity for spontaneous social behavior. She also received only one hour of "language" training each working day of the week. In contrast Washoe was encouraged to exhibit spontaneous behavior in a particularly rich environment.

Another difficulty has to do with the experimental conditions themselves. Sarah's performance with people who do not know her is less satisfactory than her performance with her trainers falling to a success rate of seventy per cent or less but nevertheless still well above chance. Of course, children's and adults' performances fall off in the same circumstances. Still, the possibility exists that Sarah reacts to nonlinguistic cues from trainers or from people who know the desired responses, just as the horse Hans did. There is even a possibility that Sarah has learned whole response patterns which she produces on cue rather than an abstract set of possibilities from which she selects according to cue.

It is this last point that causes greatest concern. Is what Sarah uses "language" in any interesting sense? Premack argues that Sarah is using language because she has mastered some of the processes Premack regards as basic language. However, the total range of those processes is severely limited, as in the number of items that are manipulated within the processes. Sarah does not attempt to make connections among the different "sentence" types: for example, to relate statements to questions, positives to negatives, and so on. Obviously, certain basic characteristics of human language are absent from the system she has acquired. Such shortcomings, however, should not be allowed to detract from Premack's accomplishment: Sarah has learned a lot about something in a very short time. In one sense we know what she learned and how she learned it, but in another sense we do not. We cannot know if she learned a form of human language unless we know what human language essentially is, and we are still not quite sure what it is.

In still another experiment a group of psychologists in Georgia have been able to teach a two-year-old female chimpanzee Lana to interact with a computer through a keyboard using a specially designed set of word characters. Lana is thereby able to get the computer to activate devices which provide her with drinks, bananas, candies, and toys. She can also show herself movies or open a window. To get what she wants, Lana must depress the correct word keys in the correct order: *please machine give banana period*, for example. Evidently Lana achieves a high degree of success (sixty-five to one hundred per cent according to task) in getting what she apparently wants, being able to find the right keys and orders in which they must be pressed and to read the messages that are presented in a special code on a screen. She is also able to read and erase incorrect messages. Intriguing though this experiment with Lana is, its results so far are much less interesting than those of the previous experiments with Washoe and Sarah. Its scope is much more limited. However, it does once again circumvent the problem of speech, and it does try to capitalize on chimpanzees' strengths rather than to exploit their weaknesses.

The Evolutionary Gap

One of the basic characteristics of human language is that its primary manifestation is through speech. Neither Washoe, Sarah, nor Lana was required to speak, so in that respect they did not manifest language behavior. It has even been claimed that any attempt, such as that by the Hayes, to teach a chimpanzee to speak is doomed to failure. According to the phonetician Philip Lieberman and his co-workers, chimpanzees, like all apes and monkeys, do not have the vocal apparatus necessary for speech.

The ability to produce the sounds of human language depends on having a bent vocal tract and the three cavities of the pharynx, mouth, and nose. A bent vocal tract is a concomitant of upright posture. A well-developed pharynx also requires that the larynx be located low in the throat. The use of the nasal cavity requires a flexible velum. To some extent chimpanzees share the upright posture of humans. However, they do not have the necessary long pharynx, their larynxes being located high in the pharynx. The flexible velum is also absent. Very young children also have high larynxes. Having a high larynx is useful in infancy, for it enables the young child to swallow and breathe at the same time without choking. As the child gets older, the larynx drops, the pharynx lengthens, and speech as we know it becomes possible. However, such a change does not occur in chimpanzees: the larynx stays high. Language in the form of speech is therefore impossible to both the newborn human child and chimpanzees of any age.

In one experiment Lieberman reproduced the possible "vowel space" of a rhesus monkey on a computer programmed to provide a description of that space. The vowel space was found to be quite limited in contrast to that available to a mature human. The deficiency resulted almost entirely from the unavailability of an adequate pharyngeal region. Lieberman concluded that the rhesus monkey lacks the full articulatory apparatus which is necessary for the production of human speech and that the human articulatory apparatus is species-specific. Only humans can talk.

This claim is not universally accepted. Another view has been expressed by Jordan, who, after an acoustical analysis of the sounds actually emitted by chimpanzees, came to conclusions different from those of Lieberman. Jordan claims that chimpanzees are capable of producing sounds in the frequency range of human speech. They do not produce such sounds because of central cognitive constraints and lack of certain developments in the central nervous system rather than because of peripheral constraints, that is, deficiencies in the morphology of the speech organs themselves.

Those investigators who have been concerned with such problems have regarded speech as a critical component in language rather than as an accidental feature. They have, for example, tended to favor the motor theory of speech perception which maintains that speech is "decoded" through some kind of reference to the articulatory motions used in its production. They have also maintained the importance of the parallel development of the anatomy of the vocal tract and of the brain itself.

The act of speaking is less critical for others in deciding what is or is not language. It is obvious that species other than the human species can manipulate both signs and symbols and engage in forms of symbolic behavior. What seems crucial for many is whether any other species has the capacity to handle the syntactic organization of human language in which a finite system of operations allows for an infinite set of possibilities for organizing individual linguistic events. They claim that only humans have this capacity. It is a species-specific capacity which results in all languages being alike in many ways, all children learning language in much the same way, all languages serving the same functions, and all languages being equally complex. Everyone learns a language and uses it in much the same way for much the same reasons and with little variation in either time or space. Human language therefore is structurally different from any kind of communication found in other species: it is qualitatively, not quantitatively, different. Eric Lenneberg, for example, has argued that any similarities noted between human language and animal communication all rest on superficial intuition. They are spurious rather than real, logical rather than biological.

Acceptance of uniqueness, of course, can lead to investigations of language for what it is like in its internal structuring independent of any other considerations, for example, of the functions it fulfills. The most comprehensive approach to comparing animal communication with human language requires consideration of functions as well as forms. One such attempt led to a number of conclusions. The first is that language requires a delay between stimulus and message; otherwise it is simply a rather uninteresting reflex system. Language allows for reference to past and future events as well as to present ones: it allows for more than naming. Language allows for reflection, for hypothesis formation, and for imagination. Language has its own principles of arrangement, that is, its characteristic syntactic basis. It has a full range of sentence types, for example, statements, questions, negations, and commands. The vocabulary also falls into a wide range of categories. Finally, children learn to control all this complexity effortlessly. In contrast, the performances of Washoe and Sarah fall short on every account.

The experiments with Washoe and Sarah cannot tell us what language is. Nor can experiments with the speech capacities of various vocal tracts. Such experiments may show us what kinds of limits prevail in certain species and in certain conditions. Definitions of language can be made deliberately to exclude or to include certain kinds of behavior: the narrower the definition the more exclusive it will be; the wider the more inclusive. If language must have a speech component, must allow anything in the conceptual world to be talked about, must be efficient yet have a certain amount of redundancy, must allow for two-way communication among users, and must have a syntactic base, then language is unique to the human species. (But then it would not be possessed by all humans, the congenitally deaf and dumb, for example. What would they have?) If language is a system for manipulating symbols rather than objects, then many species have a language. Since different investigators draw the line between these two extreme positions in different places, they come to very different conclusions.

The Origin of Language

A final word about the possible origins of language is in order. For a long time discussions of the possible origins of language have been almost taboo. What could one possibly say that was not speculative? After all, the various theories deserved the names they were given: *Bow-Wow* arising from onomatopoeia; *Pooh-Pooh* arising from emotional expressions; *Ding-Dong* arising from natural resonance; *Yo-He-Ho* arising from physical labor; *Ha-Ha* arising from laughter; and *Sing-Song* arising from singing and chanting. Recently, the topic has become discussable once more in an attempt to define issues. Of course, the issues are still somewhat unclear, since, as we have just indicated, they depend upon an adequate definition of what it is that has evolved, that is, what language "really" is. If language is speech-based, then some consideration must be given to the development of the articulatory apparatus. If it depends on the capacity of the brain, then the issues have to do with the evolution of the brain. If it depends on a feature such as the development of an innovation like duality, then the question is how such an innovation occurred.

From a series of experiments based on measurements of a fossil skull and computer simulation of the vocal tract possibilities which that skull apparently allowed, Lieberman and his co-workers claim that the Neanderthals, who existed about 100,000 years ago, did not have the same vocal tract possibilities as humans today. Neanderthals could have had only a limited phonetic repertoire: possibly five vowels, six consonants, and likely no oral-nasal contrast within any system that might have existed. Their phonetic capability was better than today's primates but far short of current human capability. Allied to a brain which was also underdeveloped, this restriction would have allowed for some kind of language ability, but one falling far short of that needed to speak any human language we know today.

However, these conclusions have been questioned on the grounds that the particular fossil used, the La Chappelle-aux-Saints fossil, was hardly a typical Neanderthal specimen, being that of an "old" man of between forty and fifty who had suffered from arthritis of the jaws, spine, and perhaps lower limbs. Neanderthal social organization also seems to have required the availability of a more elaborate system of communication than that which the experimental results would allow for: the La Chappelle-aux-Saints fossil was found in a ceremonial burial spot surrounded by implements and a food supply. Neanderthals were not semi-brutes. They seem rather to have had brains quite adequate for language. However, the various controversies are still not completely resolved. Suffice it to say that at some time in the evolution of the human race, anatomical and brain structures had to develop to a point which would allow both speech and the control of symbolic processes. The precise time at which this development occurred is still not clear.

The position which focuses on the problem of duality holds that development as critical in allowing languages to be the creative systems which they are. Duality allows a limited number of sounds to be combined and recombined in different meaning units and then these meaning units to be combined independently of the combinations of sounds so as to express meanings and combinations of meanings apparently *ad infinitum*. Again both articulatory skills and the development of the brain are prerequisites. But duality itself had to come about as a specific innovation. The parsimonious view is that it occurred once and once only and was then diffused. It did, after all, give humans a remarkable advantage over all other species. But how it occurred and when it occurred and indeed if it occurred more than once are quite unknown and possibly unknowable.

If language was not a gift to humans from a beneficent deity—and there is no reason to suppose that it was—then everything about it has a history of development. But most of that history remains inaccessible to us. Trying to write a history of the evolution of language is a brave, perhaps foolhardy, task and therefore one which is rarely attempted. It is certainly a much more difficult task than interpreting the results of teaching chimpanzees forms of human language; the likelihood of being quite wrong in the conclusions that are reached is also considerably greater.

References

Sebeok (1968) provides an overview of various issues in animal communication, and Manning (1972) an introduction to animal behavior in general. Russell and Russell (1971) and Wilson (1972) are useful introductory articles. For Goodall's work see Lawick-Goodall (1971). Some representative ethological views may be found in Ardrey (1961, 1966), Lorenz (1966), Morris (1967), and Tiger and Fox (1971). Alland (1972) and Pfeiffer (1969) present a different viewpoint. Chomsky's criticism of the level of generality of connections is in his (1967).

Lorenz (1962) describes his work with jackdaws. Russell and Russell (1971) review experiments with dolphins. Frisch (1950, 1953, 1962, 1967) and Lindauer (1961) are basic sources of information on the bee dance. For criticisms of the interpretations offered by Frisch see Esch (1967), Johnson (1967), and Wenner (1962, 1964, 1967).

Hockett discusses the design features of language in his (1958, 1963), and Hockett and Altmann (1968) propose some revisions.

Clever Hans is discussed in Pfungst (1911). Kellog (1968) and Kellog and Kellog (1933) describe the attempt to raise Gua. Hayes (1951) and Hayes and Hayes (1951) describe the attempt to raise Viki. Washoe's accomplishments are described in Gardner and Gardner (1969, 1971). Bronowski and Bellugi (1970) offer some criticisms of the Gardners' work. Sarah's accomplishments are described in Premack (1970a, 1970b, 1971) and Premack and Premack (1972). Rumbaugh, Gill, and Glaserfeld (1973) report on Lana. Linden (1974) argues that the work with the apes is of "revolutionary" importance.

For a comparison of the phonetic ability of primates and adult and newborn humans see Lieberman (1968), Lieberman and Crelin (1971), Lieberman, Crelin, and Klatt (1972), and Lieberman, Klatt, and Wilson (1969). Jordan (1971) offers a different view. Lenneberg (1969) takes particular issue with the relevance of animal experiments to understanding human language. Hockett (1960) and Hockett and Ascher (1964) offer an account of how the feature of duality might have arisen, and Swadesh (1971) is a highly speculative modern account of the origin of language.

9

The
Historical
Context

Language Change

So far we have been concerned almost exclusively with language as it currently exists and as it is constrained in use in various contexts. Little reference has been made to any changes which might occur in language and in the uses of language over the years. The concern has therefore been almost entirely synchronic, and diachronic issues have been almost entirely disregarded. Even the discussions of the developmental and biological contexts tended to deal with stages in the development of language rather than with the continuous course of development. The changes and limits that were noted as occurring in linguistic behavior or linguistic capacity were related directly to changes or limits in the growth and development of organisms' physical and cognitive capacities. The emphasis was on correlations at discrete stages. The actual ultimate behavior or capacity was assumed to be fixed. In the case of children it was regarded as adult linguistic competence, the end point to which all children were somehow progressing and which takes the same form everywhere. In the case of the animals being taught "language," it was again the maximum capacity for language-like behavior which the animal could be demonstrated to possess. In the case of the ancestors to human kind it was a capacity which depended either on brain size or on articulatory capability. Language, however, is not unchanging. The purpose of this chapter is to look at some ways in which languages change and to consider why any language should change.

The first observation to be made is that it is not transparently obvious that languages do indeed change. People from an isolated speech community who have not traveled and who have had little contact with the outside world could well believe that their language is the same as that of their distant ancestors if thoughts on such a topic were ever to cross their minds. Even travel, contact with others, and education are no guarantee of a different view. They can lead people to become familiar with other dialects and languages, but that familiarity can be achieved quite independently of any feeling that the dialects and some of those other languages may be related in interesting ways. After all, it took people many thousands of years to see how closely humans and apes were related. If some still believe that a language like English has not changed much over the centuries, they may be excused for holding that belief, for the evidence to demonstrate that many changes have occurred is not plain for all to see.

Of course, the evidence does exist. That is, certain language phenomena exist today, and the only reasonable explanation for their existence is that languages change. Systematic dialect differences are one kind of evidence. They suggest a process of diffusion from a common source. The peculiarities of the English spelling system are another; it is only reasonable to suppose that the inventors of the spelling system produced a more "logical" system than the one we use today. Our present "illogical" spellings therefore may indicate that sounds other than those which are represented today were once represented by the spellings. Pairs of words like *phone-phonic, wide-width, sign-signature, deep-depth,* and *know-acknowledge,* which show close meaning and spelling relationships between the members of each pair but rather different pronunciations, suggest that changes in pronunciation have occurred, particularly when further instances of exactly the same relationships also exist. However, not all spellings can be used in this way: words like *delight, doubt,* and *debt* and doublets like *flower* and *flour* and *son* and *sun* show still other influences in their spellings.

Certain old documents look as though they were written in some kind of English and look even more like English when scribal practices have been normalized. More recent documents, letters, texts, and poems contain puns and rhymes which work only if the language were once a little different. For example, William Shakespeare rhymed *prove* with *love* and Alexander Pope rhymed *obey* with *tea.* Sometimes there are even direct comments on the language describing situations which were apparently quite different from those which exist today, for example, comments by early dictionary makers and spelling reformers.

Any familiarity with the languages of Europe also soon reveals that English shows some interesting resemblances not only to German but also to French and even to Latin and Greek, and, in a much more general way, to Irish, Russian, and even Sanskrit. In fact the more one looks, the more resemblances there are to be found. There must have been either extensive borrowing back and forth, or the resemblances must have a deeper historical origin. Relationships do exist among the different kinds of phenomena. The issues then become those of describing the relationships and explaining how and why things are not how they used to be—and perhaps some day will not be what they are now.

As we shall see, we can say a great many things about language change; however, there are also serious limitations on what can be said. Two very important limitations are that accepted methods for reconstructing previous forms of a language can reliably "recover" only a small part of any language and that the maximum recovery time is approximately five thousand years when the evidence is plentiful. In many instances the recovery time may be reckoned only in hundreds of years not thousands because the evidence is scanty. The fragmentary and accidental nature of linguistic evidence accounts for most of the difficulty in reconstructing the past. Written records are sparse and not always usable; some, for example, the Mayan hieroglyphs, are still undeciphered. Languages and entire language families must have lived and died without either descendants or records, leaving voids that cannot be bridged. The sometimes fast pace of change itself and the effects of borrowing have produced myriads of small holes and gaps that allow even the best reconstructed language to be seen only as a fluttering shadow of what it must have been. As we indicated in the previous chapter, humans have had some capacity for language for at least twenty times longer than the maximum recovery time just indicated. The processes of change are usually studied over periods of much less than five thousand years, often as little as several hundred. Consequently, considerable caution is necessary in evaluating sweeping claims made about language change.

Two further cautions are necessary. The first is the inherent bias many people have toward regarding the present forms of a language as somehow the "best." Linguists try to avoid this bias, usually maintaining that no basis exists for making such value judgments, but labels such as *Modern English, Middle English,* and *Old English* may produce effects not intended. Likewise terms like *archaism* or *older form* seem scarcely more appropriate than the term *living fossil* in biology; each reveals a subtle bias toward the new and innovative rather than an acceptance of a particular bit of behavioral adaptation that has proved its survival value. Cockroaches are also "living fossils": they are no less real for that fact. The second caution is somewhat related. Some languages are genuine fossils, for example, Akkadian and Beothuk. They failed to survive, having no modern "descendants." We know them only from records. But a language like Latin is not a fossil in the same sense: it is not dead. French is the Latin spoken today in France, and Italian the Latin spoken today in Italy. Just as Old English eventually became Middle English and then Modern English, so Latin eventually became French and Italian in France and Italy. Only in the sense that no one today speaks the Latin of Caesar's Rome or the Old English of Alfred's West Saxon kingdom are Latin and Old English "dead" languages.

These last observations should remind us of an important difference between linguistic change and biological evolution. A few thousand years is far too short a time for the biological evolution of an entirely new species. However, it provides ample time for a language to differentiate into numerous languages whose speakers find each other mutually unintelligible. It may be tempting to claim that a study of language change allows one to see the evolutionary process at work in a speeded-up way. But, just as we must be cautious in seeing language change in purely evolutionary terms, so we must also be cautious in drawing conclusions about evolutionary processes from language change.

It may even be possible to observe linguistic change in progress. For a long time linguists thought that only the effects of linguistic change could be observed: change was not noticeable until after it had occurred. Recently, as we saw in a previous chapter, evidence has been brought forward which appears to demonstrate that ongoing change can be observed. For example, there is an ongoing change in New York City speech leading to the pronunciation of more and more r's after vowels, and there is in English almost everywhere a continued raising of the tense vowels. The evidence for these conclusions comes from the use of new techniques which allow for the recording of contextual variants of linguistic forms. The linguist then makes inferences concerning the variation which are diachronic as well as synchronic.

Before looking at how language changes and speculating as to why it does, we should first of all indicate some kinds of changes which occur. These kinds of changes will be described mainly in the terms which linguists use to account for the phenomena. The examples will also be useful in later showing the main methods that linguists use for reconstructing previous stages of a language.

Evidence of Change

It is useful to discuss changes within the four basic categories of change in pronunciation, grammar, vocabulary, and style. Not all the categories are equally amenable to historical investigation, and the major linguistic focus has actually been on changes in pronunciation. Grammatical changes have been much more difficult to handle with available methods. Vocabulary changes arise from different sources and often create serious obstacles to the study of sound change when borrowing may be involved. This difficulty has even led some linguists to declare that since each word really has its own special history, it is hardly possible to offer an account of sound change which is both concise and comprehensive.

Stylistic changes are the most difficult of all changes to discuss since an adequate account would require the existence of a wide range of historical records. Historical records tend to be not only fragmentary but also either uninteresting linguistically (statements of military accounts, for example) or deliberately formal and artistic (as in the case of inscriptions, poems, and official documents). Informal documents such as personal records and letters are much less common, particularly for the remote past when literacy was uncommon and writing materials were scarce and impermanent.

Considerable pronunciation changes can occur. Vowel sounds can change in a number of ways: for example, they can be raised, fronted, backed, centered, or diphthongized. Each of the following examples provides a rough approximation in parentheses of the older sound of the vowel in the word: raising in *beet* (*bait*); fronting in *man* (*hot*); backing in *stone* (*father*); centering in *son* (*pull*); and diphthongization in *bite* (*beet*). Vowels may also change under the influence of following vowels or vowel-like sounds in a process called umlaut. Originally *mice*, *feet*, and *geese* were two-syllable words. The second syllable in each word contained a front vowel, and the frontness feature of the second vowel spread over to the first vowel which was not itself a front vowel. *Mouse, foot,* and *goose* remained unaffected, being monosyllabic. Later, other sound changes further increased the vowel differences in each pair.

Vowels may be entirely lost. The spellings *evening, business, every,* and *Wednesday* indicate earlier pronunciations with three syllables rather than two in each word. This kind of loss is more noticeable in British English than North American English. In Britain *secretary* and *necessary* are likely to be pronounced with three syllables each rather than with four as in North America, and *medicine* with two rather than with three. Dropping vowels and whole syllables is quite a common practice. It is quite usual today to hear words such as *almost, except, about, enough,* and *eleven* pronounced as *'most, 'cept, 'bout, 'nough,* and *'leven.*

Vowel and consonant changes also interact in interesting ways. Sometimes a consonant is lost and the loss is marked by a vowel change. English *igh* spellings as in *night, bright,* and *light* are good examples. An old consonant represented by the *gh* was lost, and the vowel *i* became long and tense and eventually diphthongized. Vowels may also lengthen in certain positions relative to a particular consonant or consonants, or they may shorten. Consequently, we find pairs of words in English like *wise-wisdom, keep-kept, clean-cleanse, moon-Monday,* and *steal-stealth* in which the different vowels in each pair have arisen from a common source vowel (largely retained in the spellings) according to the number of consonants following the original vowel. Umlaut and such combinatorial changes can result in considerable differentiations of an original vowel: *whole, heal,* and *health* once had the same vowel (*hāl,* the vowel of *father*), as did *foul, defile,* and *filth* (*fūl,* much like the vowel of *fool*).

Consonant changes often involve some kind of assimilation to the environment. A voiceless consonant may become voiced in a voiced environment. The *d*-like pronunciations observed in the middle consonants of *water, better,* and *butter* in many dialects of English is an example. The *s-z* alternations in *goose-gosling* and *house-husband* are further examples of voicing. Devoicing is apparent in the final consonants of German words like *Staub, Kind,* and *Tag* pronounced as though they ended in *p, t,* and *k* respectively (compare *Stauben, Kinder,* and *Tage* with *b, d,* and *g*). *Ole* for *old* and *tes'* for *test* are also assimilations but ones resulting in complete loss since the assimilation is to "silence." *Wanna* for *want to* and *gimme* for *give me* also show complete loss; *hafta* for *have to* shows only assimilation. One special kind of assimilation is palatalization when a consonant and a following front vowel assimilate to each other often to form a new sound: Old English *ciese* became *cheese, gearn* became *yarn,* and *drencean* became *drench.* There is also assimilation by articulatory position as in the "not" prefix in *intolerable* (*in-*), *impossible* (*im-*), *incongruous* (*ing-*), *irrelevant* (*i-*), and *illegible* (*i-*).

Two or more consonants in a cluster may change together. *Ship* was once pronounced as though it were *skip* and *fish* as though it were *fisk.* The original Old English *skirt* became *shirt,* and our present *skirt* was a later borrowing from the Danish invaders after the earlier change of *skirt* to *shirt.* A three-consonant cluster may reduce to one or two consonants: *godspell* to *gospel.* A two consonant cluster may reduce to a single consonant: words such as *write, gnaw, knee, ring* (*hring*), and *loaf* (*hlāf*) were once each pronounced with two initial consonants. Consonants may also be added: the *p* in *empty,* the *d* in *thunder,* and the *b* in *humble* (compare *humility*). They also sometimes change positions with vowels or other consonants in a process called metathesis: *brid* became *bird* and *hros* became *horse* (compare *walrus* "whale horse"); *aks* and *waps* alternate with *ask* and *wasp* in some dialects; and pronunciations like *revelant* and *prehaps* occur instead of *relevant* and *perhaps.* Metathesis seems particularly to involve combinations with either *r* or *l.*

Grammatical changes can be of various kinds too. The inflectional systems of words often show easily noticeable changes. For example, the inflectional system of English has been much reduced over the last thousand years. Today, English nouns and verbs have very few inflections and most adjectives none at all. At the same time a complicated system of verb phrases has developed, as have systems of relative clauses, noun modification, and noun compounding, intricate patterns for the use of *be, have,* and *do* both as full verbs and auxiliary verbs, and complex forms of negation. However, since the grammar of a language is its creative component, grammatical changes never seem to fall into the neat categories used for sound changes. The interrelationships are such that almost any change seems to be related in some way to almost any other change.

Vocabulary changes in a number of ways. One way is very obvious. The denotations of words change: today's houses, windows, lights, and so on are not yesteryear's. *Pen* today means something different from *pen* in 1930 and something different from *pen* in 1830; only in reference to a quill pen is part of the original menaing retained: Latin *penna* "feather." Such changes are external to language. The kinds of change which interest linguists are not changes of that kind. They are internal, meaning changes which result in words having their meanings narrowed, broadened, elevated, or degraded: narrowing *meat* ("food") and *deer* ("animal"); broadening *dog* ("hound"), *alibi* ("claim to be elsewhere"), and *virtue* ("manly courage"); elevation in *earl* ("warrior") and *chivalry* ("way with horses"); and degradation in *wench* ("girl"), *knave* ("boy"), and *lust* ("desire"). Weakening of meaning also occurs: *terribly, very,* and *awfully* have little intensifying force left in most usages, and adjectives such as *marvelous, delightful, super,* and *stupendous* have a shop-worn quality about them.

The vocabulary of a language may also change as a result of borrowing from other languages. American English has borrowed many place names from American Indian languages: *Michigan, Illinois, Oshkosh, Mississippi,* and so on. Other European languages particularly French, German, Latin, and Greek have been used as sources for English, particularly French after the Norman Conquest of England in 1066 and during the centuries of close Anglo-French contact that followed. French borrowings are so numerous that they have even affected the stress system for polysyllabic words in English. Borrowings tend to show cultural contact; people do not usually borrow words when they have readily available words for the objects or concepts to be named. So French borrowings into English cluster round government (*government, crown, duke, prince, state*), law (*justice, verdict, prison, judge, crime*), war (*battle, soldier, siege, danger, march*), religion (*religion, divine, angel, saint, pray, virtue, vice*), and at a later period luxuries (*lingerie, chemise, perfume, rouge, champagne, deluxe*). Borrowings from Danish are much nearer the hearth and home and reflect a different sociocultural relationship: *egg, gate, birth, sky, ugly, crawl, skin, skirt, give, take, call,* and even the pronouns *they, them,* and *their.*

Stylistic changes may be observed for writing through an examination of literary texts: King Alfred's prose in the *Anglo-Saxon Chronicle* is very different from that of John Lyly's *Euphues*; Matthew Arnold's *Essays in Criticism* very different from Edward Gibbon's *The History of the Decline and Fall of the Roman Empire*; and all are different from the prose of the novels of either Ernest Hemingway, William Faulkner, or James Joyce. But specifying exactly how each is different from the other is no easy task. Stylistics, the study of style, is still a fairly new area in language studies. Until stylistic analysis is better developed it is difficult to make any fine-grained attempt to specify either what "style" itself consists of or how one style is different from another. That there is something that can be called style is not in dispute.

Reconstructing the Past

The kinds of changes presented in the preceding section are changes that can be fairly easily observed. There are even written data to attest to most of them. But such data do not exist for the great majority of languages. Consequently, if linguists wish to make statements about language forms that were presumed to exist in the past they must have available a method, or methods, for recovering, or reconstructing, those forms. Linguists have developed two basic methods to accomplish their task: the method of internal reconstruction and the comparative method.

The method of internal reconstruction uses data from within a single language. It requires the investigator to look for peculiarities in the distribution of grammatical forms and sounds and to seek reasons for the peculiarities. For example, the existence of pairs of words like *sane-sanity, weep-wept, wise-wisdom,* and *lose-lost* may be interpreted as indicating that changes have occurred in English which have led to the differences that we notice today. The method of internal reconstruction is an attempt to see these changes in reverse so as to arrive at the ancestral forms which underlie both *sane* and *sanity,* both *weep* and *wept,* and so on. Internal reconstruction is very limited in its usefulness because of the restricted and often fragmentary data on which it depends. Its results are much "shallower" than those provided by the comparative method. However, they provide many of the forms on which the comparative method depends for its success. The comparative method requires the availability of the ancestral form underlying *weep* and *wept* rather than *weep* and *wept* themselves.

The main method used in reconstruction is the comparative method. This method allows the linguist to reconstruct ancestral forms using data from two or more languages. These ancestral forms are usually called protoforms. The linguist uses phonetic correspondences among genuine cognates from the languages to make hypotheses concerning the protoforms of the cognates. False cognates and borrowings must be recognized and rejected. The method allows the linguist to construct protoforms for the linguistic forms in a group of related languages. The protoforms are the forms from which the various forms existing in the group have been derived through regular processes, but the actual processes themselves are sometimes quite different for each individual language in the group. The method may also be used for work on grammatical and vocabulary changes. When correspondences exist throughout the sounds, grammars, and vocabularies of two or more languages, it is possible to establish a protolanguage, the ancestral language of the two or more languages. Together these languages may be said to form a "family" of languages, for example, Indo-European. English belongs to the Indo-European family, as do such languages as Russian, Hindi, Italian, Persian, and Gaelic.

Both methods assume the regularity of sound change. That is, the working hypothesis behind both methods is that every instance of a particular sound in a particular phonological environment will behave like every other instance of that sound in the same environment. If one changes all will change, because sound laws admit of no exceptions. This Neogrammarian principle of the regularity of sound change is the cornerstone of historical linguistics. There is nearly always an additional claim that the only relevant environments are phonological environments, that is, that the location of a particular sound in a certain word or grammatical structure is irrelevant so far as sound change is concerned. Only the distribution of a sound in relation to other sounds is important. When apparent exceptions to this principle occur, as, for example when we have the particular pronunciations of *great, steak, break,* and *yea* that we have in English (rather than pronunciations with the vowel of *eat*), then some kind of interdialect borrowing must have occurred or some rare sporadic change, another instance of the "leakage" in grammars that Sapir mentioned.

One important consequence of regular sound change is that various relationships among words and grammatical units are concealed. Sound change is disruptive to that extent. Because it is disruptive people make conscious attempts to undo the damage they perceive to exist, the damage of apparent purposeless variation. Analogical extension is the clearest example of one such attempt: irregularities resulting from sound change are smoothed out by extending regular patterns to cover irregular cases, particularly when the irregularities are infrequent: the English strong verb system has been much weakened through the analogical extension of patterns from the weak verb system. A kind of paradox results: sound change is regular and outside conscious control, but its consequence is irregularity; analogical change is irregular and purposeful but brings about only a superficial regularity in a small part of whatever system it affects.

The alternative hypothesis to that which holds change to be regular is one which credits each word with its own unique history. In this view change results from interdialect borrowing mixed with analogical extension. Since such borrowing and extension can cut freely across complete systems of sounds, words, and grammar, some systematic patterns will be apparent, but so will many unique instances. This hypothesis rejects the notions that languages are essentially "pure" rather than "mixed," that the processes of change are extremely regular, and that change itself is gradual. Evidence from mixed language situations, for example, from India where Dravidian retroflexed stops have spread into the Indo-European languages, from pidgin and creole languages, and from specific language families, particularly Romance, gives some support to this different view.

However, linguists in general have not accepted it, preferring to believe that language change is regular. While the alternative view is acknowledged to be attractive for the fluidity and flexibility it allows—in contrast to the very static regularist view—it makes claims about change which are less powerful and less interesting. The empirical evidence that is available also provides no reason for abandoning the more challenging hypothesis.

Linguists acknowledge that the Stammbaumtheorie of language relationships with its "family tree" view of those relationships, its clear differentiations, and its static quality has serious limitations, but they still prefer it to the Wellentheorie, for example. This latter "wave" theory attempts to explain how languages influence each other and "flow" into each other. It ignores discreteness to a considerable extent and tends to focus on bits and pieces rather than on whole systems. Like all dynamic models, the Wellentheorie is extremely difficult to formalize. It tends to satisfy intuition rather than intellect, and linguists, in spite of what a number of them may have said, still prefer to react to what is in their heads rather than to what is in their hearts.

Describing Change

In presenting some of the evidence for change, we could not escape using a vocabulary which also described or classified certain kinds of changes. The only way to avoid some form of classification is to present data in a random fashion. It is now appropriate to present a more systematic description of types of change prior to giving some consideration to the reasons for change.

Phonetic changes can occur over a period of time. These changes often result in very noticeable dialect differences, particularly when vowel quality is involved. Such changes as tensing, lengthening, nasalization, and centering of vowels are possible without any accompanying changes in the overall system of relationships among the sounds, that is, in the phonemic system itself. Likewise, the loss of a vowel or a consonant, or the substitution of one sound for another in a specific environment does not affect the overall system: it affects only the distribution either of phonemes in individual words (for example, the different pronunciations which exist of the first vowels of *either* and *apricot*) or of phonemes in relation to each other (for example, the *k* is no longer pronounced in *knee*). If all the vowels in a system are raised and if the highest vowels diphthongize, then considerable phonetic change will have occurred in the system. However, if the number of phonemic contrasts remains the same and the same words contrast as minimal pairs, there will have been no phonemic change. Only the actual phonetic realizations of the phonemic differences have changed.

Phonemic change occurs when phonetic changes result in a different set of contrasts in the phonemic system. The two basic processes of phonemic change are split and merger. When split occurs, a contrast emerges where one did not previously exist. Words with *f* and *v*, *s* and *z*, and the voiceless *th* (*thin*) and voiced *th* (*then*) could not contrast by means of these sounds alone in Old English since the members of each pair were allophonic variants of single phonemes. But a contrast developed as a result of phonemic split: *fat* and *vat, sip* and *zip* and *thigh* and *thy*. Merger occurs when a contrast is lost. *Beet* and *beat* and *meet* and *meat* have not always been homophones. The spellings attest to a former distinction which was lost through phonemic merger.

On the whole languages do not appear to "favor" merger because its consequence is homophony as words previously clearly distinguished by their component sounds lose their distinctiveness. Sometimes the result is that one of the homophonous pair of words drops out of the language completely or becomes very specialized. In this way possible ambiguity is avoided. An example from English is the word *quean* with the meaning of "harlot." The vowels of *quean* and *queen* merged to produce an intolerable ambiguity. In one dialect of French, the words *cattus* ("cat") and *gallus* ("rooster") became homophones. Speakers of the dialect turned to various other words (*faisan, vicaire, bigey*, and *put*) in order to eliminate possible ambiguity. Homophony that is not ambiguous may be tolerated, particularly if the homophonous words are members of different form classes, that is, one is a noun and the other an adjective, or some such difference. English has a considerable amount of homophony: *peace* and *piece, son* and *sun, male* and *mail, deer* and *dear*, and *their* and *there*, for example. Sometimes the homophony is very limited in that one of the words has a very restricted use: for example, two English verbs came together as *let* as a result of vowel merger and one of them (meaning "hinder") is found today only in the expressions *without let or hindrance* in legal writing and *a let ball* in tennis (which, therefore, on linguistic evidence appears to be a game with a long history).

Phonetic systems change very slowly. Even the Great Vowel Shift in fifteenth- and sixteenth-century English, which involved the raising of all tense vowels and the diphthongization of the two highest of these, did not change the number of phonemic contrasts among English vowels to any appreciable extent. Other changes, such as vowel lengthening and shortening, have had more profound effects on the system. Change is also slow because of the internal strength that every system possesses; it is a set of relationships which are mutually supportive and resistant to outside pressures. Change is likely to occur in a way that can be described as "hole-filling"; a phoneme develops to fill a gap in the overall system: for example, the sound represented by the middle consonant in *vision* in English seems to have developed partly to fill a hole (but has done so only partially because the sound occurs almost exclusively between vowels unlike other consonant sounds which can occur in a much wider variety of contexts). The systematic extension of a feature from one subset of phonemes to another is another form of change: for example, the extension at one time of the voiceless-voiced contrast already existing in English stops to English fricatives. Simply adding or removing phonemes, as it were at random, does not occur. The overall system is crucially important.

Of course, an emphasis on systems is not without its difficulties. It raises the question of locating the precise time at which one system actually gives way to another. At what point in time did two allophones actually split or two phonemes merge? While such an issue is different from explaining why the particular split or merger occurred, it is scarcely less baffling. That it is perhaps unanswerable may well be an artifact of the methods of reconstruction that are used. Methods which require static models, the use of invariant data, and categorial decisions are perhaps inadequate to provide answers to some of the questions that might legitimately be raised. Different methods—for example, methods which could handle variable data and coexisting phonemic systems—might be able to provide answers to such questions. But then, too, they might not necessarily produce such interesting answers to other questions. To a considerable extent though the question is moot: there are currently no really adequate methods in existence to handle such data and such systems.

Changes in grammar can be described in a variety of ways. Changes in the forms of words can be traced, particularly changes involving inflectional or derivational markings. Different form classes may become more or less marked morphologically. English has become less marked as nouns, verbs, and adjectives have reduced or lost their inflectional endings. German has not experienced the same kind of drastic reduction. The marking processes used may themselves reflect sound change, analogical extension, borrowing, or any combination of these. In extreme cases the morphological changes which occur can be related to language typology. A particular language as a whole may be described as moving from analytic to synthetic, or isolating to agglutinative in type, or in the opposite direction.

This wider view also compels a consideration of syntactic devices: verb systems, devices for negation, clause types, patterns of compounding, methods of coordination and subordination, and so on. Consequently, it is sometimes possible to describe the development of a determiner system, passive constructions, noun compounding possibilities, question types, phrasal verb systems, and so on. Sometimes such descriptions may try to indicate how a particular language has developed certain inner resources over a period of time in order to produce the resulting subsystem. At a more abstract level some attempt may even be made to describe how certain meanings were expressed at different times or, conversely, what a particular word or group or words meant, or how a particular construction type functioned at a specific time.

Descriptions of grammatical change are much more difficult to formulate than descriptions of phonological change. Grammar is far more complex than phonology. The grammatical system of a language offers speakers the possibility of saying anything that can be said. The building blocks are of all shapes and sizes, the processes for using the blocks intricate, and the permutations endless. It is this creativity that is the problem. Just about everything in the grammatical system can affect everything else. No part is entirely discrete: clause formation cannot be described independently of clause negation; negation cannot be described independently of the verb system; and the verb system cannot be described independently of clause formation. Everything touches on everything else in some way.

A language is also related to its speakers. Over the years words change their meaning in response to cultural and social changes. We earlier noted *pen* as an example. Likewise, British *robin* and *penny* have different meanings from the trans-Atlantic equivalents. New words are also invented or borrowed for new things in the culture, and internal resources must develop to accommodate the need to express new meanings. For example, in English such processes as compounding (*airport, fingerprint, speedway, minibus*), creation from existing roots (*hydroplane, psychosomatic*), extending of derivations (*nationhood, finalize*), blending (*smog, motel*), and idiom formation (*give up, take over, pull a fast one*) are among those which keep the meaning system open. Still larger units may change in ways that are meaningful. Stylistic changes occur as a result of changes in who says what to whom for what reason and in what way. Such changes are necessarily extremely difficult to describe. They require the investigator to make assumptions about the data which may not be adequately testable. They also require considerable knowledge of how particular cultures "work." So the danger of providing inaccurate descriptions is much greater than when the investigator works on the history of specific sound changes.

The precise form a particular description takes is not without its problems because the form is a direct reflection of a particular view of what grammars and languages are. Sound changes may be described simply in phonetic terms. In contrast, a description of sound change couched in terms of phonemic split and merger acknowledges that phonemes are important organizational units in sound systems. A description which refers to the distinctive features of sounds embodies still another set of assumptions. In addition, one which describes sound changes in terms of changes in markedness or the addition, loss, or rearrangement of rules adds a further dimension: change is described in terms of either a reduction or an addition of markedness or of rule addition or loss. In this last case the description refers to abstract entities and is far removed from a description couched in simple phonetic terms.

Different descriptions of the same events are possible. The processes by which Old English changed eventually into Modern English can be described in a great variety of ways, even if only one part of the total change, sound change, is chosen.

Each method of description is a kind of notational variant of another, that is, it is a different way of saying the same thing with no substantive difference. A notational variant of a statement is a variant which can be produced by following some simple rules for converting one statement into another. For example, statements about phonemes and distinctive features can generally be translated fairly easily back and forth. Descriptions themselves, however, are not explanations. They do not account for change: they merely describe it. If phoneme a splits to b and c, or x and y merge to z, that is a description only. If a sound system is changed when a "rule" is added, we cannot say that the addition of the rule caused the change: effects cannot also be their own causes. It may be of interest then to turn our attention to some possible causes of change.

Accounting for Change

Many explanations of change have been offered over the years, a good number by people with only a marginal interest in language. Generally the explanation is designed to fit a particular set of beliefs its author is advancing. Hence esthetic, racial, sociopolitical, geographical, and historical theories have been extended to cover language change: a language changes to become more pleasing to its speakers, or because of the particular combination of racial characteristics in its speakers, or because of a combination of social and political factors, or as a consequence of changes in climate, or through historical accident or change. Usually a single cause is advanced and change in one part of language is regarded as a kind of mainspring to change in all parts. Even more reputable theories of change tend to be expressed this way, that is, to be "single cause" explanations.

It is not surprising that linguists have criticized this kind of dilettante interest in language change. Some have gone so far as to say that the causes of language change lie entirely outside of linguistics: they are unknown and possibly unknowable. Linguists therefore should busy themselves with other matters. Still another view is that language change is an inherently uninteresting topic because it is essentially nonfunctional and completely without purpose. It is no more interesting a topic for investigation than is measuring how wide trouser legs are any particular year, or counting how many buttons jackets have, or estimating how long men's hair is. A concern for the causes of change is not really part of serious linguistic endeavor. Of course, to accept these views would be to close off any discussion of the causes of change at the outset. While we may not be certain about the causes, there are still some very plausible explanations that are worth entertaining.

The first kind of plausible explanation attempts to relate change to the relative ease of doing certain kinds of things. It is based on the belief that people tend to exert only the effort that is necessary to achieve a particular objective. According to this argument, this principle of least effort applies just as much in language as it does in life. In sound change there are many examples of sounds assimilating or weakening, of clusters simplifying, and of various kinds of loss of sounds which appear to support this principle. We also say things like *I'll, she'd, 'bout,* and *'most,* and have shortened words like *omnibus, taxicab,* and *telephone* to *bus, taxi* or *cab,* and *phone.* It is certainly easier for us today to say *knee* and *gnaw* without pronouncing the *k* and *g* that were once pronounced. But was it easier for speakers of Old English, and was it this factor that led eventually to the dropping of the initial stops in these words? Since there are also numerous examples of the opposite kinds of phenomena, for example, dissimilation, that is, of two sounds becoming less alike, an argument that rests on ease alone is not particularly persuasive. Each language must preserve a certain amount of redundancy if it is to function efficiently. Consequently, least effort in one part of the system is likely to be offset by the need for more effort in other parts. Of course, as the focus of the effort must continually shift, the result would be a state of constant change in the language as a whole. As with most theories that attempt to account for change, this theory deals almost exclusively with sound change. It is much less useful in accounting for change in other parts of the overall system.

A recent variation of the notion of ease as being important in change is the argument for the use of "naturalness" in explanations. This position holds that language rules and processes work on natural classes of entities: a natural class is a class in which all the members share a property not shared by the members of any other class. The property cannot merely be that in a particular set of circumstances it is useful to be able to treat the members as a class. In sound change this concept of naturalness is sometimes related to the concept of markedness: marked sounds are those which have a conspicuous "something extra" to distinguish themselves from equivalent "neutral" unmarked sounds: for example, fricatives are marked in relation to stops. Change is seen to result from natural classes of sounds losing markedness characteristics. But the opposite process is also found: stops also become fricatives, as they did in the Old High German consonant shift in which *p* became *pf, t* became *ts,* and so on. Once again there must be a limit to the extent of such processes. The principle of distinctiveness on which sound systems are based depends to a considerable extent on markedness, so markedness cannot be eliminated entirely. Each language must retain a certain level of markedness to remain functionally adequate. While certain changes may be described in terms of markedness, a tendency to reduce markedness cannot itself be the causal factor.

At still another level of abstraction is the theory that linguistic systems have an internal drive toward symmetry and economy. However, all languages have unsymmetrical features. This lack of symmetry together with the drive for symmetry brings about change. Consequently, holes are filled in systems, anomalies are removed, and the phonological space inside a system is constantly readjusted as various "sounds" move around in that space. There are "push chains" and "drag chains" as sounds either push or drag other sounds when they move. The pushing and dragging cause the sounds to change. Any readjustment is geared toward achieving maximum differentiation within the space that is available for the particular kind of system which seeks that space. There is some phonetic plausibility for certain aspects of such a theory, since the need to differentiate sounds is a real one. It is particularly important that phonemic contrasts which carry a high functional load, that is, which serve to keep a great many pairs of words from becoming homophonous, be maintained unambiguously. For example, words differentiated in English by the *p-b* contrast are much more numerous than those differentiated by the *sh-zh* contrast (*fishin'* and *fission*). It also makes sense that the best system for such differentiation will be the most economical one. The central problem is that it is impossible to account for change within a system by staying entirely within that system. To do so is to give the system a life of its own, a gift which must always be suspect. Analogic creation, of course, is an extra-systemic attempt to produce some kind of economy and eliminate a perceived lack of symmetry. But what causes the initial asymmetry and lack of economy that brings about change? Once change occurs to restore the symmetry, why should further change be necessary? Something else must be affecting the sound system. Again, too, there is the very serious problem of extending this theory into other parts of the language than the sound system.

Explanations which apply some general principle which is external to language look attractive. One such principle is that change occurs because of "drift." A language is an abstraction which "exists" only in the heads of many different speakers at one time. They must produce realizations of that abstraction time and time again in their daily living. This continual need to produce abstractions as realities leads to subtle statistical variations which ultimately bring about change. In this view changes in performance eventually lead to changes in competence. To argue, as has been done, that various performances of a symphony do not change the score, so performance cannot really affect competence is to use both a false analogy and to make too much of a competence-performance distinction. Language and symphonic scores are very different and the competence-performance distinction is no more than a hypothesis itself, as yet unproved. Plausible evidence can also be cited in support of performance affecting competence. The reproduction of the same bit of information either successively by one speaker or by a succession of speakers does show changes. Systems also do not reproduce themselves exactly. Since language changes themselves seem to be neither for the better nor for the worse, any purposefulness in change can be ignored. And since all systems have much the same tasks to perform, both the redundancy and the level of economy in the system will stay constant.

Explanations that rely on drift do encounter some difficulties. They suggest that change is haphazard, but we know that it is not. Classes of sounds change rather than individual sounds, so drift itself has systematic characteristics. Left unanswered is the question of why it should show such characteristics. Second, change seems to be cumulative: drift generally has a "direction," that is, changes of particular kinds go on and on and on. For example, there appear still to be vowel changes occurring in Modern English that are reminiscent of the Great Vowel Shift. A theory which maintains that individual speakers produce language as it were out of the isolation of their own heads and mouths fails to account for such a fact.

Still another theory claims that languages must be learned and that it is the learning of languages by successive generations of speakers which produces change. Generally this theory is related to a specific theory of what a language is, a set of abstract rules. Children must learn these rules by some kind of extrapolation from the data that are available to them by using learning principles which are innate. The data have a certain variability, but children construct a maximally efficient grammar to reduce such variability to a minimum. Since these maximally efficient grammars vary from generation to generation, the language as a whole changes.

This theory has considerable appeal. However, it asserts that what must be learned are rules, and yet we still have no clear idea what these rules are like. It also pays little heed to the many different kinds of linguistic variation that are acknowledged to exist both within society and within individuals. It overemphasizes variation between succeeding generations and almost totally ignores any other kind of variation. Moreover, the concept of "succeeding generations" is itself suspect. Succeeding generations may most easily be observed within nuclear family units, but they are not always clear even there. They do not exist except as quite arbitrary distinctions in the larger society in which people are born and die all the time. Peer influences on children's language are also considerably stronger than parental influences during most of the period of language learning.

Still another view of linguistic change recognizes the inherent variation within any language and attempts to relate change to that variation. The variation need not necessarily arise from any kind of substratum effect, that is, some kind of residual effect produced when one language is abandoned by a group of speakers for another, so that French has Celtic and Germanic strata and English has Celtic and Romance strata. The presence of these strata brings about conditions for continued change. Rather, this view maintains that languages are heterogeneous rather than homogeneous in their structures, that is, that various patterns or systems coexist and that speakers are quite capable of dealing with the resulting heterogeneity.

Change begins as variation and is continued as variation. A particular change may begin anywhere. Whether it is propagated depends on how it is viewed in the wider social context. Is it associated with certain groups (regional, social class, ethnic, age) or activities and adopted at large because it is perceived to be socially desirable? Or is it rejected as undesirable? So far as social class is concerned, "upper"-class varieties are usually preferred to "lower"-class varieties, as numerous studies have shown. However, a desire to assert regional, social class, ethnic, or age identity can also have the opposite effect: language can be used to indicate parochialism, minority values, youthfulness, and the like. A particular change may also be part of a larger pattern of change which is occurring in the language. But whether it "goes anywhere" or whether it is interfered with in some way (for example, by analogical creation, hypercorrection, and even spelling pronunciation) will be determined partly by what the change is felt to indicate. Its diffusion or extension will depend on social and psychological factors not just on linguistic factors alone. Change has its external as well as its internal causes.

There is undoubtedly no single cause of linguistic change. Certainly it is difficult to see how one could exclude a variety of factors from any account. Performance is involved, so physical factors must be accommodated; however, it is difficult to see them as the prime cause. The mind is involved to the extent that it must be in a position initially to learn and later to control the kinds of language data that exist within the best system it can construct. But *best* will also require judgments to be made which involve society and depend on the speaker's place within society. And language itself is imperfect and variable. Like change in general, linguistic change is complex rather than simple to describe, and, as we have seen, almost impossible to explain adequately. Sound change is only a small part of linguistic change. It is the most investigated part, but the findings of those investigations are not at all conclusive. What emerges once more is the need to understand the complex interrelationships among the various parts of language and between a language and its users.

The Future of Language

It is an inescapable fact that living languages change. They also change in many different ways. The ways themselves are natural because language itself is a naturalistic phenomenon. However, a particular change is largely unpredictable, but only in the sense that one may be unable to say with confidence whether *x* will change at all, or, if it does, whether it will change to *y* rather than to *z*. But if *x* does change, it will not change to *a* or *b* because change can proceed only within certain parameters. To use a specific example, the vowel in *bag* may come to sound like that of *beg* in some dialects, but nowhere can it come immediately to sound like that of *boog*. If *boog* were to replace *bag* as the name of an object, that replacement would be of one word by another and not a replacement of one sound by another. It has even been argued that no process or linguistic formalism can be used in discussing language change unless it is demonstrably necessary in synchronic work. Such a constraint serves to limit speculation in historical work. This limitation is reasonable in that just as any stage of a language must be amenable to synchronic description, so successive stages should be relatable through processes and formalisms that resemble those used in synchronic work. One negative result of the limitation is that it minimizes the effects that diachronic work can have on synchronic work. It is not unlikely that the resolution of diachronic problems will help linguists decide how to resolve synchronic problems. The limitations may be bidirectional rather than unidirectional.

Change may not be directionless. There do seem to be tendencies and trends. Whether these exist because of certain principles of "ease" or "naturalness"— possibly competing with the maintenance of a necessary redundancy—or because each language has a particular drive or direction of its own is impossible to say. Of course, given the shallow time depth we have over which we can study change the tendencies and trends may be insignificant, little more than local wrinkles on the vast plane of time. We can be fairly sure that little in the past has been done consciously to speed up or slow down change. But such a situation could change: it is difficult to predict the consequences for the spoken language of the spread of literacy and compulsory education, the development of the mass media, and rise of nationalism and internationalism. Will they hasten change or slow it down? And how would anyone know? How does one measure the pace of change?

Finally, we must consider how language change relates to evolutionary change. Once more we are confronted with the "shallowness" of historical data on the one hand and the difference in kind between animal speciation and linguistic differentiation on the other. It may not be very revealing at all to discuss language change within the framework of evolutionary theory. If we wish to do so, then the question whether some languages are more advanced than others in terms of their comparative evolution arises. Species are sometimes said to be more advanced or less advanced than other species. Can languages be described in the same way? Both negative and affirmative answers are possible. The negative answer is possible if every language is considered to provide its speakers with everything they need so far as communication is concerned. Moreover, all languages seem equally hard to describe, appear to be learned in much the same way, and share the same fundamental properties. The positive answer is possible if the uses to which particular groups put their languages are considered and then these uses are scaled. A language used by millions of people in a complex array of activities is in this sense more "developed" and more "highly valued" than one spoken by a few thousand people engaged in subsistence living. All languages are definitely not equal in this last sense. However, to relate this inequality to evolutionary advancement is to extend evolutionary theory in ways not originally intended. But if, as some would maintain, human beings by their intellects, their languages, and their cultural developments have taken themselves somehow partially outside natural evolutionary development, the extension may be justified.

References

Two basic texts are those of Anttila (1972) and Samuels (1972). Keiler (1972) is a useful collection of papers. Shorter discussions of issues are contained in Kiparsky (1970, 1971). Labov (1972c) discusses ongoing changes in language.

10

Language in Context

Generalizations and Universals

One of the most important reasons for studying language is to find out what exactly it is. Language is a worthy object of study for this reason alone, as an end in itself. Since language is also in some sense a unique phenomenon, the properties which make it unique are of considerable interest. How does language differ from all other systems of communication? Finally, language is used by people, and the two—language and people—are not separable, although attempts to separate them are made from time to time. Language must be constrained in some way by the capacities which people have and by the functions which they make it serve.

Linguists have always been interested in making generalizations about language. Leonard Bloomfield, regarded by many as the seminal figure in structural linguistics in North America, believed that it was possible to make useful inductive generalizations about language. If linguists worked with enough languages, they would find certain kinds of phenomena occurring time and time again and they might expect the same phenomena to recur in still other languages to which they gave their attention. They might also expect their investigative procedures to keep on working. Languages resemble each other in certain ways. They have phonemes, morphemes, and grammatical structures. They depend on contrasts between units to make distinctions. They have word classes such as "nouns" and "verbs." They have ways of stating, asking, commanding, and requesting. Dual systems of sounds and meanings coexist, regularity is the rule, and irregularity the exception.

The assumption that all languages are alike in many different respects is basic to work in linguistics. It is even behind the attempts to describe a language like English as though it were Latin or Greek, a holdover from the eighteenth century which still persists today. But it is also behind the descriptions given by linguists of any school or tradition. Structuralists believe that all languages exhibit the kinds of structures they regard as essential to language. So do generativists. No linguist begins the task of describing phenomena without some assumptions—and most bring many assumptions to the task. And that is how it must be, for working without assumptions would be working in the dark. The important thing to recognize in evaluating any work is the particular lights that were used to illuminate parts of that darkness—the various lights that were used are the assumptions. They might reveal interesting areas or not, but what they never do is light up the whole.

The emphasis on looking exclusively at language itself for generalizations has led to a search for what are called language universals, that is, those properties which all, or most, languages exhibit. These properties are more specific than such general characteristics as system, duality, contrast, and so on. These last characteristics define language itself. The properties, or the universals, are of interest because there seems to be no reason for them other than accident (all languages share certain characteristics by chance), or monogenesis (all languages are alike because of descent from a common ancestor), or design (all languages are alike because it is the nature of language itself that they must be so). Linguists favor the last reason. They do not disavow the second, but since there is no conclusive proof either for or against monogenesis, they find it relatively uninteresting. The first reason is rejected as quite improbable given the weight of the evidence against chance.

The anthropological linguist, Joseph Greenberg, has long been interested in language universals largely of a statistical variety. He has listed numerous ways in which all languages resemble each other. One kind of universal is the *if-then* variety: if a language has one characteristic, then it must also have another. For example, according to Greenberg, if a language has inflections, then it also has derivations; if verbs agree with subjects or objects in gender, then they also agree in number; if a language has a dual (a way of grouping things by two), then it also has a plural; if a language has a category of gender, then it also has one of number; if adjectives follow nouns, then the adjectives must carry all the inflections of the nouns they follow; if descriptive adjectives generally precede nouns then none will follow, but if they generally follow the nouns, then some may also precede; and so on.

There are also greater-than-chance possibilities: languages with normal subject-object-verb order are overwhelming postpositional, employing suffixes to express relationships rather than independent prepositions. (In comparison, languages with dominant verb-subject-object order are *always* prepositional.) In declarative sentences subjects almost always precede objects; languages with dominant verb-subject-object sentences have the adjectives after the nouns with overwhelmingly more than chance frequency; and so on. To these universals we can add further ones such as nasal vowels are overall less frequent in a language than oral vowels, with the actual inventory of nasal vowels never exceeding that of oral vowels. And, finally, the whole phoneme inventory of a language must fall in a range of between ten and seventy phonemes with the greatest distribution round the midpoint of that range, that is, around forty. One characteristic shared by all these universals is that they are formal in the sense that they make reference to the linguistic forms in the actual sentences which people use, that is, the "surface structures." They do not refer either to the functions of language or to any characteristic of speakers and communication.

The Chomskian revolution in linguistics shifted the interest in universals somewhat without, for a while at least, introducing any more concern than had existed for functions, speakers, and communication. If anything, in asserting that language is completely species-specific and uniquely structured, Chomsky tended to separate form and function, speech and speaking, and language and communication more sharply than they had been separated, just as he separated body and mind, deep structure and surface structure, and competence and performance. Chomsky distinguishes two kinds of universals: substantive universals and formal universals. Substantive universals are certain general characteristics which all languages can share. All languages must be built up from a selection from an inventory of possible distinctive features of sound; all languages will use a selection from a set of categories such as noun and verb and will have ways of referring to the properties of objects (for example, "male" and "animate") and to objects, feelings, behaviors, and so on. On the other hand, formal universals are the general principles which govern the workings of the grammars of all languages. For example, the fact that transformations apply to structures not words, converting one structure into another through addition, deletion, and rearrangement, rather than one arrangement of words into another arrangement, is an important formal universal. The necessity of rule sequencing and rule cycling and the very notion of rule itself are other formal universals. Since, according to Chomsky, formal universals are everywhere the same in language, all languages are cut to the same pattern. However, in that languages differ in their choice of substantive universals, they may differ considerably from one to another. A knowledge of formal universals is also innate in language learners; their task is to work out from the data around them which substantive universals and what other local conditions operate in the particular languages they are to learn.

Chomsky's ideas concerning universal grammar produced considerable changes in linguistic investigation. New areas of concern were opened for exploration and old areas were reexamined in a completely new light. However, since Chomsky also stressed, as his predecessors had done, the centrality of the linguistic system in his investigations of language and the uniqueness of language in the world, many potentially revealing areas of investigation remained closed to investigation or were ceded to others as rather uninteresting "performance" areas.

It is also possible to approach the problem of making generalizations about language at a much more all-encompassing level. The approach which makes use of design features does just that: it forces investigators to try to relate language to other systems of communication and raises the issue of the kinds of continuity that exist in such systems between animals and humans. The chimpanzee experiments are of particular interest in this respect. In the area of language development the work of people like Piaget also places language development and even the nature of language itself into a wider framework than the one language provides for itself. However, an extreme emphasis on this approach, as in Skinner's attempts to explain language phenomena, makes what is special about language disappear into the generalities of some other theory, in this case learning theory, with little gained and much lost.

The central problem in describing language in context must be to describe the appropriate contexts. Too broad a context leads to very weak, possibly vacuous, statements. Too narrow a context, particularly the narrowest context of all, language described in terms of itself, leads to very strong statements which must always be weakened as more and more data are brought to bear on the issues. It also often ignores factors which could conceivably produce more elegant explanations because such factors are foreclosed from consideration by the constraints of the theory which has been adopted.

The study of language and the study of mankind should proceed concurrently. Language is powerfully constrained by people themselves—by their capacities, their interests, and their needs. To ignore such factors in linguistic investigation is to opt for a study of form without function, of system without substance, and of competence without performance. Language is every bit as much function, substance, and performance as it is form, system, and competence. It is an artifact of linguistic history that one set of concerns has been elevated at the expense of the other. Further advances in linguistics must be based on a recognition of what has happened and a broadening rather than any further narrowing of the scope of linguistic investigation.

Physical Factors

A study of the physical factors associated with language indicates the importance of the speaking-listening channel in human communication and of the constraints which the use of this channel imposes on language itself. The channel has an enormous capacity, but effective use requires languages to employ easily pro-duceable and discriminable sounds to overcome its "noise" and to keep the bur-den of production and reception of the necessary contrasts within manageable bounds. The intrinsic characteristics of the ears and the mouth have helped lan-guage to be what it is and set limits to what language can become. The upright posture of human beings, the position of the human larynx, and the development of the human brain, particularly its lateralization of function, are physical factors that must be considered if one is to understand the relationship which exists be-tween speech and language. If language is partly speech, then those physical factors which affect speaking and listening cannot be ignored.

Speech signals must also be transmitted. Their ultimate point of origin in the brain is still unclear since language itself cannot be localized with any degree of certainty. However, speech events must be organized in certain ways to be realized. Language has been said to provide a window into the mind, but certain facts about neurological functioning suggest that it is a one-way window at times, viewing being possible only in the other direction: language events must be or-ganized in specific ways because human neuroanatomy requires such organiza-tion. Likewise, the speed of the operations involved in speaking and listening can be no faster than the speed required for certain muscles to work. Of course, this fact itself does raise a very important issue: it is well known that certain types of language performance are carried out much faster than these speeds, a very potent argument for considering that those kinds of performance are not gov-erned by the physical requirements of speaking.

A consideration of physical factors also sheds light on problems related to the ability of very young children to acquire language and to the possibility of animals' being able to acquire language, if speech is regarded as basic to language. Many investigators regard speech in this way, but language generally transcends speech, particularly in mature adults. The speed of language functioning is one transcending characteristic. The use of written forms of language with the concomitant processing of language through the eyes rather than through the ears may be another. But all such possibilities may depend on the prior existence of speech or of a suitable codification of speech. We must not forget that even the sign language of the deaf depends on the prior existence of speech, as do all writing systems. To say that language may transcend speech is also to acknowledge the fundamental importance of speech to language.

Language is not entirely an abstraction, although it is useful at times to consider it to be so. To treat language apart from its physical characteristics is to ignore how these characteristics constrain the forms it can take. Although we know little about how people store their "knowledge" of language, stored it must be. How it is stored, why it is stored in the way it is stored, and how retrieval from storage is carried out are important issues. To say they are not *linguistic* issues is to define the range of linguistic concerns in a very narrow way. No theory of language can be correct if it runs counter to any evidence which exists on these matters; that evidence must be allowed to constrain any linguistic theory which claims to be comprehensive.

Psychological Factors

Language is used by people who have brains and minds as well as mouths and ears. The distinction between brain and mind is not as clear as the distinction between mouth and ear. Perhaps the distinction is not even necessary since the brain-mind problem may be regarded as a philosophical or semantic one rather than as an empirical one. What is clear is that language is centrally organized in the head rather than peripherally organized at the mouth or ears.

This central organization has its own constraints, those relating to attention, perception, memory, and the actual production and processing of language. Experimentation has produced various findings about general human constraints in these processes, quite often from studies which have had little or nothing to do with language itself. We therefore know a considerable amount about some of the processes that must operate within the "black box." We know considerably less about the psychological reality of specific linguistic events and processes. Psychological investigation is still in its infancy. Progress depends to some extent on achieving a consensus about what language is and what the essential components of any language are. It also depends on knowing which claims to test and how best to test them. One important consequence of the work done so far, though, is that investigators tend to make less strong claims than they once did and to be much more cautious in how they go about their work. Over the years the issues have also become more complex rather than less.

If language is used by speakers whose heads control their mouths and ears, then what is in those heads is important to linguists. There is a growing realization that investigations which focus on language alone will not allow anyone to say very much of interest about the insides of heads. To decide to look only one way, through the window of the mind, from language into the head, is to cut oneself off rather deliberately from possible sources of knowledge.

Communication Factors

Language is also used by speakers for thinking and for communicating with each other. Again, there are serious problems in arriving at a full understanding of the relationships between language and thought. It may never be possible to settle definitively the various issues raised by Sapir and Whorf on the one hand and Piaget, Vygotsky, and Luria on the other. We can be sure that much language-related activity occurs in ways which are presently inaccessible to investigation by the kinds of methods with which we are familiar. The mind still works in mysterious ways, and thinking is at the center of many of the mysteries. Perhaps thinking will eventually be given an explanation in physical terms. Perhaps not. Certainly any explanation must go much deeper than statements that thinking is a kind of covert activity in the larynx. But it cannot be so deep as to leave thinking something entirely mystical. The key issue is finding a productive middle ground through asking the right questions and devising ways to find answers to those questions.

Already we know certain things about thinking. It is extremely fast and minimally redundant in many of its forms. In some forms it even seems to be independent of language, for example, musical and artistic "thinking." In some forms it is like the language used by intimates in familiar contexts. That this is so should not be surprising since thought is obviously the most intimate of all language uses: while thinking, a person must assume that much can remain unsaid and still be understood. Occasionally, too, it helps to say a few things out loud, for example, either for immediate confirmation of a resolution or to make a denial explicit.

The same principle controls much communication among individuals—only certain things need to be said. Language also has a variety of functions and particular linguistic forms are put to a number of uses. They are also put to use in circumstances in which other kinds of communication are occurring and which require speakers to make choices according to their intent. A greeting exchanged on the street will therefore be very different linguistically from a speech at the United Nations and cocktail party chatter will be very different from courtroom jousting. Different forms will be used, different assumptions will be made about who knows what, who can speak, and what are acceptable responses; and the same linguistic act, for example, the act of keeping silent, may bring about entirely different consequences in different circumstances.

The users of a language know how to use language in these different ways. Admittedly, they do not show the same uniformity in such usage that they do in pronouncing *cat*, or in forming plurals, or in using *cat* in a sentence with *chase* and *dog*. But the uniformity in usage is sufficiently widespread in any language to be best regarded as systematic. Participants in language acts are generally quite aware of deviations from accepted usage and treat them as violations of accepted rules of behavior. While linguists need not necessarily investigate everything that is systematic about language and language use, those who have given their attention to linguistic function as well as linguistic form have often found the insights which they have gained to be invaluable in coming to a better understanding of both.

Language is one of human kind's most important characteristics. It is certainly the most useful tool people possess. Attempting to study the forms the tool may take, apart from any uses which it has, may lead to a great deal of success initially, for undoubtedly a great deal can and should be said about its forms. But tools exist to be used. And what they are used for is no less important than what they are!

Developmental Factors

Language must also be learned. The process of language acquisition may shed some light on what language is. The extreme positions of maintaining either that knowledge of language is somehow innate in children at birth or that language is learned exactly as everything else is learned have little to offer. Neither produces very interesting questions and conclusions. Each is an assertion which tends to close off inquiry rather than to encourage further investigation.

Any study of language acquisition in children must relate that acquisition to the physical, cognitive, and social development of children. How do children develop physically and what are the resulting constraints on their linguistic capability? How does cognitive development affect what children can do with the language data that surround them? What is the course of development of the social functions of speech in children? What do children use language for? Answers to these questions require some prior understanding of the physical, cognitive, and social factors which affect language so that investigators can have some hope of demonstrating how what is ultimately achieved was achieved.

A concentration on the acquisition of linguistic forms alone or the effectiveness of certain learning paradigms in achieving results can produce findings but only ones with limited usefulness. As we have indicated, functions are at least as important as forms, and many factors affect learning. An approach to problems of language acquisition which respects the complexities of both linguistic form and language function and of the learning environment is far more likely to produce long lasting results than one which oversimplifies and produces powerful theories which new data quickly destroy.

Likewise, it may also be possible to learn something about language from experiments that attempt to teach varieties of language to animals and from studies of systems of animal communication. It may well be that the human language is qualitatively different from any kind of animal communication and that experiments seeking to teach animals to communicate with humans can produce only very limited results. However, any assistance such experimental work provides in arriving at a better understanding of language must be welcomed. At the moment a number of open questions exist; they require answers when such answers are possible or rephrasing of the questions when they are not. Only when the answers are known will we be able to say whether they were worth all the effort expended to get them.

Functional Factors

Language is used in many different contexts for a wide variety of purposes. Language forms reflect rather than determine what people can say. What they can say is governed to a considerable extent by factors such as age, sex, social relationship, professional affiliation, knowledge of subject matter, and so on. People choose language forms to reflect the degree of conscious of subconscious awareness of such factors which particular contexts require. They learn the skills to do this during the process of language acquisition and social acculturation.

Language has also many different functions. It can be used for private thought, for phatic communion, for various kinds of social interaction, or, when turned onto itself as subject matter, for a metalanguage, as in linguistics. People must learn the language varieties appropriate to each function in the culture in which they live. The functions themselves are almost certainly universal.

No language is completely homogeneous. Regional and social differences and the range of functional choices ensure variation. Every speaker must become accustomed to that variation, and most learn to handle variation without much difficulty. Variation is of special linguistic interest because of the clues it contains as to what speakers are able to do with language data. While we may find it useful for some purposes to consider a language to be an abstract system, we must not forget that people unhesitatingly cope with a wide variety of instances of real language in their everyday living.

Historical Factors

Every language has a history. It is a product of countless thousands of years of change and variation. Change and variation are extremely difficult to study with the linguistic models and techniques that are available. The models are designed almost exclusively for synchronic work in language situations deliberately conceived to be static and unvarying. The techniques also allow for only a very shallow time depth to historical work. However, diachronic processes are dynamic, and human language has had a much longer history than the one which can be reconstructed. Consequently, our knowledge of language history is limited.

The course of linguistic change is not easy to predict because the processes of change are not always clear. This situation exists partly because of the shallow time depth just mentioned and partly because we are still searching for a full definition of language itself. In the absence of such a definition we cannot always be sure what kinds of changes we must explain. Any attempt, too, to consider change within an evolutionary framework is fraught with the difficulty of specifying the exact parallels between language change and the evolution of species. It is certainly possible to make analogies between the two, but analogies can be totally misleading.

Change does occur. Its course seems unpredictable, but not totally unpredictable because it must proceed within certain constraints. It is possible to describe many of those constraints once problems related to the shallowness of the time perspective are acknowledged. Whether languages get better or worse as a result of change requires some measure of language efficiency. Measures which relate improvement to certain political, social, scientific, and literary factors and to the numbers of people who speak different languages do suggest that noticeable differences exist among languages. Some of these differences may even be considered to demonstrate that certain languages are "better" than others in specific ways.

Most language change seems to be unprincipled in the sense that no reasons exist for particular changes; sound change is particularly unprincipled. It is not surprising therefore that aimless "drift" has appeared to be the rule rather than the exception in change. However, humans are tinkerers: analogical extension, certain kinds of language engineering, and deliberate fossilization, as in writing systems, tend to undo what sound change does by producing regularity out of irregularity, but do so by introducing irregularities of their own. Deliberate borrowing and mixing also may occur concurrently. The total result is much the same mixture of regularity and irregularity as before.

The result once more therefore is variation. Language is not static and uniform: it is so only in grammar books. In actual use language is dynamic and highly variable. Language change also ensures a continuation of language variation.

Language and Linguistics

As we indicated in the first chapter, linguists have often concerned themselves with a very narrow range of problems when they study language. They also pursue their interests using a limited set of procedures regardless of the "school" to which they belong. Consequently, they look for contrastive units and distributions, for qualitative differences rather than quantitative ones, and for the strongest statements they can make about relationships. Language phenomena are assumed to have their own independent existence.

The result is descriptions of language which tend to ignore nonlinguistic data. Phonemic systems are discussed and compared with only occasional reference to anything but the simplest phonetic principles. Sentences are asserted to be the fundamental units of language, even though most language exchanges demand use of units larger than the sentence, the individual sentences themselves making sense only in context. Languages are said to change in certain ways, for example, through rule addition, loss, or rearrangement, but little justification is given for the use of the concept of "rule" itself in such statements, and the process of change is apparently assumed to go on largely in a vacuum. Language variation is described in terms of variables derived from studies of groups of people, but the linguistic behavior of individual speakers is left unconsidered. Is speech behavior systematic in groups *and* individuals? It would be quite possible to find much less systematic behavior in individuals than in groups. Individuals are notoriously hard to assess.

Since linguists work almost exclusively with language data, their explanations must be offered in terms of those data. If linguists keep only certain possibilities in mind, then they must couch their explanations in terms of those possibilities. For example, if they observe limits on phonetic output and are committed to expressing all conclusions in the form of rules, they may declare that the limits result from "conspiracies" of rules. But such a solution may be quite inadequate, merely describing what happens in a way which the theory allows but essentially doing so by a kind of ad hocness that a comprehensive investigation should seek to avoid. Simpler, more adequate solutions demand an awareness that people are not equipped to deal with too much variety in the stimuli which they confront: they cannot handle too many possibilities all at once. Language stimuli are no different. Language has evolved in ways which have maintained certain limits to the variety of structures which can be manifested for no other reason than it must continue to be a viable instrument for communication.

A concentration on linguistic phenomena alone also strengthens any desire to regard language as a unique phenomenon. Instead of attempting to consider how language is related to other phenomena, many linguists have stressed the uniqueness of language and have proceeded to express all their findings in terms which emphasize uniqueness. It is, of course, quite possible to proceed in this way, but it is not the only way of proceeding. The dangers of an exclusive approach are many. That language is unique is a hypothesis to be tested rather than a fact to be asserted. Parsimony requires a sharing of principles found to be generally useful in science. It does not require each discipline to create its own principles: ad hocness should be the last resort of a discipline rather than its first recourse.

Language in Context

Language behavior is part of human behavior and must be related to other forms of human behavior and to human capacities. The most parsimonious approach to language is one which seeks to relate specific aspects of language behavior and language capacity to related aspects of general human and animal behavior and capacity. The strongest hypothesis is that there are no fundamental differences between the two, that is, that the differences which do exist are quantitative rather than qualitative. The onus is on linguists to demonstrate qualitative differences conclusively: they cannot simply assert that such differences exist and then feel no obligation to prove the assertion. Today, as more and more linguists examine their assumptions, they are forced to consider possibilities which they had previously been able to ignore. The broadening of linguistic activity which has resulted in recent years is one of the main sources of the current vitality of linguistics.

Language provides for information flow. The term *information* has a very useful technical sense, but it can also be used nontechnically. Language is one of the systems that allow humans to gain and exchange information. People live in settings which must be maintained, and that maintenance requires various kinds of information to flow. An overall ecological framework exists encompassing people, settings, and information. This framework maintains itself in and through a set of relationships. Language is one member of that set, all the members of which have a mutual dependence. Language can be most revealingly investigated if it is regarded as interdependent rather than independent.

Any study of language in the context of information exchange also leads to a consideration of how systems maintain themselves. On the one hand, they tend to disintegrate unless they are constantly used and refurbished. On the other, they have their own internal regulatory mechanisms which help them to achieve a kind of homeostasis. It is possible to relate language change and variation and the various language encounters of everyday living to these processes.

Linguists no longer seek a theory of syntax or a theory of phonology but a theory of language. Such a theory would be concerned with language functions as well as language forms, with function considered as least as important as form. Language events would also be considered to have physical and social determinants as well as mental ones. Language would be regarded as speech in the broadest definition possible of speech, that is, in a definition which includes speaking to communicate ideas. The most interesting statements about language would be held to be those which said something important about how language functions within the general framework of human behavior; less interesting statements would be those concerned exclusively with linguistic forms. The latter kinds of statement would still be necessary; however, they would not be regarded as sufficient. The theory would deal not with language in isolation but with language in context.

References

For Bloomfield's views on induction see his (1933). Greenberg (1963) contains much material on universals. Chomsky's views on universal grammar are contained in his (1972); Bach (1974) discusses these views at some length in his final chapter.

Bibliography

Abercrombie, David. 1965. *Studies in Phonetics and Linguistics.* London: Oxford University Press.

Adams, Parveen, editor. 1972. *Language in Thinking.* London: Penguin.

Alland, Alexander, Jr. 1972. *The Human Imperative.* New York: Columbia University Press.

Allen, H. B., and G. N. Underwood, editors. 1971. *Readings in American Dialectology.* New York: Appleton-Century-Crofts.

Anttila, Raimo. 1972. *An Introduction to Historical and Comparative Linguistics.* New York: Macmillan.

Ardrey, Robert. 1961. *African Genesis.* New York: Dell.

———. 1966. *The Territorial Imperative.* New York: Dell.

Argyle, M., and J. Dean. 1965. "Eye Contact, Distance and Affiliation." *Sociometry,* vol. 28, pp. 289-304. In Laver and Hutcheson (1972), pp. 301-16.

Austin, J. L. 1962. *How to Do Things with Words.* Cambridge, Mass: Harvard University Press.

Bach, Emmon. 1974. *Syntactic Theory.* New York: Holt, Rinehart, and Winston.

Bailey, Charles-James N. 1973a. "The Patterning of Language Variation." In Bailey and Robinson (1973), pp. 156-86.

———. 1973b. *Variation and Linguistic Theory.* Washington, D.C.: Center for Applied Linguistics.

Bailey, Richard W., and Jay L. Robinson, editors. 1973. *Varieties of Present-day English.* New York: Macmillan.

Bar-Adon, Aaron, and Werner F. Leopold, editors. 1971. *Child Language: A Book of Readings.* Englewood Cliffs, N.J.: Prentice-Hall.

Barnes, Douglas, James Britton, and Harold Rosen. 1971. *Language, the Learner and the School.* Revised edition. London: Penguin.

Basso, K. H. 1972. " 'To Give up on Words': Silence in Western Apache Culture." In Giglioli (1972), pp. 67-86.

Berlin, Brent, and Paul Kay. 1969. *Basic Color Terms: Their Universality and Evolution.* Berkeley: University of California Press.

Bernstein, Basil B. 1961. "Social Structure, Language and Learning." *Educational Research,* vol. 3, pp. 163-76.

———. 1971. "Language and Socialization." In Minnis (1971), pp. 227-45.

Bever, Thomas G. 1965. "Is Linguistics Empirical?" *Psychological Review,* vol. 72, pp. 493-500.

———. 1970. "The Cognitive Basis for Linguistic Structures." In *Cognition and the Development of Language,* edited by John R. Hayes. New York: Wiley. Pp. 279-352.

Bever, Thomas G., Jerry A. Fodor, and William Weksel. 1965. "On the Acquisition of Syntax: A Critique of 'Contextual Generalization'." *Psychological Review,* vol. 72, pp. 467-82. In Bar-Adon and Leopold (1971), pp. 263-78.

Birdwhistell, Ray L. 1970. *Kinesics and Context: Essays on Motion Communication.* Philadelphia: University of Pennsylvania Press.

Bloom, Lois. 1970. *Language Development: Form and Function in Emerging Grammars.* Cambridge, Mass.: M.I.T. Press.

———. 1973. *One Word at a Time.* The Hague: Mouton.

Bloomfield, Leonard. 1933. *Language.* New York: Holt.

Boggs, Stephen T. 1972. "The Meaning of Questions and Narratives to Hawaiian Children." In Cazden, John, and Hymes (1972), pp. 299-327.

Boomer, D. S., and J. D. M. Laver. 1968 "Slips of the Tongue." *British Journal of Disorders of Communication,* vol. 3, pp. 2-12.

Braine, Martin D.S. 1963a. "On Learning the Grammatical Order of Words." *Psychological Review,* vol. 70, pp. 323-48. In Bar-Adon and Leopold (1971), pp. 242-63.

———. 1963b. "The Ontogeny of English Phrase Structure: The First Phase." *Language,* vol. 39, pp. 1-13. In Bar-Adon and Leopold (1971), pp. 279-89.

———. 1965. "On the Basis of Phrase Structure: A Reply to Bever, Fodor, and Weksel." *Psychological Review,* vol. 72, pp. 483-92.

Bronowski, J., and Ursula Bellugi. 1970. "Language, Name, and Concept." *Science,* vol. 168, pp. 669-73.

Brown, Roger. 1958. *Words and Things.* Glencoe, Ill.: The Free Press.

———. 1973. *A First Language: The Early Stages.* Cambridge, Mass.: Harvard University Press.

Brown, Roger, and Ursula Bellugi. 1964. "Three Processes in the Child's Acquisition of Syntax." *Harvard Educational Review,* vol. 34:2, pp. 133-51. In Bar-Adon and Leopold (1971), pp. 307-18.

Brown, Roger, Courtney B. Cazden, and Ursula Bellugi. 1967. "The Child's Grammar from I to III." In *1967 Minnesota Symposium on Child Psychology,* edited by J. P. Hill. Minneapolis: University of Minnesota Press. Pp. 28-73. In Bar-Adon and Leopold (1971), pp. 382-412.

Brown, Roger, and M. Ford. 1961. "Address in American English." *Journal of Abnormal and Social Psychology* vol. 62, pp. 375-85. In Laver and Hutcheson (1972), pp. 128-45.

Brown, Roger, and A. Gilman. 1960. "The Pronouns of Power and Solidarity." In *Style in Language,* edited by T. A. Sebeok. Cambridge, Mass.: M.I.T. Press. Pp. 253-76. In

Fishman (1970), pp. 252-75, Giglioli (1972), pp. 252-82, and Laver and Hutcheson (1972), pp. 103-27.

Brown, Roger, and Camille Hanlon. 1970. "Derivational Complexity and Order of Acquisition in Child Speech." In *Cognition and the Development of Language*, edited by J. R. Hayes. New York: Wiley. Pp. 11-53.

Brown, Roger, and David McNeill. 1966. "The 'Tip of the Tongue' Phenomenon." *Journal of Verbal Learning and Verbal Behavior*, vol. 5, pp. 325-37.

Bruner, Jerome S., Jacqueline J. Goodnow, and George A. Austin. 1956. *A Study of Thinking*. New York: Wiley.

Burling, Robbins. 1970. *Man's Many Voices: Language in its Cultural Context*. New York: Holt, Rinehart and Winston.

———. 1973. *English in Black and White*. New York: Holt, Rinehart and Winston.

Carmichael, L., H. P. Hogan, and A. A. Walter. 1932. "An Experimental Study of the Effect of Language on the Reproduction of Visually Perceived Forms." *Journal of Experimental Psychology*, vol. 15, pp. 73-86.

Carroll, John B., editor. 1956. *Language, Thought, and Reality: Selected Writings of Benjamin Lee Whorf*. New York: Wiley.

Carroll, John B., and Joseph B. Casagrande. 1958. "The Function of Language Classifications in Behavior." In *Readings in Social Psychology*. Third edition, edited by E. E. Maccoby, T. M. Newcomb, and E. L. Hartley. New York: Holt, Rinehart and Winston. Pp. 18-31.

Cazden, Courtney B. 1972. *Child Language and Education*. New York: Holt, Rinehart and Winston.

Cazden, Courtney B., Vera P. John, and Dell Hymes, editors. 1972. *Functions of Language in the Classroom*. New York: Teachers College Press.

Cherry, E. C. 1963. "Some Experiments on the Recognition of Speech with One and with Two Ears." *Journal of the Acoustical Society of America*, vol. 25, pp. 975-79.

Chomsky, Carol S. 1969. *The Acquisition of Syntax in Children from 5 to 10*. Cambridge, Mass.: M.I.T. Press.

Chomsky, Noam. 1957. *Syntactic Structures*. The Hague: Mouton.

———. 1959. "Review of B. F. Skinner, *Verbal Behavior*." *Language*, vol. 35, pp. 26-58.

———. 1965. *Aspects of the Theory of Syntax*. Cambridge, Mass.: M.I.T. Press.

———. 1966. *Cartesian Linguistics: A Chapter in the History of Rationalist Thought*. New York: Harper and Row.

———. 1967. "The General Properties of Language." In Darley (1967), pp. 73-81.

———. 1972. *Language and Mind*. Enlarged edition. New York: Harcourt Brace Jovanovich.

Cicourel, Aaron V. 1973. *Cognitive Sociology*. London: Penguin.

Clifton, C., Jr., I. Kurcz, and J. J. Jenkins. 1965. "Grammatical Relations as Determinants of Sentence Similarity." *Journal of Verbal Learning and Verbal Behavior*, vol. 4, pp. 112-17.

Dale, Philip S. 1972. *Language Development: Structure and Function*. Hinsdale, Ill.: The Dryden Press.

Darley, Frederic L., editor. 1967. *Brain Mechanisms Underlying Speech and Language*. New York: Grune and Stratton.

Denes, Peter B., and Elliot N. Pinson. 1963. *The Speech Chain: The Physics and Biology of Spoken Language*. Bell Telephone Laboratories.

Deutsch, Martin, Irwin Katz, and Arthur R. Jensen, editors. 1969. *Social Class, Race, and Psychological Development*. New York: Holt, Rinehart and Winston.

DeVito, Joseph. 1970. *The Psychology of Speech and Language: An Introduction to Psy-*

*cholinguistics.*New York: Random House.

———, editor. 1973. *Language: Concepts and Processes.* Englewood Cliffs, N.J.: Prentice-Hall.

Dillard, J. L. 1972. *Black English: Its History and Usage in the United States.* New York: Random House.

Dingwall, William Orr, editor. 1971. *A Survey of Linguistic Science.* University of Maryland: Linguistics Program.

Downing, John. 1970. "Children's Concepts of Language in Learning to Read." *Educational Research,* vol. 12, pp. 106-12.

Duncan, Starkey. 1972. "Some Signals and Rules for Taking Speaking Turns in Conversations." *Journal of Personality and Social Psychology,* vol. 23, pp. 283-92.

Eifermann, R. R. 1961. "Negation: A Linguistic Variable." *Acta Psychologica,* vol. 18, pp. 258-73.

Epstein, W. 1969. "Recall of Word Lists Following Learning of Sentences and of Anomalous and Random Strings." *Journal of Verbal Learning and Verbal Behavior,* vol. 8, pp. 20-25.

Ervin-Tripp. S.M. 1969. "Sociolinguistics." In *Advances in Experimental Social Psychology,* vol. 4, edited by L. Berkowitz. New York: Academic Press. Pp. 93-107. In Pride and Holmes (1972), pp. 225-40.

———. 1973. "Some Strategies for the First Two Years." In Moore (1973), pp. 261-86.

Esch, Harald. 1967. "The Evolution of Bee Language." *Scientific American,* vol. 216, pp. 96-104.

Evans, Richard I. 1973. *Jean Piaget: The Man and His Ideas.* New York: E. P. Dutton.

Eysenck, H. J. 1971. *The IQ Argument: Race, Intelligence and Education.* New York: Library Press.

Falk, Julia S. 1973 *Linguistics and Language.* Lexington, Mass.: Xerox.

Farb, Peter. 1974. *Word Play: What Happens When People Talk.* New York: Alfred A. Knopf.

Fischer, John L. 1958. "Social Influences on the Choice of a Linguistic Variant." *Word,* vol. 14, pp. 47-56. In Bar-Adon and Leopold (1971), pp. 147-53.

Fishman, Joshua A., editor. 1970. *Readings in the Sociology of Language.* The Hague: Mouton.

Flavell, John H. 1963. *The Developmental Psychology of Jean Piaget.* Princeton: D. Van Nostrand.

Fodor, Janet Dean. 1970. "Formal Linguistics and Formal Logic." In Lyons (1970b), pp. 198-214.

Fodor, J., and M. Garrett. 1966. Some Reflections on Competence and Performance." In Lyons and Wales (1966), pp. 133-79.

Frake, C. O. 1964. "How to Ask for a Drink in Subanun." *American Anthropologist,* vol. 66, pp. 127-32. In Giglioli (1972), pp. 87-94 and Pride and Holmes (1972), pp. 260-66.

Frisch, Karl von. 1950. *Bees: Their Vision, Chemical Senses, and Language.* Ithaca, New York: Cornell University Press.

———. 1953. *The Dancing Bees: An Account of the Life and Senses of the Honey Bee.* New York: Harcourt, Brace and World.

———. 1962. "Dialects in the Language of the Bees." *Scientific American,* vol. 207, pp. 78-87.

———. 1967. *The Dance Language and Orientation of Bees.* Cambridge, Mass.: Harvard University Press.

Fromkin, Victoria A. 1968. "Speculations on Performance Models." *Journal of Linguistics*, vol. 4, pp. 47-68.

———. 1973. "Slips of the Tongue." *Scientific American*, vol. 229, pp. 110-17.

Fromkin, Victoria A., and Robert Rodman. 1974. *An Introduction to Language*. New York: Holt, Rinehart and Winston.

Fry, D. B. 1970. "Speech Reception and Perception." In Lyons (1970b), pp. 29-52.

Gardner, Beatrice T., and R. Allen Gardner. 1971. "Two-way Communication with an Infant Chimpanzee." In *Behavior of Nonhuman Primates*, edited by Allan Schrier and Fred Stollnitz. New York: Academic Press. Pp. 117-84.

Gardner, Howard. 1973. *The Quest for Mind: Piaget, Levi-Strauss, and the Structuralist Movement*. New York: Alfred A. Knopf.

Gardner, R. Allen, and Beatrice T. Gardner. 1969. "Teaching Sign Language to a Chimpanzee." *Science*, vol. 165, pp. 664-72.

Garrett, M., T. Bever, and J. A. Fodor. 1966. "The Active Use of Grammar in Speech Perception." *Perception and Psychophysics*, vol. 2, pp. 149-62.

Geertz, Clifford. 1960. *The Religion of Java*. Glencoe, Ill.: The Free Press.

Geschwind, Norman. 1973. "The Brain and Language." In Miller (1973), pp. 61-72.

Ghiselin, Brewster. 1955. *The Creative Process*. New York: Mentor Books.

Giglioli, Pier Paolo, editor. 1972. *Language and Social Context*. London: Penguin.

Gleason, H. A., Jr. 1961. *An Introduction to Descriptive Linguistics*. Revised edition. New York: Holt, Rinehart and Winston.

Gleason, Jean Berko. 1973. "Code Switching in Children's Language." In Moore (1973), pp. 159-67.

Gleitman, Lila R., and Henry Gleitman. 1970. *Phrase and Paraphrase: Some Innovative Uses of Language*. New York: W. W. Norton.

Goffman, Erving. 1955. "On Face-work: An Analysis of Ritual Elements in Social Interaction." *Pscyhiatry*, vol. 18, pp. 213-31. In Laver and Hutcheson (1972), pp. 319-46.

———. 1957. "Alienation from Interaction." *Human Relations*, vol. 10, pp. 47-60. In Laver and Hutcheson (1972), pp. 347-63.

———. 1971. *Relations in Public*. New York: Basic Books.

Gordon, David, and George Lakoff. 1971. "Conversational Postulates." In *Papers from the Seventh Regional Meeting of the Chicago Linguistic Society*. Chicago: Chicago Linguistic Society. Pp. 63-84.

Gough, P. B. 1965. "Grammatical Transformations and Speed of Understanding." *Journal of Verbal Learning and Verbal Behavior*, vol. 4, pp. 107-11.

Greenberg, Joseph H. 1963. *Universals of Language*. Cambridge, Mass.: M.I.T. Press.

Greene, Judith. 1972. *Psycholinguistics: Chomsky and Psychology*. London: Penguin.

Grice, H. P. 1971. "Utterer's Meaning, Sentence-Meaning, and Word Meaning." In *The Philosophy of Language*, edited by J. R. Searle. London: Oxford University Press. Pp. 54-70.

Gumperz, John. 1971. *Language in Social Groups*. Stanford: Stanford University Press.

Gumperz, John, and Jan-Petter Blom. 1971. "Social Meaning in Linguistic Structures: Code-switching in Norway." In Gumperz (1971), pp. 274-310.

Hall, Edward T. 1959. *The Silent Language*. New York: Doubleday.

———. 1966. *The Hidden Dimension*. New York: Doubleday.

Halliday, M. A. K. 1973. *Explorations in the Functions of Language*. London: Edward Arnold.

Harrison, Randall P. 1974. *Beyond Words: An Introduction to Nonverbal Communication*. Englewood Cliffs, N.J.: Prentice-Hall.

Haugen, Einar. 1966. "Dialect, Language, Nation." *American Anthropologist,* vol. 68, pp. 922-35. In Pride and Holmes (1972), pp. 97-111.

Haugen, Einar, and Morton Bloomfield, editors. 1974. *Language as a Human Problem.* New York: W. W. Norton.

Hayes, Catherine. 1951. *The Ape in our House.* New York: Harper and Row.

Hayes, Keith J., and Catherine Hayes. 1951 "Intellectual Development of a Home-raised Chimpanzee." *Proceedings of the American Philosophical Society,* vol. 95, pp. 105-9.

Hebb, Donald O. 1949. *The Organization of Behavior: A Neurophysiological Theory.* New York: Wiley.

Herrnstein, Richard. 1973. *IQ in the Meritocracy.* Boston: Atlantic-Little Brown.

Hess, R. D., and V. C. Shipman. 1967. "Cognitive Elements in Maternal Behavior." In *1967 Minnesota Symposium on Child Psychology,* edited by J. P. Hill. Minneapolis: University of Minnesota Press. Pp. 57-81.

Hockett, Charles F. 1954. "Two Models of Grammatical Description." *Word.* vol. 10, pp. 210-31.

———. 1958. *A Course in Modern Linguistics.* New York: Macmillan.

———. 1960. "The Origin of Speech." *Scientific American,* vol. 203, pp. 89-96.

———. 1963. "The Problem of Universals in Language." In Greenberg (1963), pp. 1-22.

Hockett, Charles F., and S. A. Altmann. 1968. "A Note on Design Features." In Sebeok (1968), pp. 61-72.

Hockett, Charles F., and Robert Ascher. 1964. "The Human Revolution." *Current Anthropology,* vol. 5, pp. 135-47. Comments and replies, pp. 147-68.

Householder, Fred W. 1952. "Review of Zellig S. Harris, *Methods of Structural Linguistics.*" *International Journal of American Linguistics,* vol. 18, pp. 260-68.

Hubel, David H. 1963. "The Visual Cortex of the Brain." *Scientific American,* vol. 209, pp. 54-62.

Hubel, David H., and T. N. Wiesel. 1962. "Receptive Fields, Binocular Interaction and Functional Architecture in the Cat's Visual Cortex." *Journal of Physiology* (London), vol. 160, pp. 106-54.

Huxley, Renira, and Elisabeth Ingram, editors. 1971. *Language Acquisition: Models and Methods.* New York: Academic Press.

Hymes, Dell. 1962. "The Ethnography of Speaking." In *Anthropology and Human Behavior,* edited by T. Gladwin and W. C. Sturtevant. Washington, D.C.: Anthropology Society of Washington. Pp. 13-53. In Fishman (1970), pp. 99-138.

———. 1964. "Introduction: Toward Ethnographies of Communication." *American Anthropologist,* vol. 66, pp. 12-25. In Giglioli (1972), pp. 21-44.

———. 1971. "Competence and Performance in Linguistic Theory." In Huxley and Ingram (1971), pp. 3-28.

———. 1972. "Introduction." In Cazden, John, and Hymes (1972), pp. xi-lvii.

———. 1974. *Foundations in Sociolinguistics: An Ethnographic Approach.* Philadelphia: University of Pennsylvania Press.

Jakobson, Roman. 1960. "Linguistics and Poetics." In *Style in Language,* edited by T. A. Sebeok. Cambridge, Mass: M.I.T. Press. Pp. 350-77.

———. 1968. *Child Language, Aphasia and Phonological Universals.* The Hague: Mouton.

———. 1971. "The Sound Laws of Child Language and Their Place in General Phonology." In Bar-Adon and Leopold (1971), pp. 75-82.

Jefferson, Gail. 1972. "Side Sequences." In Sudnow (1972), pp. 294-338.

Jenkins, James J. 1969. "Language and Thought." In *Approaches to Thought,* edited by J. F. Voss. Columbus, Ohio: Charles E. Merrill. Pp. 211-37.

Jensen, Arthur R. 1972. *Genetics and Education*. New York: Harper and Row.
———. 1973. *Educability and Group Differences*. New York: Harper and Row.
Johnson, Dennis L. 1967. "Honey Bees: Do They use the Direction Information Contained in Their Dance Maneuver?" *Science*, vol. 155, pp. 844-47.
Johnson-Laird, P. N. 1969a. "On Understanding Logically Complex Sentences." *Quarterly Journal of Experimental Psychology*, vol. 21, pp. 1-13.
———. 1969b. "Reasoning with Ambiguous Sentences." *British Journal of Psychology*, vol. 60, pp. 17-23.
———. 1970. "The Perception and Memory of Sentences." In Lyons (1970), pp. 261-70.
Joos, Martin. 1962. *The Five Clocks*. Bloomington: Publications of the Research Center in Anthropology, Folklore, and Linguistics, no. 22.
Jordon, J. 1971. "Studies on the Structure of the Organ of Voice and Vocalization in the Chimpanzees." *Folia Morphologica* (Warsaw), vol. 30, pp. 97-126, 222-48, 323-40.
Keenan, E. L. 1971. "Two Kinds of Presupposition in Natural Language." In *Studies in Linguistic Semantics*, edited by C. J. Fillmore and D. T. Langendoen. New York: Holt, Rinehart and Winston. Pp. 45-54.
Keiler, Allan R., editor. 1972. *A Reader in Historical and Comparative Linguistics*. New York: Holt, Rinehart and Winston.
Kellog, Winthrop N. 1968. "Communication and Language in the Home-raised Chimpanzee." *Science*, vol. 162, pp. 423-27.
Kellog, Winthrop N., and Louise A. Kellog. 1933. *The Ape and the Child*. New York: McGraw-Hill.
Key, Mary R. 1972. "Linguistic Behavior of Male and Female." *Linguistics*, no. 88, pp. 15-31.
Kim, Chin-Wu. 1971. "Experimental Phonetics." In Dingwall (1971), pp. 17-135.
Kimura, Doreen. 1967. "Functional Asymmetry of the Brain in Dichotic Listening." *Cortex*, vol. 3, pp. 163-78.
Kiparsky, Paul. 1970. "Historical Linguistics." In Lyons (1970b), pp. 302-15.
———. 1971. "Historical Linguistics." In Dingwall (1971), pp. 576-649.
Klima, E. S., and Ursula Bellugi. 1966. "Syntactic Regularities in the Speech of Children." In Lyons and Wales (1966), pp. 183-219 and Bar-Adon and Leopold (1971), pp. 412-24.
Knapp, Mark L. 1972. *Nonverbal Communication in Human Interaction*. New York: Holt, Rinehart and Winston.
Labov, William. 1966. "The Effect of Social Mobility on Linguistic Behavior." *Sociological Inquiry*, vol. 36, pp. 186-203.
———. 1969. "Contraction, Deletion, and Inherent Variability of the English Copula." *Language*, vol. 45, pp. 715-62. Also in Labov (1972a), pp. 65-129.
———. 1970. *The Study of Nonstandard English*. Urbana, Ill.: National Council of Teachers of English.
———. 1972a. *Language in the Inner City: Studies in the Black Vernacular*. Philadelphia: University of Pennsylvania Press.
———. 1972b. "Rules for Ritual Insults." In Sudnow (1972), pp. 120-69.
———. 1972c. *Sociolinguistic Patterns*. Philadelphia: University of Philadelphia Press.
Labov, William, Paul Cohen, Clarence Robins, and John Lewis. 1968. *A Study of the Nonstandard English of Negro and Puerto Rican Speakers in New York City: Phonological and Grammatical Analysis*. Vol. 1, Cooperative Research Project 3288. Washington D.C.: Office of Education.
Ladefoged, Peter. 1967. *Three Areas of Experimental Phonetics*. London: Oxford University Press.

Lakoff, Robin. 1972. "Language in Context." *Language,* vol. 48, pp. 907-27.
————. 1973. "Language and Woman's Place." *Language in Society,* vol. 2:1. pp. 45-79.
Lambert, Wallace E. 1972. *Language, Psychology, and Culture.* Stanford: Stanford University Press.
Lane, Harlan. 1965. "Motor Theory of Speech Perception: A Critical Review." *Psychological Review,* vol. 72, pp. 275-309.
Langacker, Ronald W. 1973. *Language and Its Structure: Some Fundamental Linguistic Concepts.* Second edition. New York: Harcourt Brace Jovanovich.
Laver, John. 1970. "The Production of Speech." In Lyons (1970b), pp. 53-75.
Laver, John, and Sandy Hutcheson, editors. 1972. *Communication in Face to Face Interaction: Selected Readings.* London: Penguin.
Lawick-Goodall, Jane Van. 1971. *In the Shadow of Man.* London: William Collins.
Lehiste, Ilse. 1970. "Temporal Organization of Spoken Language." *Ohio State University Working Papers in Linguistics,* vol. 4, pp. 95-114.
Lenneberg, E. H. 1962. "Understanding Language Without Ability to Speak: A Case Report." *Journal of Abnormal Social Psychology,* vol. 65, pp. 419-25.
————. 1967. *Biological Foundations of Language.* New York: Wiley.
————. 1969. "On Explaining Language." *Science,* vol. 164, pp. 635-43.
Lettvin, J. Y., H. R. Maturana, W. S. McCulloch, and W. H. Pitts. 1959. "What the Frog's Eye Tells the Frog's Brain." *Proceedings of the Institute of Radio Engineers,* vol. 47, pp. 1940-51.
————. 1961. "Two Remarks on the Visual System of the Frog." In *Sensory Communication,* edited by Walter A. Rosenblith. Cambridge, Mass.: M.I.T. Press. Pp. 757-76.
Liberman, A. M. 1957. "Some Results of Research on Speech Perception." *Journal of the Acoustical Society of America,* vol. 29, pp. 117-23.
Liberman, A. M., F. S. Cooper, K. S. Harris, P. F. MacNeilage, and M. Studdert-Kennedy. 1967. "Some Observations on a Model for Speech Perception." In Wathen-Dunn (1967), pp. 68-87.
Liberman, A. M., P. Delattre, and F. S. Cooper. 1952. "The Role of Selected Stimulus-Variables in the Perception of the Unvoiced Stop Consonants." *American Journal of Psychology,* vol. 65, pp. 497-516.
Lieberman, Philip. 1967. *Intonation Perception and Language.* Cambridge, Mass.: M.I.T. Press.
————. 1968. "Primate Vocalizations and Human Linguistic Ability." *Journal of the Acoustical Society of America,* vol. 44, pp. 1574-84.
Lieberman, Philip, and Edmund S. Crelin. 1971. "On the Speech of Neanderthal Man." *Linguistic Inquiry,* vol. 2, pp. 203-22.
Lieberman, Philip, E. S. Crelin, and D. H. Klatt. 1972. "Phonetic Ability and Related Anatomy of the Newborn and Adult Human, Neanderthal Man, and the Chimpanzee." *American Anthropologist,* vol. 74, pp. 287-307.
Lieberman, Philip, D. H. Klatt, and W. A. Wilson. 1969. "Vocal Tract Limitations on the Vowel Repertoires of Rhesus Monkey and Other Nonhuman Primates." *Science,* vol. 164, pp. 1185-87.
Liles, Bruce, L. 1975. *An Introduction to Linguistics.* Englewood Cliffs, N.J.: Prentice-Hall.
Lindauer, Martin. 1961. *Communication among Social Bees.* Cambridge, Mass.: Harvard University Press.
Linden, Eugene. 1974. *Apes, Men, and Language.* New York: Saturday Review Press.
Lindsay, Peter H., and Donald A. Norman. 1972. *Human Information Processing: An Introduction to Psychology.* New York: Academic Press.

Lorenz, Konrad. 1952. *King Solomon's Ring*. London: Methuen.
———. 1966. *On Aggression*. New York: Harcourt, Brace.
Luria, A. R. 1971. "The Directive Function of Speech in Development and Dissolution." In Bar-Adon and Leopold (1971), pp. 185-200.
Lyons, John. 1970a. *Noam Chomsky*. New York: Viking.
———. editor. 1970b. *New Horizons in Linguistics*. London: Penguin.
Lyons, John, and R. J. Wales, editors. 1966. *Psycholinguistic Papers: The Proceedings of the 1966 Edinburgh Conference*. Edinburgh: Edinburgh University Press.
MacCorquodale, K. 1969. "B. F. Skinner's *Verbal Behavior:* A Retrospective Appreciation." *Journal of the Experimental Analysis of Behavior*, vol. 12, pp. 831-41.
———. 1970. "On Chomsky's Review of Skinner's *Verbal Behavior*." *Journal of the Experimental Analysis of Behavior*, vol. 13, pp. 83-99.
McDavid, Raven I., Jr. 1949. "Postvocalic /-r/ in South Carolina: A Social Analysis." *American Speech*, vol. 23, pp. 194-203.
McMahon, I. E. 1963. "Grammatical Analysis as Part of Understanding a Sentence." Unpublished Doctoral Dissertation, Harvard University.
McNeill, David. 1966. "Developmental Psycholinguistics." In Smith and Miller (1966), pp. 15-84.
———. 1970. *The Acquisition of Language: The Study of Developmental Psycholinguistics*. New York: Harper and Row.
Malinowski, Bronislaw. 1923. "The Problem of Meaning in Primitive Languages." In *The Meaning of Meaning*, by C. K. Ogden and I. A. Richards. London: Kegan Paul. Pp. 451-510. In Laver and Hutcheson (1972), pp. 146-52.
Manning, Aubrey. 1972. *An Introduction to Animal Behavior*. Second edition. Reading, Mass.: Addison-Wesley.
Martinet, André. 1964. *Elements of General Linguistics*. London: Faber and Faber.
Meltzer, Nancy S., and R. Herse. 1969. "The Boundaries of Written Words as Seen by First Graders." *Journal of Reading Behavior*, vol. 1, pp. 3-14.
Miller, Casey, and Kate Swift. 1973. "One Small Step for Genkind." In DeVito (1973), pp. 171-82. (Reprinted from *The New York Times Magazine*, April 16, 1972.)
Miller, George A. 1951. *Language and Communication*. New York: McGraw-Hill.
———. 1956. "The Magical Number Seven Plus or Minus Two: Some Limits on Our Capacity for Storing Information." *Psychological Review*, vol. 63, pp. 81-97.
———. 1962. "Some Psychological Studies of Grammar." *American Psychologist*, vol. 17, pp. 748-62.
———, editor. 1973a. *Communication, Language, and Meaning: Psychological Perspectives*. New York: Basic Books.
———. 1973b. "Nonverbal Communication." In Miller (1973), pp. 231-41.
Miller, George A., and Stephen Isard. 1963. "Some Perceptual Consequences of Linguistic Rules." *Journal of Verbal Learning and Verbal Behavior*, vol. 2, pp. 217-28.
Miller, George A., and K. E. McKean. 1964. "A Chronometric Study of Some Relations Between Sentences." *Quarterly Journal of Experimental Psychology*, vol. 16, pp. 297-308.
Minnis, Noel, editor. 1971. *Linguistics at Large*. New York: Viking.
Mishler, Elliot G. 1972. "Implications of Teacher Strategies for Language and Cognition: Observations in First-Grade Classrooms." In Cazden, John, and Hymes (1972) pp. 267-98.
Moore, Timothy E., editor. 1973. *Cognitive Development and the Acquisition of Language*. New York: Academic Press.

Morris, Desmond. 1967. *The Naked Ape.* New York: McGraw-Hill.

Nottebohm, F. 1970. "Ontogeny of Bird Song." *Science*, vol. 167, pp. 950-56.

Pfeiffer, John E. 1969. *The Emergence of Man.* New York: Harper and Row.

Pfungst, O. 1911. *Clever Hans: The Horse of Mr. Van Osten.* New York: Holt.

Piaget, Jean. 1950. *The Language and Thought of the Child.* London: Routledge and Kegan Paul.

————. 1972. "Language and Thought from the Genetic Point of View." In Adams (1972), pp. 170-79.

Pickford, Glenn R. 1957. "American Linguistic Geography: A Sociolinguistic Appraisal." *Word*, vol. 12, pp. 211-33.

Pittenger, Robert E., Charles F. Hockett, and John J. Danehy. 1960. *The First Five Minutes.* Ithaca: Paul Martineau.

Pollack, I., and J. Pickett. 1964. "The Intelligibility of Excerpts from Conversations." *Language and Speech*, vol. 6, pp. 165-71.

Premack, Ann James, and David Premack. 1972. "Teaching Language to an Ape." *Scientific American*, vol. 227, pp. 92-99.

Premack, David. 1970a. "The Education of Sarah." *Psychology Today*, vol. 4, pp. 54-58.

————. 1970b. "A Functional Analysis of Language." *Journal of the Experimental Analysis of Behavior*, vol. 14, pp. 107-25.

————. 1971. "Language in Chimpanzee?" *Science*, vol. 172, pp. 808-22.

Pribram, K. H. 1969. "The Neurophysiology of Remembering." *Scientific American*, vol. 220, pp. 73-86.

Pride, J. B., and Janet Holmes, editors. 1972. *Sociolinguistics: Selected Readings.* London: Penguin.

Reid, J. F. 1966. "Learning to Think about Reading." *Educational Research*, vol. 9, pp. 56-62.

Richardson, Ken, and David Spears, editors, 1972. *Race and Intelligence: The Fallacies behind the Race-IQ Controversy.* Baltimore: Penguin.

Robins, R. H. 1968. *A Short History of Linguistics.* Bloomington: Indiana University Press.

Robinson, W. P. 1971. "Social Factors and Language Development in Primary School Children." In Huxley and Ingram (1971), pp. 49-66.

————. 1972. *Language and Social Behavior.* London: Penguin.

Robinson, W. P., and S. J. Rackstraw. 1972. *A Question of Answers.* London: Routledge and Kegan Paul.

Rose, Steven. 1973. *The Conscious Brain.* New York: Alfred A. Knopf.

Rosten, Leo. 1968. *The Joys of Yiddish.* New York: McGraw-Hill.

Rumbaugh, Duane M., Timothy V. Gill, and E. C. von Glaserfeld. 1973. "Reading and Sentence Completion by a Chimpanzee (Pan)." *Science*, vol. 182, pp. 731-33.

Russell, Claire, and W. M. S. Russell. 1971. "Language and Animal Signals." In Minnis (1971), pp. 159-94.

Russell, G. W. E. 1898. *Collections and Recollections, by One Who Has Kept a Diary.* London: Harper and Brothers.

Sachs, J. S. 1967. "Recognition Memory for Syntactic and Semantic Aspects of Connected Discourse." *Perception and Psychophysics*, vol. 2, pp. 437-42.

Samuels, M. L. 1972. *Linguistic Evolution: With Special Reference to English.* London: Cambridge University Press.

Sapir, Edward. 1921. *Language: An Introduction to the Study of Speech.* New York: Harcourt, Brace and World.

Saussure, Ferdinand de. 1959. *Course in General Linguistics.* New York: Philosophical Library.

Savin, H. B., and E. Perchonock. 1965. "Grammatical Structure and the Immediate Recall of English Sentences." *Journal of Verbal Learning and Verbal Behavior,* vol. 4, pp. 348-53.

Scarr-Salapatek, Sandra. 1971. "Race, Social Class and IQ." *Science,* vol. 174, pp. 1285-95.

Schegloff, Emanuel A. 1972. "Notes on a Conversational Practice: Formulating Place." In Sudnow (1972), pp. 75-119 and Giglioli (1972), pp. 95-135.

Searle, John R. 1969. *Speech Acts: An Essay in the Philosophy of Language.* Cambridge: Cambridge University Press.

———. 1972. "What Is a Speech Act?" In Giglioli (1972), pp. 136-54.

Sebeok, Thomas A., editor. 1968. *Animal Communication: Techniques of Study and Results of Research.* Bloomington: University of Indiana Press.

Shankweiler, Donald. 1971. "An Analysis of Laterality Effects in Speech Perception." In *Perception of Language,* edited by David L. Horton and James J. Jenkins. Columbus, Ohio: Charles E. Merrill. Pp. 185-200.

Shipley, Elizabeth F., Carlota S. Smith, and Lila R. Gleitman. 1969. "A Study of the Acquisition of Language: Free Responses to Commands." *Language,* vol. 45, pp. 322-42.

Sinclair, Hermine. 1971. "Sensorimotor Action Patterns as a Condition for the Acquisition of Syntax." In Huxley and Ingram (1971), pp. 121-35.

Sinclair-de Zwart, Hermine. 1969. "Developmental Psycholinguistics." In *Studies in Cognitive Development: Essays in Honor of Jean Piaget,* edited by David Elkind and John H. Flavell. New York: Oxford University Press. Pp. 315-36. In Adams (1972), pp. 266-76, 364-73.

———. 1973. "Language Acquisition and Cognitive Development." In Moore (1973), pp. 9-25.

Skinner, B. F. 1957. *Verbal Behavior.* New York: Appleton-Century-Crofts.

Sledd, James, and Wilma R. Ebbit, editors. 1962. *Dictionaries and That Dictionary.* Chicago: Scott, Foresman.

Slobin, Dan I. 1966. "Grammatical Transformations in Childhood and Adulthood." *Journal of Verbal Learning and Verbal Behavior.* vol. 5, pp. 219-27.

———. 1968. "Early Grammatical Development in Several Languages, with Special Attention to Soviet Research." Working Paper No. 11, Language-Behavior Research Laboratory, University of California, Berkeley.

———. 1971a. "Developmental Psycholinguistics." In Dingwall (1971), pp. 298-410.

———. 1971b. *Psycholinguistics.* Glenview, Ill.: Scott, Foresman.

Smith, E. M., H. O. Brown, J. E. P. Toman, and L. S. Goodman. 1947. "The Lack of Cerebral Effects of *d*-tubocurarine." *Anesthesiology,* vol. 8, pp. 1-14.

Smith, Frank, and George A. Miller, editors. 1966. *The Genesis of Language: A Psycholinguistic Approach.* Cambridge, Mass.: M.I.T. Press.

Sperry, R. W. 1964. "The Great Cerebral Commissure." *Scientific American,* vol. 210, pp. 42-52.

Sperry, R. W., and M. S. Gazzaniga. 1967. "Language Following Surgical Disconnection of the Hemispheres." In Darley (1967), pp. 108-21.

Stevens, K. N., and M. Halle. 1967. "Remarks on Analysis by Synthesis and Distinctive Features." In Wathen-Dunn (1967), pp. 88-102.

Stewart, William A. 1967. "Sociolinguistic Factors in the History of American Negro Dialects." *The Florida FL Reporter,* vol. 5:2, pp. 1-7. In Allen and Underwood (1971), pp. 444-53.

———. 1968. "Continuity and Change in American Negro Dialects." *The Florida FL Reporter,* vol. 6:1, pp. 3-4, 14-16, 18. In Allen and Underwood (1972), pp. 454-67.

Studdert-Kennedy, M., A. M. Liberman, K. S. Harris, and F. S. Cooper, 1970. "Motor Theory of Speech Perception: A Reply to Lane's Critical Review." *Psychological Review*, vol. 77, pp. 234-49.

Studdert-Kennedy, M., and D. Shankweiler. 1970. "Hemispheric Specialization for Speech Perception." *Journal of the Acoustical Society of America*, vol. 48, pp. 579-94.

Sudnow, David, editor. 1972. *Studies in Social Interaction*. New York: Free Press.

Swadesh, Morris. 1971. *The Origin and Diversification of Language*. Chicago: Aldine-Atherton.

Taylor, I. K. 1966. "What Words Are Stuttered?" *Psychological Bulletin*, vol. 65, pp. 236-42.

Thorne, J. P. 1966. "On Hearing Sentences." In Lyons and Wales (1966), pp. 1-25.

Tiger, Lionel, and Robin Fox. 1971. *The Imperial Animal*. New York: Holt, Rinehart and Winston.

Turner, G. W. 1973. *Stylistics*. London: Penguin.

Turner, Roy. 1972. "Some Formal Properties of Therapy Talk." In Sudnow (1972), pp. 367-96.

Vygotsky, L. S. 1962. *Thought and Language*. Cambridge, Mass.: M.I.T. Press.

———. 1972. "Thought and Word." In Adams (1972), pp. 180-213.

Wales, R. J., and J. C. Marshall. 1966. "The Organization of Linguistic Performance." In Lyons and Wales (1966), pp. 27-95.

Wang, William S-Y. 1971. "The Basis of Speech." In *The Learning of Language*, edited by Carroll E. Reed. New York: Appleton-Century-Crofts. Pp. 267-306.

Wanner, Eric. 1973. "Do We Understand Sentences from the Outside-In or from the Inside-Out?" *Daedalus*, vol. 102, pp. 163-83.

Wardhaugh, Ronald. 1972. *Introduction to Linguistics*. New York: McGraw-Hill.

Wason, P. C. 1961. "Response to Affirmative and Negative Binary Statements." *British Journal of Psychology*, vol. 52, pp. 133-42.

———. 1965. "The Contexts of Plausible Denial." *Journal of Verbal Learning and Verbal Behavior*, vol. 4, pp. 7-11.

Wathen-Dunn, W. 1967. *Models for the Perception of Speech and Visual Forms*. Cambridge, Mass.: M.I.T. Press.

Watson, J. B. 1913. "Psychology as the Behaviorist Views It." *Psychological Review*, vol. 20, pp. 158-77.

———. 1924. *Behaviorism*. Chicago: University of Chicago Press.

Weir, Ruth. 1962. *Language in the Crib*. The Hague: Mouton.

Wenner, Adrian M. 1962. "Communication with Queen Honey Bees by Substrate Sound." *Science*, vol. 138, pp. 446-48.

———. 1964. "Sound Communication in Honeybees." *Scientific American*, vol. 210, pp. 116-24.

———. 1967. "Honey Bees: Do They Use the Distance Information Contained in Their Dance Maneuver?" *Science*, vol. 155, pp. 847-49.

Whitaker, Harry A. 1971. "Neurolinguistics." In Dingwall (1971), pp. 136-251.

Williamson, Juanita V., and Virginia M. Burke, editors. 1971. *A Various Language: Perspectives on American Dialects*. New York: Holt, Rinehart and Winston.

Wilson, Edward O. 1972. "Animal Communication." *Scientific American*, vol. 227, pp. 52-60.

Wolfram, Walt, and Ralph W. Fasold. 1974. *The Study of Social Dialects in American English*. Englewood Cliffs, N.J.: Prentice-Hall.

Zangwill, Oliver L. 1971. "The Neurology of Language." In Minnis (1971), pp. 209-26.